Royal Air Force
FIGHTER COMMA
LOSSES
of the Second World War

Volume 1
Operational Losses: Aircraft and Crews
1939–1941

Revised and Updated

Royal Air Force
FIGHTER COMMAND
LOSSES
of the Second World War

Volume 1
Operational Losses: Aircraft and Crews
1939–1941

Revised and Updated

NORMAN L R FRANKS

MIDLAND
An imprint of
Ian Allan Publishing

First published 1997
Second edition 2008

Copyright © 1997, 2008 Norman L R Franks

ISBN 978 1 85780 286 3

Design concept and editonal layout
© Midland Publishing Limited
and Stephen Thompson Associates

Published by Midland Publishing
Midland Publishing is an imprint of Ian Allan Publishing Ltd
Riverdene Business Park, Hersham, Surrey KT12 4RG

Printed in England by Ian Allan Printing Ltd

North American trade distribution:
Specialty Press Publishers & Wholesalers Inc
39966 Grand Avenue, North Branch, MN 55056, USA
Telephone: 651 277 1400 Fax: 800 895 4585
Toll free telephone: 800 895 4585

Contents

Acknowledgements

The staff of the Air Historical Branch, especially to Graham Day who has helped in a very great way to finding missing serial numbers and airmen's names and fates. To the staff of the Public Archives, Kew. In addition to those who helped with the original first edition back in 1997, much help came from many sources following its publication, many from northern Europe, over whose countries much of the air battles were fought. So thank you, Henk Welting, Xavier Nedelec, Hans Onderwater, Betty Clements, Tony Wood, Graham Pitchfork, Peter Hall. And also the great help given by Wojtek Matusiak and my friend Andy Saunders.

Bibliography

1941, The Turning Point: Parts 1 and 2, John Foreman; Air Research, 1993–1994.
Aces High: Chris Shores and Clive Williams; Grub Street, 1994.
The Battle of Britain Then and Now: Winston Ramsey (Ed.); After the Battle Publications, 1982.
Battle of Britain: The Forgotten Months: John Foreman; Air Research, 1988.
British Military Aircraft Serials 1878–1987: Bruce Robertson; Midland Counties Publications, 1987.
The Canadian Years (242 Squadron): H Halliday; Canada's Wings Inc, 1982.
A Few of the Many: Dilip Sarkar; Ramrod Publications, 1995.
Fighter Squadron (19 Squadron): Derek Palmer; 1990.
Fighter Squadrons of the RAF: John Rawlings; MacDonald & Jane's, 1969.
Fledgling Eagles: Chris Shores, Brian Cull, C-J Ehrengardt, H Weiss and B Olsen; Grub Street, 1991.
High Blue Battle: D McIntosh; Spa Books, 1990.
Ku Czci Poleglych Lotnikov 1939–1945, R Gretzyngier, W Matusiak, W Wójcik & J Zieliński; Agencja Lotnicza Altair, 2006.
Lions Rampant: Douglas McRoberts; William Kimber, 1985.
Mnozi Nedoleteli: Frantisek Loucky; Vojsko, 1989.
RAF Squadrons: Wing Commander C G Jefford MBE RAF; Airlife Publishing Limited, 1988.
RCAF Overseas: three volumes; Oxford University Press; 1944, 1945, 1949.
Twelve Days in May: Brian Cull, B Lander and H Weiss; Grub Street, 1995.
Squadron Codes Z937-56: Michael JF Bowyer and John DR Rawlings; Patrick Stephens Limited, 1979.
The Story of 609 Squadron: Frank Ziegler and Chris Goss; Crecy, 1993.
We Never Slept: The Story of 605 (County of Warwick) Squadron, 1926–1957: Ian Piper; Piper 1996.

Plus the following published by Air-Britain (Historians) Ltd:
Fleet Air Arm Aircraft 1939 to 1945: Ray Sturtivant ISO with Mick Burrow; 1995.
The K File, The Royal Air Force of the 1930s: James J Halley MBE; 1995.
Royal Air Force Aircraft L1000 to N9999: James J Halley; 1993.
Royal Air Force Aircraft P1000 to R9999: James J Halley MBE; 1996.
Royal Air Force Aircraft T1000 to T9999: James J Halley; 1981.
Royal Air Force Aircraft V1000 to W9999: James J Halley; 1983.
Royal Air Force Aircraft X1000 to Z9999: James J Halley; 1984.
Royal Air Force Aircraft AA100 to AZ999: James J Halley; 1985.
Royal Air Force Aircraft: BA100 to BZ999: James J Halley; 1986.
Squadrons of the Royal Air Force and Commonwealth 1918–1988: James J Halley; 1988.

Introduction

This book lists the operational losses sustained by RAF Fighter Command from September 1939 until the end of December 1941. It does not list non-operational losses, such as crashes or training accidents. However, some of the crashes listed might have been caused by accidents but if they occurred while the pilot was flying on an operational sortie, they are generally listed.

For the most part they show an aircraft lost and whether or not a pilot was lost too; where an aircraft was not written off, although perhaps damaged, but the pilot was wounded seriously enough to be taken away from operations, then this too is deemed a 'loss' to the Command and therefore listed.

The central source of information came from Fighter Command's Combats and Casualty Record (AIR 16) at the Public Record Office and the squadron operational record books (ORBs), the Forms 540 and 541s, to be found in AIR 27 at Kew. Additional information came from the Ministry of Defence casualty records, also various Fighter Command files within AIR 16.

This original source information was supplemented and added to by referring to a number of my research notes made over the years and through interviews with a number of former fighter pilots over the last 30 years.

There are also a number of publications in which the authors have covered a good deal of ground in this sphere, to either a greater or lesser degree. The bibliography lists those that have been found to be most useful in the compiling of this volume.

There is no real way of knowing if all aircraft and pilots lost in France or in Norway have been listed, simply because many records for this period are incomplete due to a number of causes. However, those shown are the losses that are known. Likewise, the Battle of Britain period has thrown up anomalies, most of which relate to a hard-pressed RAF with greater priorities than the paperwork. Indications are given with some entries to show problems of identifying particular incidents or aircraft.

The presentation should present few problems to readers, especially those already familiar with Bill Chorley's *Royal Air Force Bomber Command Losses of the Second World War*, a series published by sister company Midland Counties Publications. Reference to the Glossary of Terms on page 8 should ease the necessary use of abbreviations.

While there has been a conscious attempt to follow a similar layout to that series, the world of fighters and bombers is very different, not least in the number of souls involved and in the way sorties were administered and charted.

Losses are presented in date order within each section with the first column quoting the unit that the aircraft was operating with at the time. For some of the losses quoted, especially in the Battle of France and Battle of Britain phases, the operating unit may not have been the de facto 'owning' unit – again a reflection of the chaotic and ever-changing times. The second column gives the aircraft type and below that the pilot/crew.

Column three gives the aircraft serial number, where known. Question marks here either are used to cast doubt on the serial number quoted (perhaps with an explanation in column four) or to show that no identity is known. Sometimes an individual code letter, or code-letter grouping will be given as well as, or in place of, a serial number. While squadron two-letter groupings were worn plus individual letters (eg 'KW-Z' of 615 Squadron) only where the squadron two-letter grouping is confirmed as being worn by the aircraft involved, is this given in full. A review of two-letter squadron code groupings can be found in Appendices A, B, C and D. Below the serial number and/or code comes an indication of the status of the crew following the loss. 'Safe' is self-explanatory, 'Wounded' (WIA) denotes physical harm suffered in battle while 'Injured' is used to denote pre- or post-battle harm, eg injury in a forced-landing etc. 'Wounded' and 'Injured' are often further detailed in column four. 'Missing' usually indicates an unknown fate, while 'SI' refers to *slightly injured*. 'PoW' denotes that the airman became a prisoner of war. Where the aircrew gave their lives, this is marked '+'. As will be seen frequently from column four, the men of Fighter Command were often in their teens or early twenties when asked to pay the ultimate price.

Column four gives further supporting material to the loss. Mostly this starts with the nature of the sortie followed by combat details. Where the airmen listed had other incidents that appear in this volume they are given by date. If the aircraft was repaired and re-entered service, brief details are sometimes given, mostly centring around its ultimate fate. Details of known burials in Europe have also been provided, with the age of the aircrew involved, if known.

Names, especially place names, were occasionally mis-spelled in the official records (not surprisingly, as correct spelling was not at the top of the priority list for the personnel involved). Where a name or place was clearly incorrect, it has been corrected in this text. However, some mis-spellings may remain as in the original source material.

As with sister publication *Royal Air Force Bomber Command Losses of the Second World War*, comments, additions and corrections are welcomed via the publisher for *Fighter Command Losses of the Second World War* and they will appear in an appendix within Volume 2, which will cover the years 1942–1943.

Norman L R Franks
Bexhill on Sea, East Sussex   July 2007

Glossary of Terms

AA	Anti-Aircraft
A/C	Aircraft
AC1	Aircraftman First Class
AC2	Aircraftman Second Class
A/F	Airfield
AFC	Air Force Cross
AFM	Air Force Medal
AG	Air Gunner
AI	Air Interception
AM	Air Ministry
A/S	Anti-Shipping
ASR	Air Sea Rescue
BEM	British Empire Medal
CBE	Commander of the Order of the British Empire
CGM	Conspicuous Gallantry Medal
Circus	Bombers heavily escorted by fighters to bring enemy fighters into combat
Cpl	Corporal
CO	Commanding Officer
CWGC	Commonwealth War Graves Commission
DCM	Distinguished Conduct Medal
DFC	Distinguished Flying Cross
DFM	Distinguished Flying Medal
DoW	Died of Wounds
DoI	Died of Injuries
DSO	Distinguished Service Order
EA	Enemy Aircraft
FAA	Fleet Air Arm
FFAF	Free French Air Force
FL	Force-landed
F/L	Flight Lieutenant
F/O	Flying Officer
F/S	Flight Sergeant
FTR	Failed to Return
Fw	Feldwebel
FW	Focke-Wulf
G/C	Group Captain
He	Heinkel
HMS	His Majesty's Ship
Hptm	Hauptmann
IAZ	Inner Artillery Zone
JG	Jagdgeschwader
Jim Crow	Fighter recce sortie over English Channel
Ju	Junkers
KBE	Knight of the British Empire
KIA	Killed In Action
KIFA	Killed In Flying Accident
LAC	Leading Aircraftman
LG	Landing Ground
Lt	Lieutenant
MBE	Member of the Order of the British Empire
MC	Military Cross
Me	Messerschmitt*
MID	Mentioned in Dispatches
Mid.	Midshipman
MM	Military Medal
MTB	Motor Torpedo Boat
MU	Maintenance Unit
NCO	Non-commissioned Officer
NJG	Nachtjagdgeschwader
NKG	No Known Grave
Non-Op	Non-operational
OBE	Officer of the Order of the British Empire
Oblt	Oberleutnant
Ofw	Oberfeldwebel
ORB	Operational Record Book
OTU	Operational Training Unit
PAF	Polish Air Force
P/O	Pilot Officer
PoW	Prisoner of War
Pte	Private
RAAF	Royal Australian Air Force
RAF	Royal Air Force
Ramrod	Similar to Circus, but with intention of destroying a target
RCAF	Royal Canadian Air Force
Recce	Reconnaissance
Rhubarb	Freelance fighter sortie against targets of opportunity
RN	Royal Navy
RNAF	Royal Norwegian Air Force
RNethAF	Royal Netherlands Air Force
RNVR	Royal Navy Volunteer Reserve
RNZAF	Royal New Zealand Air Force
Roadstead	Low level attack on coastal shipping
Rodeo	Fighter sweep without bombers
SAAF	South African Air Force
Sgt	Sergeant
S/L	Squadron Leader
SoC	Struck off Charge
SOS	Save Our Souls (distress message)
Sub-Lt(A)	Sub Lieutenant (Air)
Sqn	Squadron
Sweep	General term for fighters operating over enemy territory with or without bombers; bomber support
T/o	Take-off
Uffz	Unteroffizier
UK	United Kingdom
US	United States
USAAF	United States Army Air Force
VC	Victoria Cross
WAAF	Women's Auxiliary Air Force
W/C	Wing Commander
W/O	Warrant Officer
W/01	Warrant Officer First Class
W/02	Warrant Officer Second Class
*	Bar
+	Fatal Casualty

* The argument about 'Bf' or 'Me' as the prefix for the Messerschmitt 109 and 110 fighters has generally settled upon them being Bayrische Flugzeugwerke (ie Bf) designs. The German Air Ministry (Reichs-luftfahrtministerium – RLM) marks the transition from 'Bf' to 'Me' between the unsuccessful Bf162 Jaguar (whose number was subsequently allocated to the He162 Volksjäger) and the Me 163 Komet. However, all of this was lost on those serving in the RAF and other armed forces and the aircraft were universally regarded as 'MEs' and for this series these types will be recorded in that vein, ie Me109s and Me110s.

Chapter 1

The 'Phoney War'

At the beginning of September 1939, Fighter Command had 37 operational fighter squadrons on strength, although a number were in the process of forming, others would be formed before the end of the year.

The Commander-in-Chief of Fighter Command, Air Marshal Sir Hugh Dowding, had long been campaigning for more squadrons, knowing that he would lose a number that were earmarked for France if war came, while others might be sent to Norway. The Air Staff had decided that 50 front-line fighter squadrons would be adequate to defend Britain against an aerial assualt from Germany, so on the eve of war, Dowding was already 13 squadrons below this set figure.

The Air Staff calculations had embraced the concept that, as in the First World War, France would hold the front battle line, supported by the British. Therefore, any attacks upon Britain from the air would have to come from Germany direct, and this being the case, they would not be able to have fighter escort due to the range. Although the Germans, like the British and French, had been experimenting with twin-engined long-range fighters (the Me110, the Blenheim If and the Potez 63), it was thought that RAF fighters would not have great problems if Me110s were sent as escort, and that mainly it would be unescorted bombers that would need to be intercepted and engaged.

During the last week of August 1939, with war imminent, Fighter Command's 37 operational squadrons at its disposal were as follows:

Squadron	Base	Aircraft type
Royal Air Force Squadrons:		
1	Tangmere	Hurricane I
3	Biggin Hill	Hurricane I
17	North Weald	Hurricane I
19	Duxford	Spitfire I
23	Wittering	Blenheim If
25	Northolt	Blenheim If
29	Debden	Blenheim If
32	Biggin Hill	Hurricane I
41	Catterick	Spitfire I
43	Tangmere	Hurricane I
46	Digby	Hurricane I
54	Hornchurch	Spitfire I
56	North Weald	Hurricane I
64	Church Fenton	Blenheim If
65	Hornchurch	Spitfire I
66	Duxford	Spitfire I
72	Church Fenton	Spitfire I

Squadron	Base	Aircraft type
73	Digby	Hurricane I
74	Hornchurch	Spitfire I
79	Biggin Hill	Hurricane I
85	Debden	Hurricane I
87	Debden	Hurricane I
111	Northolt	Hurricane I
151	North Weald	Hurricane I
213	Wittering	Hurricane I
Special Reserve Squadrons:		
501	Filton	Hurricane I
504	Hucknall	Hurricane I
Auxiliary Air Force Squadrons:		
600	Northolt	Blenheim If
601	Hendon	Blenheim If
602	Abbotsinch	Spitfire I
603	Turnhouse	Spitfire I
604	Hendon	Blenheim If
605	Tangmere	Blenheim If
607	Usworth	Gladiator I
609	Yeadon	Spitfire I
611	Duxford	Spitfire I
615	Kenley	Gladiator I

In the final hectic seven days prior to the actual declaration on 3 September 1939, a number of squadrons were repositioned to their immediate war stations. Movements up to mid-September 1939 were as follows: on 27 August No. 504 went to Digby, No. 609 to Catterick; 2 September Nos 3 and 17 to Croydon, No. 601 to Biggin Hill, No. 604 to North Weald, No. 615 to Croydon; 4 September No. 87 to France; 7th September No. 602 to Grangemouth; 9 September No. 1 to France along with No. 73 and No. 85; 15 September No. 25 to Filton.

Nos 1 and 73 Squadrons formed part of the British Advanced Air Striking Force (fighter cover for the Battle and Blenheim squadrons of the AASF), and Nos 85 and 87 were part of the Air Component of the British Expeditionary Force (BEF), attached to the British Army in the field. Although these and other units which were eventually sent to France were technically no longer under strict Fighter Command control, the following lists will include all known aircraft lost on operations while in France, in Part II of Chapter 1.

Further moves in the opening weeks of the war saw No. 504 go to Debden on 9 October (with a detachment to Wattisham) and No. 607 to Acklington on 10 October (with a detachment to Drem).

Details of the individual losses for this initial period of the war, commence overleaf.

Part I

UK Operations – September 1939 to May 1940

6 September 1939

56 Sqn	Hurricane I P/O M L Hulton-Harrop	L1985 +	Patrol. Accidentally attacked and shot down by No. 74 Sqn Spitfires near Ipswich.
56 Sqn	Hurricane I P/O F C Rose	L1980 Safe	As above. Repaired and lost when HMS *Glorious* was sunk on 8 June 1940. See 18 May 1940.

1 October 1939

615 Sqn	Gladiator II P/O J C M Hanbury	N2314 +	Night patrol. Flew into the ground at Holmwood Common, Surrey.

11 January 1940

66 Sqn	Spitfire I Sgt D Stone	N3036 Safe	Damaged by return fire from a He111 of KG26 over North Sea. Written off.

18 January 1940

43 Sqn	Hurricane I Sgt H J Steeley	L1734 +	Collision over convoy patrol. Crashed over Broomhill, Northants. Age 23.
43 Sqn	Hurricane I Sgt E G P Mullinger	L2066 +	As above: age 24. Now buried at Chevington cemetery, Northumberland.

9 February 1940

43 Sqn	Hurricane I F/O M K Carswell	L1744 'A' Safe	Patrol. Crashed into the sea following engine trouble off Coquet Island during combat with He111 – rescued. See 1 June and 2 September 1940.

16 February 1940

79 Sqn	Hurricane I F/O J J Tarlington	L1699 +	Missing from convoy patrol over North Sea. Ditched north of Reculver, Kent. Australian.

21 February 1940

43 Sqn	Hurricane I F/O J W C Simpson	L1729 'S' Safe	Convoy patrol. Crashed on take-off at Acklington. See 19 July 1940.
616 Sqn	Spitfire I F/L A N Wilson	K9810 +	Hit the sea on convoy patrol off Hornsea, North Sea.

22 February 1940

602 Sqn	Spitfire I S/L A D Farquhar	K9962 Safe	Scramble. After combat with He111, pilot landed to secure prisoners and crashed. A/c repaired and put back into service. See 4 September 1940.

28 February 1940

611 Sqn	Spitfire I Sgt A E A Bruce	L1051 +	Convoy patrol. Crashed into the sea near East Dudgeon Lightship.

29 February 1940

152 Sqn	Spitfire I S/L F W C Shute	K9898 +	Scramble. Missing over North Sea, engine failure, c.1530 hrs.

2 April 1940

151 Sqn	Hurricane I P/O H C F Fenton	L1799 +	Convoy patrol. Crashed into sea off the East Coast – pilot drowned.

152 Sqn	Gladiator II ?	N5646 Safe	Ditched off NE coast – engine failure. Pilot rescued, No record in Sqn ORB.
504 Sqn	Hurricane I F/O D Phillips	L1951 Wounded	Convoy patrol. Ditched after combat with He115 over North Sea, c.1400. Pilot wounded in leg and rescued.

3 April 1940

41 Sqn	Spitfire I F/O E N Ryder	N3114 Safe	Scramble. Ditched off Whitby after combat with He111, but rescued. See 27 September 1940 and 31 October 1941.

9 April 1940

229 Sqn	Hurricane I Sgt G L Dent	L1790 +	Convoy patrol. Crashed in sea 25 miles off Grimsby – engine failure. Body recovered; Cavenham cemetery, aged 25.

16 April 1940

43 Sqn	Hurricane I F/O P Folkes	N2550 +	Convoy patrol. Crashed early pm.

11 May 1940

54 Sqn	Spitfire I P/O J D B McKenzie	N3187 +	Scramble 1825. Lost over Channel. NKG. New Zealander, aged 25.

S/L John W Donaldson DSO DFC, OC 263 Sqn, lost in the sinking of HMS *Glorious* on 8 June 1940. Seen here with Joan Sanders, sister of J G Sanders DFC (615 Sqn) and future wife of R P R Powell DFC (111 Sqn).

Part II

Operations over France – September 1939 to May 1940

31 October 1939

| 73 Sqn | Hurricane I
Sgt H G Phillips | ? 'B'
Injured | Patrol. Baled out after being hit by flak over Bouzanville-Saarguemines area am. |

2 November 1939

| 87 Sqn | Hurricane I
P/O C C D Mackworth | ?
Safe | Patrol. Force-landed at Seclin after combat with He111. See 14 May 1940. |

8 November 1939

| 73 Sqn | Hurricane I
P/O R F Martin | L1959
Safe | Patrol. Force-landed on Esch airfield, Luxembourg, after suffering oxygen problems – interned but pilot escaped and returned to France. |
| 73 Sqn | Hurricane I
P/O C Wright | ?
Safe | Hit by French AA whilst chasing a Do17; crash-landed on fire, hood jammed. |

10 November 1939

| 87 Sqn | Hurricane I
P/O H J R Dunn | L1619
Safe | Patrol. Force-landed in Belgium after combat with EA and interned. Pilot escaped 27 November. |

14 November 1939

| 87 Sqn | Hurricane I
F/O R L Glyde | L1628 'O'
Safe | Force-landed in La Panne, Belgium. Interned but escaped 27 November. See 13 August 1940. |
| 87 Sqn | Hurricane I
S/L W E Coope | L1813
Safe | Force-landed at Koksijde, Belgium, and interned but escaped 27 November. See 15 April and 4 June 1941. |

23 November 1939

| 1 Sqn | Hurricane I
F/O C D Palmer | L1925
Safe | Patrol. Crash-landed near Moiremont after combat with Do17. See 2 April and 17 May 1940. |

9 December 1939

| 87 Sqn | Hurricane I
Sgt F V Howell | ?
Safe | Force-landing in Belgium. Pilot managed to get back across the frontier before the police arrived. |

18 December 1939

| 615 Sqn | Gladiator I
P/O S M Wickham | N5582
+ | Escort (for leave boat from Boulogne). Stalled and crashed at St Inglevert; buried at Douai, France. |

22 December 1939

| 73 Sqn | Hurricane I
Sgt R M Perry | N2385
+ | Patrol. Crashed at Altroft in combat with Me109s of III/JG53. Buried at Chambières French National Cemetery, Metz. |
| 73 Sqn | Hurricane I
Sgt J Winn | L1967
+ | Patrol. Crashed Homburg-Budange in same fight. Buried in Metz. |

12 February 1940

| 87 Sqn | Hurricane I
Sgt P F H Thurgar | L1613 'L'
+ | Crashed at Plechatel, France. Cause unknown. Buried Château Renault. |

2 March 1940

1 Sqn	Hurricane I P/O J S Mitchell	L1971 +	Patrol. Shot down in combat near Metz by Do17, *c.*1105. Buried in Chambières French National Cemetery. New Zealand pilot, aged 21.
1 Sqn	Hurricane I F/L H M Brown	L1843 Safe	Damaged by Do17. Crash-landed near Fénétrange. See 20 April 1940.
73 Sqn	Hurricane I F/O E J Kain	L1808 Safe	Patrol. Crash-landed near Metz after combat with Me109. A/c eventually returned to service. See also 26 March 1940.
73 Sqn	Hurricane I Sgt D A Sewell	L1958 Safe	Ditto.

12 March 1940

73 Sqn	Hurricane I P/O L G Bishop	N2364 +	Patrol. Dived into ground neat St Privot, Moselle. Oxygen failure. Canadian with the RAF.
73 Sqn	Hurricane I Sgt L J W Humphris	L1962 Safe	Lost – crashed near Metz.

22 March 1940

73 Sqn	Hurricane I	?	Lost in combat with Me109s near Bouzanville.

26 March 1940

73 Sqn	Hurricane I F/O E J Kain	L1766? Safe	Baled out near Saalautern after combat with III/JG53 (L1766 was written off in a crash 5 October 1940, with 6 OTU). See 2 March and 7 June 1940.

29 March 1940

73 Sqn	Hurricane I P/O J G Perry	P2570* +	Patrol. Shot down near Epiny by Me109 of 9/JG53. Buried at Chambières French National Cemetery, Metz. Aged 22. *According to AM Form 1582.

2 April 1940

1 Sqn	Hurricane I P/O C D Palmer	N2326 Safe	Patrol. Shot down by Werner Mölders of III/JG53 and baled out. See 23 November 1939 and 17 May 1940.

7 April 1940

73 Sqn	Hurricane I F/O G F Brotchie	? Sl/WIA	Baled out after combat with Me109 flown by Wolfgang Lippert, I/JG53.

18 April 1940

85 Sqn	Hurricane I ?	L1637 ?	Crashed in forced-landing and a/c abandoned in May.

20 April 1940

1 Sqn	Hurricane I F/O I G Kilmartin	L1843 Safe	Scramble. Crash-landed near Paris after combat with Ju88. Cat B.

21 April 1940

73 Sqn	Hurricane I P/O P B Walker	? WIA	Combat with JG53 and force-landed severely damaged.
85 Sqn	Hurricane I ?	N2363 ?	Damaged on landing; abandoned May.

23 April 1940

73 Sqn	Hurricane I Sgt C N S Campbell	P2576 Sl/WIA	Patrol. Baled out during combat with JG53. Landed in Luxembourg but managed to get back across border.
73 Sqn	Hurricane I Sgt T B G Pyne	N2391 Sl/WIA	Force-landed west of Merzig after combat with JG53; splinter wounds to one arm and shoulder. See 14 May 1940.

9 May 1940

87 Sqn	Hurricane I P/O H J R Dunn	N2362	Damaged during combat with Do17; injured. Overturned on landing and pilot suffered a cut head.

F/O Les Clisby DFC, 1 Sqn France, killed in action on 14 May 1940.

Part III

Norway – April to June 1940

With the German invasion of Norway on 8/9 April 1940, Dowding was requested to provide a fighter squadron to assist in the defence of Narvik. No. 263 Squadron, equipped with Gloster Gladiator biplane fighters was assigned, and on the 22nd, eighteen pilots and their aircraft were onboard the carrier HMS *Glorious*. She sailed for Norway the following day. Taking off from the carrier's deck and led by a FAA Blackburn Skua, the aircraft landed on the frozen Lake Lesjaskog, about 50 miles south of Åndalsnes. Several days of desperate fighting were to follow – not just with the enemy, but the bitter conditions as well.

Having lost most of its aircraft within a few days, the squadron was re-equipped and set out on a second expedition in May. A second RAF squadron, No. 46, joined the Norwegian campaign via HMS *Glorious* and encountered strong opposition and severe ground conditions but managed to successfully land their Hurricanes on the carrier. HMS *Glorious* and her escorting destroyers HMS *Acasta* and HMS *Ardent* were intercepted by the German battlecruisers *Gneisenau* and *Scharnhorst* on 8 June. The German vessels sunk all three ships with a huge loss of life; only two pilots from No. 46 survived whereas those from No. 263, who also landed on the carrier, were decimated.

25 April 1940

263 Sqn	Gladiator II	?	Patrol. Forced-landed with engine trouble – a/c bombed on the ground *c*.1105 and destroyed.
	Sgt Forrest	Safe	
263 Sqn	Gladiator IIs	N5588, N5589, N5628, N5632, N5634, N5635, N5639, N5641, N5680, N5720, N5915 & poss N5633. Known losses on Lake Lesjaskog, bombed by enemy aircraft. N5628 salvaged and is displayed at RAF Museum, Hendon. N5641 was also salvaged and restored post-war.	

26 April 1940

263 Sqn	Gladiator II P/O M A Craig-Adams	N5647 Safe	Patrol, baled out after engine trouble. Some remains salvaged in May 2002. See 22 May 1940.
263 Sqn	Gladiator II	N5909	Bombed on ground at Åndalsnes.

21 May 1940

263 Sqn	Gladiator II P/O W P Richards	N5697 +	Patrol. Crashed near Torskenfjord in bad weather; buried at Harstad, Norway.
263 Sqn	Gladiator II F/L R L Mills	N5693 Injured	Ditto.

22 May 1940

263 Sqn	Gladiator II P/O M A Craig-Adams	N5719 +	Shot down south of Søvegan in combat with He111 of 5/KG26, *c*.1045. Body recovered in 1946 and buried in Narvik cemetery. See 26 April 1940.
263 Sqn	Gladiator II Sgt B E P Whall	N5698 Safe	Baled out west of Harstad after combat with Do17, *c*.1645. See 18 August and 7 October 1940.

26 May 1940

263 Sqn	Gladiator II	N5705 N5714	Damaged and abandoned at Bodo and Bardufoss.

27 May 1940

263 Sqn	Gladiator II F/L C B Hull	? WIA	Crashed after combat with Ju87s and Me110s near Bodøhalvøya, 0830. See 7 September 1940.
263 Sqn	Gladiator II Lt A Lydekker FAA	? WIA	Force-landed following combat 0830, and later written off.

16

29 May 1940

46 Sqn	Hurricane I P/O J F Drummond	L1988 Safe	Baled out after combat with bombers at 0305 (Arctic daylight). See 10 October 1940.
46 Sqn	Hurricane I F/O J W Lydall	L1816 +	Shot down in combat with He111s near Beisfjord. Buried Narvik.
46 Sqn	Hurricane I P/O N L Banks	L1794 +	Ditto.

2 June 1940

46 Sqn	Hurricane I ?	N2543 Safe	Abandoned after undercarriage collapsed on landing at Skaanland.
263 Sqn	Gladiator II P/O J L Wilkie	N5893 +	Shot down in combat with Me110 flown by Helmut Lent, ZG76, east of Rombaksfjord, pm. Buried at Narvik. New Zealand pilot, aged 20, born in Australia.

8 June 1940 — The following aircraft and pilots were lost in the sinking of HMS *Glorious*.

46 Sqn   F/L C R D Stewart   F/O R M J Cowles   F/O P J Frost
F/O H H Knight   F/O M C F Mee   P/O L G B Bunker
Sgt E Shackley   Sgt B L Taylor

Hurricane Is   L1793, L1804, L1805, L1806, L1815, L1853, L1961, L1980, P2632, P2633

263 Sqn   S/L J W Donaldson DSO DFC
F/L A T Williams   F/O H T Grant-Ede DFC   F/O H F Vickery (NZ)
F/O L R Jacobsen   F/O S R McNamara   P/O J Falkson
P/O P H Purdy DFC   P/O M A Bentley   Sgt E F W Russell

Gladiator IIs   N5681, N5695, N5699, N5723, N5906, N5907, N5908

Other 263 Squadron Gladiator II losses in Norway:
N5720, N5725, N5894, N5898, N5904, N5905

Hurricane of 73 Sqn in France, its serial number, P2541, chalked on the propeller blade. This was one of dozens of aircraft lost or abandoned in France during the retreat.

Chapter 2

The Battle of France – 10 to 20 May 1940

Once again, due to the nature of the operations, withdrawals and retreat, it has not been possible to identify all aircraft and pilot losses. A number of records were destroyed or lost in the final evacuation. It has been possible to establish a list of 'lost' Hurricanes from those known to have been despatched to France and did not return, often without further details recorded. The Hurricanes that were recorded as lost or abandoned in France do not signify a particular pilot loss.

As soon as the German *Blitzkrieg* was unleashed, Fighter Command was asked to send reinforcements into the battle zone. Dowding knew full well that if he sent his precious fighters away from the defence of the mainland, when it came to the Battle of Britain, his fighting strength could have been seriously compromised. Nonetheless, Dowding was overruled. In an attempt to keep a nucleus of each squadron in England, he only allowed individual flights to leave for France. Once the flights had been united, they were to form a squadron formation in France; this did not work well as pilots in their composite squadrons were unfamiliar with each other and did not benefit from their previous collaboration.

In all, some 452 Hurricanes were sent to France (Dowding absolutely refused permission for Spitfires to operate from France). Of this number only 66 returned to Britain. Of the 386 known to have been lost in France, no fewer than 178 were abandoned or destroyed through lack of repair. Of this number, the Air Component lost 203 Hurricanes between 10 to 20 May, but only some 75 to direct combat actions.

10 May 1940

1 Sqn	Hurricane I F/L P R Walker	N2382 'B' Safe	Patrol. Force-landed east of Verdun after combat with Do17 of III/KG2, 0530 am.
1 Sqn	Hurricane I F/O R L Lorimer	L1689 Safe	Patrol. Baled out after being hit by return fire from He111 of KG53. See 13 and 14 May 1940.
1 Sqn	Hurricane I F/O P H M Richey	L1679 'G' Safe	Patrol. Damaged in combat; force-landed at Mezières airfield and a/c destroyed by bombing on 14 May. See 11, 15 and 19 May 1940.
3 Sqn	Hurricane I F/O R B Lines-Roberts	L1923 Safe	Patrol. Crashed during forced-landing after combat with He111s near Fieffe. See 13 May 1940.
3 Sqn	Hurricane I F/O A R Ball	N2333 Safe	Patrol. Lost in darkness, headed for England and baled out near Dover.
73 Sqn	Hurricane I F/O N Orton	N2318 Safe	Patrol. Crash-landed near Conflans-en-Jarnisy after combat with Do17.
73 Sqn	Hurricane I F/L R E Lovett	P2804 Wounded	Patrol. Hit by return fire from Do17 of I/KG2 near Conflans. Force-landed on fire and exploded. See 5 and 7 September 1940.
85 Sqn	Hurricane I P/O D V G Mawhood	'VY-S' Injured	Hit by return fire from Ju88 of 8/LG1 and force-landed. Possibly L1779.
501 Sqn	Hurricane I F/O A B Angus	N2472 Safe	Patrol. Force-landed after combat with Ju88, Celles-Edcanaf area; a/c abandoned. See 16 May 1940.
607 Sqn	Hurricane I F/L J Sample	P2615 Safe	Patrol. Baled out attacking He111s of KG1 over Albert.
607 Sqn	Hurricane I F/O R F Weatherill	P2574 'G' Safe	Patrol. Force-landed after attack on He111 of KG27 – abandoned? See 18 May 1940.

No. 600 Squadron was part of Fighter Command, and on the first day of the *Blitzkrieg*, six of their Blenheim fighters were ordered to attack German aircraft that had either landed on the Dutch airfield at Waalhaven or found flying over Rotterdam. They were engaged by Me110 fighters from 3/ZG1 led by Hptm Werner Streib and five were shot down.

600 Sqn	Blenheim If S/L J M Wells Sgt J Davies Cpl B A Kidd	L6616 'R' + Evaded +	Shot down on attack against airfield at Waalhaven, Holland. NKG. Buried Rotterdam, aged 30.
600 Sqn	Blenheim If P/O R C Haine P/O M Kramer	L1517 'N' Evaded Evaded	Ditto. Crash-landed on coast near to Goeree-Overflakee.
600 Sqn	Blenheim If F/L J H C Rowe P/O R W H Echlin RCAF	L1401 'K' PoW +	Ditto. Stalag Luft III. Canadian. Buried Piershil, Protestant C/Yard, aged 36.
600 Sqn	Blenheim If F/O C R Moore Cpl L D Isaacs	L1335 'W' + +	Ditto. Both buried Rotterdam; Isaacs was aged 20.
600 Sqn	Blenheim If P/O M H Anderson LAC H C W Hawkins	L1515 'L' + +	Ditto. Both buried Spijkenisse; Anderson was aged 23.
600 Sqn	Blenheim If P/O T N Hayes Cpl G H Holmes	L1514 'O' Safe Safe	Ditto. Badly shot-up but returned to base.

11 May 1940

1 Sqn	Hurricane I F/O P H M Richey	L1685 Safe	Patrol. Shot down by Me110 – baled out, 1915 hrs. See 10, 15 and 19 May 1940.
17 Sqn	Hurricane I P/O O P DeL Hulton-Harrop	N2407 'N' PoW	Patrol. Shot down by Me109 of JG51, and baled out near Dordrecht.
17 Sqn	Hurricane I S/L G C Tomlinson	N2547 Safe	Patrol. Shot down by Me109 near the Hague; evaded and returned to UK. See 17 May 1940.
17 Sqn	Hurricane I F/L M S Donne	N2403 +	Patrol. Shot down by Me109 near Ypres and buried at Numansdorp, Netherlands. Aged 23.
17 Sqn	Hurricane I Sgt J A A Luck	P2758 PoW	Patrol. Shot down by Me109 of JG51 near Dordrecht. Kopernikus camp.
17 Sqn	Hurricane I P/O G W Slee	N2405 'Y' +	Patrol. Shot down by Me109 of JG51. Buried Gravendaal, Netherlands.
73 Sqn	Hurricane I P/O A McFadden	P2811 Safe	Shot down by Me110 of I/ZG2 and force-landed near Poilcourt. See 14 May 1940.
79 Sqn	Hurricane I F/L R Edwards	L2068 Injured	Patrol. Baled out near Mons during attack on He111; burn injuries.
79 Sqn	Hurricane I P/O L L Appleton	L2049 Safe	Damaged by return fire from He111 of KG1, force-landed at Le Touquet.
85 Sqn	Hurricane I F/L R H A Lee	N2388 'R' Safe	Patrol. Baled out after combat with Do17 near Maastricht. Escaped after capture and returned to unit. See 17 May and 18 August 1940.
85 Sqn	Hurricane I P/O J A Hemingway	L1979 'Y' Safe	Patrol. Crash-landed near Maastricht after flak hit. A/c abandoned, pm. See 18 and 26 August 1940.
607 Sqn	Hurricane I P/O P Dixon	P2573 'A' Safe	Patrol. Force-landed on French A/F out of fuel and destroyed on ground by bombing on 12 May.
607 Sqn	Hurricane I P/O T D Jay	P2571 Wounded	Damaged by return fire from He111 of I/LG1 and a/c written off.

12 May 1940

1 Sqn	Hurricane I F/O R G Lewis	L1688 Safe	Escort. Baled out after combat with Me109s of JG27 near Maastricht.
1 Sqn	Hurricane I S/L P J H Halahan	L1671 Safe	Escort. Crash-landed in Belgium after combat; A/c abandoned.
79 Sqn	Hurricane I P/O C T Parker	L2065 Safe	Patrol. Baled out after combat with Do17 of KG77; evaded through lines. See 20 May 1940.
87 Sqn	Hurricane I F/O J A Campbell DFC	L1970 +	Patrol. Shot down by Me109 of JG27 near Maastricht. Canadian, aged 27. Buried near Maastricht.
87 Sqn	Hurricane I Sgt F V Howell	L1632 Safe	Patrol. Baled out after combat with JG27 near Maastricht.
501 Sqn	Hurricane I F/O P H Rayner	L2054 'E' +	Patrol. Shot down in combat with He111s near Beauvilliers. Buried at Seuil, France. Aged 27.
501 Sqn	Hurricane I F/L E Holden	L2050 Safe	Patrol. Crash-landed after combat with Do17 of 3(F)/123 near Reims. Believed to have been abandoned.
501 Sqn	Hurricane I F/O M F C Smith	L2053 +	Shot down by Me110 of ZG2 near Mezières. Choloy War Cemetery, aged 27.
501 Sqn	Hurricane I F/O C E Malfroy	L1914 Safe	Shot down by Me110 of ZG2, crash-landed near Mezières. Abandoned. New Zealander.
607 Sqn	Hurricane I F/O W E Gore	P2572 'B' Injured	Patrol. Baled out after combat with of 4/LG1. See 28 September 1940.
615 Sqn	Hurricane I F/O L Fredman	P2564 +	Patrol. Shot down by Me109 near Liege. Buried Wihogne churchyard, Belgium. Aged 22.

Group of 79 Sqn pilots in France 1940 with French pilots (L to R): P/O L L Appleton, KIA 14 May, P/O J E R Wood, KIA 8 July, F/O D W A Stones (DFC*), F/Lt E J Davies DFC, KIA 27 June.

13 May 1940

1 Sqn	Hurricane I F/O L R Clisby DFC	L1694 'F' Safe	Patrol. Damaged upon landing to secure crew of He111. Landed near bomber and chased crew on foot! Hurricane abandoned. SE of Vouzières, 0640; A/c abandoned. See 14 May 1940.
1 Sqn	Hurricane I F/O R L Lorimer	L1681 Safe	Patrol. Force-landed between St Loupe-Terria after combat with He111s and written-off. See 10 and 14 May 1940.
1 Sqn	Hurricane I F/O B Drake	'P' Wounded	Baled out after combat with Me110 near Rethal.
3 Sqn	Hurricane I F/O A R Ball	L1901 DoW	Patrol. Crash-landed after fight with Do17 near Wavre. Captured but died of wounds 6th July 1940. See 10 May 1940.
3 Sqn	Hurricane I F/O R B Lines-Roberts	N2653 +	Patrol. Collided with N2654 returning from patrol: both exploded, 1800 hrs. Buried Cité Bonjean Military Cemetery, aged 23. See 10 May 1940.
3 Sqn	Hurricane I F/O W S C Adams	N2654 +	Ditto. Aged 33.
17 Sqn	Hurricanes N3403, N2454, N2405 and N2407 all lost or abandoned on this date.		
66 Sqn	Spitfire I F/O Brown	N3027 Evaded	Escort. Force-landed at La Zoute (Knokke-Het-Zoute), Belgium.
73 Sqn	Hurricane I P/O R A Marchand	L1673 Injured	Patrol. Crash-landed near Bétheniville after combat with Do17 and Me110s – believed abandoned. See 15 September 1940.
85 Sqn	Hurricane I S/L J O W Oliver	P2821 Safe	Patrol. Baled out after combat with Me109 of 8/JG3 over Belgium.
87 Sqn	Hurricane I Sgt F V Howell	L1930 Sl/WIA	Patrol. Shot down by Me109 and baled out. Rejoined unit 18 May. See 9 December 1939.
87 Sqn	Hurricane I ?	L1979 ?	Patrol. Shot down by Me109 near Hazebrouck.

Pilots of 1 Squadron (France) scramble for the camera (L to R): P/O B Drake (DSO DFC), F/O R L Lorimer, KIA 13 May, F/O C D Palmer, KIA 27 October 1942, F/O P P Hanks (DFC) and Les Clisby, KIA 15 May.

264 Sqn	Defiant I P/O Thomas LAC J S M Bromley	L6958 Evaded +	Patrol. Damaged by Me109 and crashed at Biesbosch, south of Rotterdam.
264 Sqn	Defiant I P/O G E Chandler LAC D L McLeish	L6960 + +	Ditto. Shot down south of Rotterdam. Buried Made-en-Drimmelen, Holland. Buried Werkendam. Both aged 20.
264 Sqn	Defiant I F/L A E Skelton P/O Hatfield	L6969 'T' PoW Evaded	Ditto. Stalag Luft III.
264 Sqn	Defiant I P/O P E J Greenhous LAC F D Greenhalgh	L6977 PoW PoW	Shot down over Dunkirk area. Stalag Luft III. Lamsdorf camp.
264 Sqn	Defiant I P/O McLeod LAC W E Cox	L6965 Evaded Evaded	Crashed at Zevenbergen.
607 Sqn	Hurricane I Sgt K N V Townsend	P2616 PoW	Patrol. Shot down near Louvain while in combat with Me109s.
615 Sqn	Hurricane I F/O P N Murton-Neale	L2035 +	Escort. Shot down by Me110 of ZG1 near Namur. Buried Courrière, SE of Namur, aged 23. CWGR notes death as 14 May.

14 May 1940

1 Sqn	Hurricane I F/L P P Hanks	N2380 'S' Safe	Patrol. Baled out after combat with Me110 of ZG26 over Sedan. Crashed at St Remy le Petit.
1 Sqn	Hurricane I F/O R L Lorimer	L1676 +	Shot down by Me110 at Sedan. See 10 and 13 May 1940.
1 Sqn	Hurricane I F/O L R Clisby DFC	P2546 +	Shot down by Me110 at Sedan, 0800. Buried Choley, France, aged 25. See 13 May 1940.
3 Sqn	Hurricane I P/O F R Carey DFM	L1932 Wounded	Shot down in combat with Do17 of 3(F)/11, crash-landed and returned to safety.
3 Sqn	Hurricane I Sgt D A Allen	L1591 +	Shot down in combat with Ju87s near Sedan. Buried Villers-Cerney, aged 20.
3 Sqn	Hurricane I P/O M M Stephens	N2546 Safe	Force-landed after combat, A/c assumed abandoned. S of Annelles.
3 Sqn	Hurricane I P/O C G StD Jeffries	L1908 Safe	Baled out near Sedan after combat with Me110s.
73 Sqn	Hurricane I Sgt T B G Pyne	P2812 +	Shot down near Namur by Me109 of JG52. Baled out but killed. Buried Choley, France, aged 24. See 23 April 1940.
73 Sqn	Hurricane I P/O V D M Roe	P2813 +	Shot down in combat with Me109s near Namur. Buried Choley, France. Aged 28.
73 Sqn	Hurricane I Sgt L G M Dibden	P2689 +	Shot down by Me109 near Sean, 1530. Buried at Choley, France. Aged 21.
73 Sqn	Hurricane I P/O A McFadden	L1891 Safe	Shot down by Do17 of KG76; crash-landed and lost. See 11 May 1940.
79 Sqn	Hurricane I P/O L L Appleton	P2537 +	Shot down in combat with Ju88 near Renaix, pm.
79 Sqn	Hurricane I P/O J E R Wood	N2490 Injured	Baled out after combat with Ju88 N of Leuze. See 8 July 1940.
87 Sqn	Hurricane I P/O P L Jarvis	L1616 +	Shot down in combat with He111s west of Maastricht, 0900.

87 Sqn	Hurricane I F/O E P Joyce	L1646 Wounded	Shot down in combat with Me110 S of Brussels, 1900. Leg amputated.
87 Sqn	Hurricane I P/O C C D Mackworth	L1834 +	Baled out after combat with Me110s – parachute caught fire. Buried at Bruyelle, Belgium. Aged 21. See 2 November 1939.
87 Sqn	Hurricane I P/O G C Saunders	L1612 DoW	Shot down by Me110 near Mainrault; died of wounds 19 May. Aged 23. New Zealander.
242 Sqn	Hurricane I F/L J L Sullivan	P2621 +	Shot down in combat with Hs123 of II(s)/LG2, near Gorrey-le-Château. Buried at Perwez, Belgium.
504 Sqn	Hurricane I P/O S A C Sibley	L1941 +	Shot down by flak near Brussels, 1230 pm.
504 Sqn	Hurricane I S/L J B Parnall	L1639 +	Shot down in combat with He111s near Louvignies, 1230. Aged 34. Buried Chaussee-notre-Dame-Louvignies, Belgium.
504 Sqn	Hurricane I F/O M E A Royce	L1950 Safe	Baled out after combat with Me110 near Louvignies.
504 Sqn	Hurricane I Sgt S Hamblett	N2492 +	Shot down by Me110 near Ath, Belgium.
504 Sqn	Hurricane I P/O B E G White	L1916 Safe	Damaged by Me109 of JG26 and written off after crash-landing.
607 Sqn	Hurricane I F/O G I Cuthbert	P2618 +	Shot down by Me109 of JG2 near Louvain, 0900. Buried Hotton, Luxembourg. Aged 28.
607 Sqn	Hurricane I F/O M H B Thompson	P2620 +	Shot down by Me109 of JG2 near Louvain. Buried Heverlee, Belgium.
607 Sqn	Hurricane I F/O A E Le Breuilly	P2713 +	Shot down by Me109 of JG2 near Gorrey-le-Château.

15 May 1940

1 Sqn	Hurricane I F/L P R Walker	L1681 Safe	Shot down by Me110 near Vouzières, crash-landed and written off. ZG26.
1 Sqn	Hurricane I F/O P H M Richey	L1943 Safe	Baled out after combat with Me110s of ZG26 near St-Hilaire-le-Grand. See 10, 11 and 19 May 1940.
3 Sqn	Hurricane I S/L P Gifford DFC	L1610 Safe	Force-landed near Wevelghem and abandoned. See 16 May 1940.
3 Sqn	Hurricane I Sgt J L C Williams	L1645 +	Shot down by Me109 of III/JG26, near Dinant. 1240 hrs.
3 Sqn	Hurricane I F/L M M Carter DFC	N2534 +	Shot down by Me110 of II/ZG76 near Vouzières. Buried Mauberge-Centre, France, aged 27.
3 Sqn	Hurricane I P/O N D Hallifax	N2422 PoW	Shot down in combat with Me110s of II/ZG76 near Zeebrugge.
73 Sqn	Hurricane I F/O N Orton	P2579 Wounded	Baled out after combat with Me110s of ZG2. See 10 May 1940 and 17 September 1941.
73 Sqn	Hurricane I Sgt L J Humphries	L1693 Wounded	Baled out after combat with Me110s of ZG2, west of Vouzières.
85 Sqn	Hurricane I F/O D H Allen DFC	P2828 Safe	Baled out after combat with Me110s of 5/ZG26 east of Ath, Belgium.
85 Sqn	Hurricane I F/O T G Pace	L1694 Injured	Crashed-landed and burned after combat with Me110s of ZG26 east of Ath. Pilot suffered burns.

85 Sqn	Hurricane I P/O J H Ashton	L1775 Safe	Baled out south of Ath after combat with Me110s of ZG26. See 27 May 1940.
87 Sqn	Hurricane I F/O T J Edwards	P2538 +	Shot down by Me110 of II/ZG76 south of Lille, 1845. NKG, aged 25.
607 Sqn	Hurricane I S/L L E Smith	P2870 +	Shot down by Me109s/AA fire, am. Possibly JG53. NKG. Aged 31.
607 Sqn	Hurricane I F/O I B N Russell	P2619 'D' Wounded	Crash-landed 1630, after combat with He111 of 9/KG51 – aircraft was abandoned. See 1 June 1940.
615 Sqn	Hurricane I F/O H N Fowler	P2622 PoW	Baled out in combat with Me109s of JG53, Dinant-Ardennes area. Escaped and returned to England.
615 Sqn	Hurricane I P/O D J Looker	P2554 Wounded	Baled out near Waterloo after hit by ground fire. See 18 August 1940.

16 May 1940

3 Sqn	Hurricane I S/L P Gifford DFC	P2825 +	Shot down in combat with Me110s of ZG1. NKG, aged 30. See 15 May 1940.
85 Sqn	Hurricane I Sgt L A Crozier	N2389 Injured	Baled out after combat with Me109 of 5/JG2 near Lille and badly burned.
85 Sqn	Hurricane I P/O M H G Rawlinson	P2535 +	Shot down in combat with Me109s of JG27. Buried Quievrain, Belgium.
85 Sqn	Hurricane I P/O H D Clark	P2824 Wounded	Crash-landed after combat with 109s of 3/JG76.
85 Sqn	Hurricane I Sgt H H Allgood	L1898 Wounded	Crash-landed after combat with 109s of 5/JG2, north-west of Lille.
85 Sqn	Hurricane I F/O M B Czernin	L1640 Safe	Crash-landed after combat with 109s of 3/JG76, 1730 pm. Abandoned. See 17 November 1940.
85 Sqn	Hurricane I F/O A B Angus DFC	L1641 +	Shot down by Me109 of JG27 SW of Lille. Buried at Fretin, France, aged 22. See 10 May 1940.
87 Sqn	Hurricane I Sgt G L Nowell	L1614 Safe	Crash-landed after combat with Do17 – abandoned. See 23 May 1940.
87 Sqn	Hurricane I Sgt A N Trice	L2000 +	Shot down by Me109 west of Mons.
615 Sqn	Hurricane I F/L L T W Thornley	N2335 +	Shot down by Me109 near Tirlemont.
615 Sqn	Hurricane I P/O T C Jackson	N2338 PoW	Ditto – baled out. Stalag Luft III camp.
615 Sqn	Hurricane I P/O B P Young	P2577 Wounded	Shot down by Me109 near Brussels and baled out badly burned.

17 May 1940

1 Sqn	Hurricane I F/O C D Palmer	P2820 Safe	Baled out in combat with Me110s of V(Z)/LG1 near Reims, 0900. See 23 November 1939.
1 Sqn	Hurricane I Sgt F J Soper	L1905 'H' Safe	Shot down by Me110 of LG1 and damaged beyond repair. See 19 May 1940 and 5 October 1941.
3 Sqn	Hurricane I F/O D A E Jones	L1609 Safe	Baled out after combat with Do17 of 5/KG76 near Merville, 1730.
3 Sqn	Hurricane I Sgt P Hillwood	L1899 Injured	Crash-landed Vitry after combat with Do17 of 5/KG76 near Cambrai and Me109 of 1/JG3. Aircraft burned.

Pilots of 17 Squadron, France 1940 (L to R): F/O W J Harper, P/O R C Whittaker (DFC) KIA 7 June 1940, Hunter, F/O R V Meredith, KIA 3 June, F/O J Jefferies (DFC) KIA 15 April 1943, P/Off K Manger (DFC), KIA 11 August 1940.

17 Sqn	Hurricane I S/L G C Tomlinson	P3277 Safe	Force-landed 1630 SE of Brussels after combat with Ju87s of IV(S)/LG1 and set on fire. Slightly injured.
17 Sqn	Hurricane I F/O A P Lines	P2822 Safe	Baled out after combat with Me109 of 8/JG26 south of Brussels.
79 Sqn	Hurricane I F/O R Herrick	L2140 PoW	Shot down by Me109 of 6/JG52 and baled out near Valenciennes. Stalag Luft III prison camp.
85 Sqn	Hurricane I P/O P P Woods-Scawen	N2319 Sl/WIA	Baled out 1600 after combat with Me109s of 1/JG3 east of Lille. See 19 May and 1 September 1940.
245 Sqn	Hurricane I P/O J S Southwell	N2501 Safe	Crash-landed near Pottignes after combat with Me109 of 8/JG26, 1900.
245 Sqn	Hurricane I Sgt R W E Jarrett	N2702 Safe	Lost course after combat with Me109 and crashed near Dieppe.
615 Sqn	Hurricane I P/O M Ravenhill	P2907 Safe	Force-landed 0545 after combat with Hs126 – out of fuel. Abandoned.

18 May 1940

1 Sqn	Hurricane I Sgt R A Albonico	L1856 PoW	Shot down by ground fire near St Quentin, 1530 hrs. Kopernikus camp.

1 Sqn	Hurricane I P/O C M Stavert	N2353 Safe	Force-landed near Condé-Vraux after combat and out of fuel. Abandoned.
3 Sqn	Hurricane I P/O P M Gardner	N2464 Safe	Force-landed south of Douai after combat with Do17 of 2/KG76. Burnt by pilot.
56 Sqn	Hurricane I F/O F C Rose	N2439 +	Shot down by Me110 of I/ZG26 near Brebières, 1530. See 6 September 1939.
56 Sqn	Hurricane I F/L I S Soden DSO	N2437 +	Shot down near Vitry by Me110 of ZG76, 1800. Buried Biache-St-Vaast, France. Aged 23.
56 Sqn	Hurricane I P/O F B Sutton	N2553 'L' Sl/WIA	Destroyed after force-landing after combat with Me109 of JG26. Vitry.
79 Sqn	Hurricane I P/O D W A Stones	P3451 Safe	Force-landed after combat with Me110 of II/ZG76, near Vitry, 1830.
85 Sqn	Hurricane I F/O D H Allen DFC	P2701 +	Shot down in combat with Me110s of ZG26, 0700. NKG, aged 22.
85 Sqn	Hurricane I F/O W N Lepine	N2425 PoW	Baled out wounded in fight with Me110s of I/ZG76 near Cambrai.
111 Sqn	Hurricane I Sgt J T Craig	L1607 Safe	Abandoned after crash-landing; hit by Me110 of I/ZG76 S of Mons, 1525. See 31 August 1940.
111 Sqn	Hurricane I F/L C S Darwood	L2051 +	Shot down by Me109 of JG26 S of Mons. Buried Longuenesse Souvenir Cemetery, St Omer. Aged 26.
145 Sqn	Hurricane I P/O M A Newling	N2600 Safe	Baled out after combat with He111 of KG4 near Brussels, 1625. See 6 July 1941.
151 Sqn	Hurricane I Sgt G Atkinson	L1850 Safe	Damaged by Me110 of II/ZG76 and force-landed near Vitry. Abandoned.
151 Sqn	Hurricane I F/O R M Milne	L1755 Safe	Ditto.
229 Sqn	Hurricane I P/O M A Bussey	P2729 PoW	Shot down by Me109 of II/JG2 west of Brussels. Stalag Luft III camp.
229 Sqn	Hurricane I P/O D deC C Gower	P2676 Safe	Baled out during combat with Me109s of II/JG2 west of Brussels, 1045.
229 Sqn	Hurricane I P/O A M Dillon	L1802 +	Shot down by Me109 of II/JG26 near Mons. Buried Bergen, Mons. Aged 18.
229 Sqn	Hurricane I F/L F E Rosier	L2142 Injured	Aircraft exploded in combat with 109s of II/JG26. Baled out but burned.
242 Sqn	Hurricane I P/O R H Weins	L1665 Injured	Crashed after combat with Me110s of I/ZG26 near Cambrai – written off.
242 Sqn	Hurricane I P/O M K Brown	N2320 Wounded	Baled out during combat with Me110s of I/ZG26. Wounded in right leg.
242 Sqn	Hurricane I F/O L E Chambers	L1922 PoW	Baled out with burns during combat with Me110s of I/ZG26. Stalag Luft III.
253 Sqn	Hurricane I P/O J T Strang	P2761 Safe	Force-landed after combat with 110s of II/ZG26, near Vitry, 1600. New Zealander with RAF.
253 Sqn	Hurricane I Sgt R A Brackley	L1655 Safe	Force-landed after combat with 109 of II/JG26 near Vitry pm. Abandoned.
253 Sqn	Hurricane I P/O D B Bell-Salter	N2545 Safe	Force-landed Vitry after combat with Me109s of II/JG26. Abandoned.
253 Sqn	Hurricane I P/O J D Ford	L1611 Safe	Baled out in combat with He111s of II/KG1. See 23 May 1940.

504 Sqn	Hurricane I F/L J S Owen	L1912 +	Baled out in combat with Me109s of I(J)/LG1 but killed in his parachute. 2100 hrs. Buried Cambrai, aged 25.
504 Sqn	Hurricane I P/O R J B Renison	L1944 PoW	Baled out during combat with Me109s of I(J)/LG north-east of Mons. Stalag Luft III prison camp.
601 Sqn	Hurricane I F/L Sir A P Hope	L2141 Safe	Force-landed near Grevillers after combat with Do17 of 2/KG76.
601 Sqn	Hurricane I S/L T L E B Guinness	L2034 Safe	Damaged in combat with He111 of KG4; left abandoned at Merville.
607 Sqn	Hurricane I F/O R F Weatherill	P2536 'R' +	Shot down by Me109 near Cambrai by Me109 of 2/JG51. Buried Cambrai, aged 24. See 10 May 1940.
607 Sqn	Hurricane I P/O A S Dini	P2797 Safe	Damaged by Me109 of II/JG26 and abandoned after crash-landing at Vitry.
607 Sqn	Hurricane I S/L W F Blackadder	P2873 Safe	Force-landed Vitry after damaged in combat with Do17 of II/KG76 and abandoned.

19 May 1940

1 Sqn	Hurricane I F/O P H M Richey	? Wounded	Baled out wounded during combat with He111s of KG27 near Château-Thierry. See 10, 11 and 15 May.
1 Sqn	Hurricane I Sgt F J Soper	L1925 Safe	Force-landed after combat with He111 of KG27 and abandoned. Also see 17 May 1940 and 5 October 1941.
3 Sqn	Hurricane I P/O J Rose	? Safe	Shot down by Me109 of I/JG/77 near Seclin and abandoned. See 25 Aug 1940.
17 Sqn	Hurricane I P/O R E Harris	N2408 +	Shot down by Me109 of LG2 near Le Cateau, 1620. Buried Noyelles sur Selle, aged 22.
17 Sqn	Hurricane I Sgt A F Pavey	N2525 PoW	Shot down by Me109 of LG2 and baled out near Cambrai.
32 Sqn	Hurricane I F/O J C Milner	N2462 PoW	Baled out after combat with Me109 of I/JG2 near Le Cateau, midday.
73 Sqn	Hurricane I P/O N C Langham-Hobart	P2543 Safe	Crash-landed after combat with Me110 of V(Z)/LG1 am and written off.
73 Sqn	Hurricane I P/O J E P Thompson	N2385 Safe	Crash-landed after combat with Me110s of V(Z)/LG1 south-east of Paris am and abandoned.
73 Sqn	Hurricane I Sgt L S Pilkington	P2539 Safe	Damaged by bomber's return fire and force-landed at base. Abandoned.
85 Sqn	Hurricane I Sgt J McG Little	P2562 +	Shot down by Me109 of 1/JG2 near Lille, 1200 hrs.
85 Sqn	Hurricane I P/O P P Woods-Scawen	P2547 Safe	Baled out after combat with Me109s of 2/JG77 near Lille. See 17 May and 1 September 1940.
85 Sqn	Hurricane I S/L M F Peacock	P2551 Safe	Baled out after combat with He111s of 6/KG4 near Seclin, 1630.
87 Sqn	Hurricane I F/O J M Strickland	P2687 Wounded	Baled out after combat with Me109 but wounded by a French bullet, am.
87 Sqn	Hurricane I P/O H J L Dunn	L1620 Injured	Baled out with slight burns after fight with Me109 of II/JG2, near Orchies.
87 Sqn	Hurricane I F/O R M S Rayner	P2683 Safe	Force-landed near Lille after combat with Me109 of JG77 – abandoned.
111 Sqn	Hurricane I S/L J M Thompson	L1733 Safe	Crash-landed after combat with Me110s of II/ZG76 nr Doullens. Abandoned.

111 Sqn	Hurricane I P/O D S H Bury	L1774 +	Shot down by fighter west of Arras. Buried Chili Trench, Gavrelle, aged 25
111 Sqn	Hurricane I P/O I C Moorwood	L1720 +	Shot down by fighter SE of Arras. Buried Sains-les-Marquion, aged 21.
145 Sqn	Hurricane I P/O K R Lucas	N2598 +	Shot down by Me109 of 3/JG27 near Arras, pm. Buried Warloy-Baillon.
213 Sqn	Hurricane I P/O L G B Stone	N2538 Safe	Force-landed, hit by French AA fire near Lille pm – A/c abandoned.
242 Sqn	Hurricane I F/O J C Milner	P2808 Safe	Force-landed after combat with 109 of 1/JG2 near Lille – abandoned.
253 Sqn	Hurricane I P/O F W Ratford	N2542 +	Shot down by Me109 of I/JG3, S of Arras pm. Buried Reincourt-les-Cagnicourt, France.
253 Sqn	Hurricane I F/L H T J Anderson	L1674 +	Shot down near Lille by Me109 of I/JG3. Buried Lille Southern Cem.
253 Sqn	Hurricane I Sgt G Mackenzie	L1667 +	Shot down by Me109 of I/JG3 near Lille. Buried Cysoing, aged 23.
504 Sqn	Hurricane I P/O J R Hardacre	P3555 Safe	Baled out after combat with Me109 of LG2 near Lille am. See 30 September 1940.
504 Sqn	Hurricane I S/L J H Hill	P3551 Wounded	Baled out after combat with LG2 near Lille. Survived assault by French civilians.
504 Sqn	Hurricane I Sgt M V Mapletoft	N2355 Wounded	Baled out after combat with Me109 of 1/JG2 west of Lille.
601 Sqn	Hurricane I F/O G N S Cleaver	P2800 Safe	Crash-landed due to debris damage in combat, 1100 – A/c abandoned. See 15 August 1940.

Hurricane L1679 of 1 Squadron, flown by F/O P H M Richey DFC. **Damaged in combat on 10 May, it was destroyed by bombing on the 14th.**

S/L A L Franks AFC, OC 610 Squadron, killed over Dunkirk on 29 May 1940. On the right is F/L A T Smith, also of 610, who died trying to land his damaged Spitfire at Hawkinge on 25 July.

601 Sqn	Hurricane I F/O T E Hubbard	P2684 Safe	Force-landed after combat with He111 near Boyelles, S of Arras. Pilot set fire to a/c. See 7 June 1940.
601 Sqn	Hurricane I F/O H J Riddle	L2081 Safe	Crash-landed after combat with Me110 II/ZG26. Abandoned. See 21 May 1940.
607 Sqn	Hurricane I S/L G M Fidler	P3535 'P' +	Shot down in combat with Me109 of LG2 pm. Buried Bachy, aged 27.
615 Sqn	Hurricane I F/O R D Pexton	N2331 Wounded	Baled out north of Cambrai after fight with Me109s of 9/JG26 east of Arras.

20 May 1940

32 Sqn	Hurricane I Sgt G North	N2583 Safe	Crash-landed SE Arras after being hit by Hs126 of 3(H)/41; A/C burnt out – 1830 hrs.
79 Sqn	Hurricane I P/O T C Parker	P2634 Safe	Shot down by ground fire over St Quentin while strafing, 1400. A/C abandoned. See 12 May 1940.
79 Sqn	Hurricane I P/O L R Dorrien-Smith	L2145 +	Shot down during ground strafe near St Quentin, 1400 hrs. NKG, aged 21.
85 Sqn	Hurricane I Sgt H N Howes	P2555 Safe	Shot down by Me110 of ZG26 and crash-landed and abandoned near Abbeville, 0930.
85 Sqn	Hurricane I S/L M F Peacock DFC	L2141 +	Ground attack. Shot down by flak along Arras road. Buried in Arras. Aged 28. See 19 May 1940.

85 Sqn	Hurricane I P/O R W Shrewsbury	P3426 +	Shot down by ground fire over Arras road pm. Aged 19.
85 Sqn	Hurricane I P/O R W Burton	P2437 +	Ditto. Buried Querrieu, aged 26.
213 Sqn	Hurricane I P/O W M Sizer	? Sl/WIA	Crash-landed near La Panne after combat with Me109s. See 31 May 1940.
504 Sqn	Hurricane I P/O B E White	? Wounded	Crash-landed after ground attack due to flak over Arras road. Abandoned.
504 Sqn	Hurricane I P/O M Jebb	P3586 Wounded	Ditto. See 15 September 1940.
601 Sqn	Hurricane I F/O G R Branch	P2699 'D' Safe	Baled out after combat with Do17 of 3(F)/10, near Izel, 0600 hrs. See 11 August 1940.
601 Sqn	Hurricane I F/O P B Robinson	P3278 Safe	Damaged by flak and force-landed at Merville. Abandoned.
607 Sqn	Hurricane I F/O R E W Pumphrey	P3448 'H' PoW	Shot down by ground fire, baled out over Arras road, 1040 am. Stalag Luft III prison camp.
615 Sqn	Hurricane I P/O V B S Verity	L2060 Safe	Crash-landed after combat with Me110s of ZG26 – A/c abandoned. See 31 May 1940.

Spitfire P9377 of 222 Squadron was shot down over Dunkirk on 1 June 1940. P/O R A L Morant crash-landed on the beach and evaded capture.

Chapter 3

Dunkirk

As the Battle of France came to a close on 20 May, Fighter Command suffered further losses in support of the planned evacuation of the British Army from Dunkirk. The first part of this chapter covers operations over France and its coast from bases in southern England up to 25 May. The subsequent losses sustained by Fighter Command for the Dunkirk period is covered between the official dates of Operation Dynamo: 26 May to 3 June 1940.

The Dunkirk operation severely tested Fighter Command – not only its fighter pilots, but also radar operators, controllers and ground crews. Fighter Command had been primarily designed for a defensive war; however, throughout the evacuation, it was asked to operate many miles from its bases over sea and, at times, outside radar and radio range. Operating time over the beaches and ports of France was limited and the Germans could often dictate when their aircraft would appear. When German formations were encountered, they often came in large numbers, far in excess of the covering Spitfires, Hurricanes and Defiants. Therefore, it was decided to send fighters over in 'wing' strength; however, this did not mean the wing operated as a single unit as RAF squadrons had not been trained to fly in large formations. As a consequence, squadrons split up and no one had overall control over them. There was no senior authoritative figure in control of the various units so squadrons had a tendency to separate and operate individually. Also, there were times when squadrons would take turns to 'lead' and a junior pilot would direct the wing to the French coast whereas a more senior and experienced leader was being led!

Although the evacuation was successful, it also cut deep into Dowding's already weakened Command. The following losses occurred during Operation Dynamo and apart from fighters, the losses were also severe in pilots, those surviving either made it back to their own lines or were captured by the enemy. It was also the first time many senior airmen – squadron and flight commanders – saw action and discovered that their tactics were outdated, therefore many valuable pilots failed to survive more than a few sorties. It was a steep learning curve and those who realised that the 'book' was flawed took control and changed tactics as the air war rapidly advanced.

Pre-Dunkirk

21 May 1940

74 Sqn	Spitfire I P/O R D Aubert	K9957 Safe	Patrol. Force-landing at Berck-sur-Mer due to fuel shortage after chasing a Ju88. Abandoned. See 25 May 1940.
253 Sqn	Hurricane I P/O D DeC C Gower	P3546 +	Patrol. Shot down by ground fire near Etaples and buried there. Aged 20. See 18 May 1940.
253 Sqn	Hurricane I S/L E D Elliott	P3552 PoW	Patrol. Shot down by ground fire. Stalag Luft III camp.
601 Sqn	Hurricane I F/O H J Riddle	L2088 Safe	Patrol over Amiens. Engine failed and crash-landed near Abbeville. A/c abandoned. See 19 May 1940.

22 May 1940

56 Sqn	Hurricane I F/O J B Wicks	N2431 Evaded	Patrol N France. Force-landed near Belgian border, returning via Dunkirk on 3 June. See 26 August 1940.
65 Sqn	Spitfire I P/O K G Hart	K9920 Safe	Patrol over Calais. Force-landing North Foreland with engine trouble – a/c burned out. See 26 May and 20 August 1940.
605 Sqn	Hurricane I F/O G W B Austin	N2349 Wounded	Patrol over Arras. Set on fire in combat with Me109s; pilot hit in left leg and baled out near Vermelles. Evacuated via Dunkirk and hospitalised.
605 Sqn	Hurricane I Sgt Moffatt	L2058 +	Patrol over Arras. Shot down by Me109.
605 Sqn	Hurricane I P/O C F Currant	P3575 Safe	Patrol over Arras pm. Force-landed in France after fight with Me109s and broke his nose. Set a/c on fire and returned by nightfall.

| 605 Sqn
F/O G F M Wright | Hurricane I | L2120
+ | Patrol over Arras. Shot down by He111. Buried
Berneville, France. Aged 36. |

23 May 1940

32 Sqn Sgt G L Nowell	Hurricane I	P3550 Wounded	Patrol over northern France. Shot down by Me109s, baled out near Arras and evacuated via Calais. See 16 May 1940.
74 Sqn S/L F L White	Spitfire I	N3243 Rescued	Patrol. Force-landed at Calais-Marck after combat with Hs126; rescued by 54 Squadron.
74 Sqn F/O V G Byrne	Spitfire I	K9867 PoW	Patrol. Shot down by ground fire over Clarmarais Wood; wounded in leg. Stalag Luft III.
92 Sqn P/O P A G Learmond	Spitfire I	P9370 +	Patrol over French coast. Shot down in flames over Dunkirk by Me109.
92 Sqn S/L R J Bushell	Spitfire I	N3194 'N' PoW	Patrol. Shot down by Me110. Later became 'Bix-X' at Stalag Luft III and murdered by the Gestapo after the 'Great Escape' in March 1944. Buried in Poznan.
92 Sqn F/O J A Gillies	Spitfire I	N3290 PoW	Patrol. Shot down by Me110. Stalag Luft III camp.
92 Sqn Sgt P H Klipsch	Spitfire I	P9373 +	Patrol. Shot down by Me110s and Wierre-Effroy, France. Spitfire was excavated in 1999 (*Time Team*).
92 Sqn F/L C P Green	Spitfire I	N3167 Wounded	Patrol. Wounded in leg during combat with Me110s. A/c damaged but was returned to service, then damaged beyond repair 26 July 1940. See 7 September 1940.
242 Sqn P/O J Benzie	Hurricane I	P2550 Wounded	Escort N France. Baled out after fight with Me109 near Ypres. See 7 September 1940.
242 Sqn F/O J W Graafstra	Hurricane I	P2809 +	Escort N France. Shot down by Me109s and buried Wancourt, aged 27.
242 Sqn P/O G A Malone	Hurricane I	P2730 +	Escort N France. Shot down by Me109s and buried Anzac Cemetery, Sailly-sur-la-Lys, France.
242 Sqn P/O J B Smiley	Hurricane I	P3392 PoW	Escort N France. Baled out after combat with Me109s. Stalag Luft III camp.
253 Sqn P/O D J Ford	Hurricane I	N2614 Safe	Patrol. Shot down in combat with Me109s. See 18 May 1940.
605 Sqn F/L P G Leeson	Hurricane I	L2121 PoW	Patrol over Ostend. Shot down by AA fire and badly wounded. In German hospital for nine months. Stalag Luft III.

24 May 1940

54 Sqn F/O T N Linley	Spitfire I	P9455 +	Patrol over Calais. Combat with Me109s and shot down.
54 Sqn Sgt J W B Phillips	Spitfire I	P9388 Safe	Patrol over Calais. Force-landed after combat with Me109s. Pilot set a/c on fire and returned safely.
74 Sqn F/O D S Hoare	Spitfire I	P9321 PoW	Patrol. Force-landed at Calais-Marck. Abandoned.
74 Sqn P/O R D Aubert	Spitfire I	P9441 +	Patrol – failed to return. See 22 May 1940.
74 Sqn F/L W P F Treacy	Spitfire I	K9992 Safe	Patrol. Shot down and returned by ship. See 27 May 1940 and 20 April 1941.

74 Sqn	Spitfire I Sgt E A Mould	K9952 Safe	Patrol. Ditto. See 28 July 1940.
92 Sqn	Spitfire I F/O P F Cazenove	P9374 'J' PoW	Patrol. Force-landed at Calais after combat with Me109s. Stalag Luft III. Recovered from beach in 1980 and is currently being restored at Duxford.
242 Sqn	Hurricane I P/O R L Hill	P3266 +	Patrol over French coast. Collided with P3272 over the English Channel.
242 Sqn	Hurricane I P/O J W Mitchell	P3272 +	Collided with P3266 (above).

25 May 1940

54 Sqn	Spitfire I Sgt F E Buckland	N3096 +	Crashed near Dunkirk. NKG.
54 Sqn	Spitfire I F/L D G Gribble	P9388 Safe	Force-landed at Dunkirk and pilot returned by ship.
151 Sqn	Hurricane I F/L F A Ives	P3319 +	Escort over St Omer. Collided with P/O Bushell over France.
605 Sqn	Spitfire I F/O G R Edge	N2557 Safe	Patrol Calais-Dunkirk late am. Hit by AA fire aircraft: Cat B damage.

Hurricane L1564 in 1938 with 111 Squadron. On 2 June 1940, P/O R R Wilson was shot down over the Channel by German fighters but baling out, Wilson landed near Manston. Unfortunately, he was killed in action on 11 August 1940.

Operation Dynamo – 26 May to 3 June 1940

26 May 1940

17 Sqn	Hurricane I F/S W T Jones	N2528 +	Patrol. In combat with Do17s and Me110s.
17 Sqn	Hurricane I F/L C F G Adye	P3483 +	Patrol. Baled out after combat with Me109s over the Channel. NKG.
19 Sqn	Spitfire I S/L G D Stephenson	N3200 PoW	Patrol. Shot down in combat. Sent to Colditz prison camp.
19 Sqn	Spitfire I P/O P V Wilson	N3237 DoW	Patrol. Baled out during combat. Died 28 May 1940.
19 Sqn	Spitfire I Sgt C A Irwin	P9305 +	Patrol – lost in combat with Me109s.
19 Sqn	Spitfire I P/O M D Lyne	L1031 Wounded	Patrol. Force-landed on Walmer beach, Deal, with bullet in knee after combat with Me109s.
19 Sqn	Spitfire I F/O G E Ball	? Wounded	Patrol. Hit in head and arm during combat with Me109s.
54 Sqn	Spitfire I P/O J L Allen DFC	N3188 Safe	Patrol. Baled out over Channel and rescued. Also see 24 July 1940.
65 Sqn	Spitfire I F/O J Welford	P9437 +	Patrol. Hit by AA fire during combat with Me109s; baled out but parachute did not have time to deploy.
65 Sqn	Spitfire I P/O K G Hart	K9912 'O' Safe	Patrol. Force-landed on beach after combat with Me109, returned by boat. A/c destroyed. See also 22 May and 20 August 1940.
145 Sqn	Hurricane I P/O P L Parrott	N2589 Safe	Patrol. Forced to land at Little Mongeham, near Dover, after damaged by He111. A/c repaired and SoC 11 February 1942. See 1 December 1940.
605 Sqn	Hurricane I P/O I J Muirhead	N2346 Safe	Patrol over Dunkirk. Shot down by Me110 and baled out. Fired on by Belgian troops but returned by ship from Ostende. Ship torpedoed: rescued and returned safely. See 7 and 15 October 1940.

27 May 1940

54 Sqn	Spitfire I F/L M C Pearson	N3030 'T' +	Patrol. Last seen chasing Ju88 over Calais. NKG.
56 Sqn	Hurricane I P/O M H C Maxwell	P3478 Safe	Patrol. Hit by Belgian AA fire whilst chasing He111 and baled out. Returned by ship. See 28 August and 30 September 1940.
56 Sqn	Hurricane I F/L R H Lee	P3311 Safe	Patrol. Shot down into the sea and rescued. See 11 May and 18 August 1940.
56 Sqn	Hurricane I F/O Fisher	P3355 Wounded	Patrol. Shot down by Me110 but returned by sea. (Several pilots were shot down or crash landed at or near Dunkirk but managed to join the evacuation of troops.)
65 Sqn	Spitfire I F/O G V Proudman	N3128 Wounded	Patrol. Hit in crossfire from Do17s and wounded in the legs. See 7 July and 11 August 1940.
74 Sqn	Spitfire I P/O P C Stevenson	L1084 Safe	Patrol. Force-landed at Dunkirk after hit by Do17; returned by ship on 31 May 1940. See 11 August 1940.
74 Sqn	Spitfire I F/L W P C Treacy	K9875 Evaded	Patrol. Lost in combat and evaded via Spain. See 25 May 1940 and 20 April 1941.

Sqn	Aircraft / Pilot	Serial / Fate	Notes
145 Sqn	Hurricane I P/O A Elson	P2723 +	Patrol. Shot down in combat with Ju88s and Me110s.
145 Sqn	Hurricane I P/O P H O'C Rainier	N2713 +	Patrol. Shot down in combat with Ju88s and Me110s.
145 Sqn	Hurricane I Sgt A Bailey	N2711 +	Ditto.
145 Sqn	Hurricane I F/O D N Forde	N2710 Safe	Patrol. Shot down by Me110 but got home by sea. See also 23 July 1941.
145 Sqn	Hurricane I P/O E C J Wakeham	P3314 Safe	Ditto. See 8 August 1940.
145 Sqn	Hurricane I P/O J H Ashton	P2723 Safe	Ditto. See 15 May 1940.
601 Sqn	Hurricane I F/O C A Lee-Steere	P3486 +	Patrol. Lost in combat; buried at Oostkerke Cemetery, Belgium. Aged 29.
601 Sqn	Hurricane I F/L Sir A Hope	P2568 'R' Safe	Patrol. Force-landed at Dunkirk and got home by sea. See 18 May 1940.
605 Sqn	Hurricane I F/O N Forbes	L2119 PoW	Escort for Blenheims to St Omer. Last seen chasing He111 near Poperinghe. Sent to Colditz.
605 Sqn	Hurricane I S/L G V Perry	P3423 +	Patrol Calais-St Omer with 17 Sqn, pm. Shot down by fighters. NKG.
605 Sqn	Hurricane I F/O P J Danielson	P3581 +	Ditto. NKG.
610 Sqn	Spitfire I F/O A R Mitchell	L1016 +	Missing over Dunkirk.
610 Sqn	Spitfire I Sgt W T Medway	L1003 +	Ditto. Buried at Oosduinkerke Cemetery, west of Nieuport, Belgium.

28 May 1940

Sqn	Aircraft / Pilot	Serial / Fate	Notes
19 Sqn	Spitfire I F/O G W Petre	L1029 Wounded	Patrol. Explosive shell hit cockpit, wounding pilot in one leg. A/c repaired and returned to service.
54 Sqn	Spitfire I P/O A C Deere	N3180 Safe	Patrol. Force-landed near Nieuport after combat with Do17; A/c burned, pilot returned by sea. See 9 July, 15, 28 and 31 August 1940.
65 Sqn	Spitfire I P/O T Smart	P9435 Safe	Patrol. Force-landed Dunkirk after hit in glycol tank by Do17. Returned by sea.
213 Sqn	Hurricane I F/L E G Winning	P3354 'E' +	Escort to St Omer. Buried Langemark near Ypres, Belgium.
213 Sqn	Hurricane I F/O T Boyd	P2717 'B' Safe	Escort. Shot down over sea and rescued. See 31 May 1940.
213 Sqn	Hurricane I Sgt S L Butterfield	P2721 Safe	Shot down by Me109. Baled out over sea, rescued by paddle steamer Royal Eagle. See 11 Aug 1940.
213 Sqn	Hurricane I P/O G C Stone	P2792 'C' +	Patrol. Body found in water, buried at sea. See 19 May 1940.
213 Sqn	Hurricane I Sgt J A Lishman	P2834 Wounded	Patrol. Shot down into the sea and wounded in the arm but rescued.
229 Sqn	Hurricane I Sgt S A Hillman	N2551 +	Patrol.
242 Sqn	Hurricane I P/O A H Deacon	N2651 PoW	Patrol. Shot down by Me109. Stalag Luft III.

Hurricane L1584. With 65 Squadron, P/O R M Mudie was shot down into the sea by JG51 on 14 July 1940. Mudie died of his injuries the next day.

242 Sqn	Hurricane I P/O D F Jones	L1746 +	Shot down by Me109. Canadian in RAF. Buried Oostduinkerke Comm Cemetery, Belgium. Aged 26.
264 Sqn	Defiant I F/L E H Whitehouse P/O H Scott	L6959 + +	Shot down by Me109. Gunner buried in Longuenesse, aged 33.
264 Sqn	Defiant I P/O A McLeod P/O J E Hatfield	L7007 + +	Shot down by Me109.
264 Sqn	Defiant I Sgt L C W Daisley LAC H Revill	L6953 + +	Shot down by Me109. Pilot buried in Wissant, France.
616 Sqn	Spitfire I Sgt M Ridley	K9947 Sl/WIA	Patrol. Badly damaged and pilot suffered a head wound. See 26 August 1940.
616 Sqn	Spitfire I S/L M Robinson	K9804 Safe	Patrol. Severely damaged by Me109 and force-landed at Manston. SoC.

29 May 1940

17 Sqn	Hurricane I P/O D W H Hanson	? Sl/WIA	Fight with Me110s over France. Shell splinters right leg.
56 Sqn	Hurricane I P/O K C Dryden	N2659 Safe	Patrol. Force-landed on beach and returned by sea.
56 Sqn	Hurricane I Sgt J W Elliott	L1972 +	Shot down over Dunkirk.
64 Sqn	Spitfire I S/L E G Rogers	L1052 +	Shot down in combat with Me109s.
64 Sqn	Spitfire I P/O R T George	K9832 +	Ditto.
64 Sqn	Spitfire I P/O H B Hackney	K9906 +	Ditto.

64 Sqn	Spitfire I	K9813	Ditto.
	F/S C Flynn	Safe	
151 Sqn	Hurricane I	P3303	Baled out over sea, rescued by a hospital ship.
	F/O K E Newton	Safe	New Zealand pilot. See 28 June 1940.
151 Sqn	Hurricane I	P3321	Ditto – rescued by a destroyer.
	P/O R N H Courtney	Safe	
229 Sqn	Hurricane I	P3489	Shot down by Me109. New Zealand pilot.
	F/L F N Clouston	+	
229 Sqn	Hurricane I	P2636	Shot down by Me109.
	F/L P E S F M Brown	+	
229 Sqn	Hurricane I	P2876	Shot down by Me109.
	Sgt J C Harrison	+	
229 Sqn	Hurricane I	N2473	Baled out after combat with Me109.
	F/O W G New	Safe	
229 Sqn	Hurricane I	N2521	Ditto.
	P/O A S Linney	Safe	
242 Sqn	Hurricane I	L1666	Damaged in combat, landed on one wheel. Repaired.
	P/O J B Latta	Safe	Canadian.
264 Sqn	Defiant I	L6957	Badly damaged by Me110. Gunner baled out when
	P/O D H S Kay	Safe	turret was hit and was lost but pilot returned safely.
	Sgt E J Jones	+	Canadian AG, buried Dunkirk, aged 31.
264 Sqn	Defiant I	L6972	Ditto – came down in sea near Dunkirk and rescued
	P/O E G Barwell	Safe	by destroyer.
	P/O J E M Williams	Safe	
264 Sqn	Defiant I	L7019	Damaged; AG wounded and baled out. A/c crashed on
	P/O R W Stokes	Safe	landing at RAF Manston.
	LAC Fairbrother	Wounded	
610 Sqn	Spitfire I	L1006 'R'	Shot down by Me109.
	F/O G M Kerr	+	
610 Sqn	Spitfire I	N3289	Ditto.
	F/O J Kerr-Wilson	+	
610 Sqn	Spitfire I	N3177 'T'	Ditto. Body washed up at Zeeland on the Dutch coast.
	S/L A L Franks	+	Sage War Cemetery, aged 32.
610 Sqn	Spitfire I	L1006 'R'	Baled out over sea, hit by AA fire – presumed drowned.
	Sgt P D Jenkins	+	

30 May 1940

609 Sqn	Spitfire I	L1086	Lost returning from patrol. Crashed in bad visibility at
	F/O G D Ayre	+	Oakley, Essex.

31 May 1940

64 Sqn	Spitfire I	K9813	Combat with Me110s. Died later and buried Edingen,
	F/S G H Hatch	PoW/+	Belgium, on 26 September 1940.
111 Sqn	Hurricane I	L1973	Wounded in ankle during combat and crash-landed at
	Sgt J Robinson	Wounded	Manston. Machine repaired and finally SoC in July 1944.
213 Sqn	Hurricane I	P9342 'L'	Came down in the sea and rescued by ship.
	S/L H D McGregor	Safe	
213 Sqn	Hurricane I	P2763 'G'	Baled out, landing on a beach and returned by sea.
	F/O K N G Robinson	Safe	

213 Sqn	Hurricane I P/O W M Sizer	P3424 'P' Safe	Crash-landed on fire near Dunkirk, and returned by sea. See 20 May 1940.
213 Sqn	Hurricane I F/O W N Gray	P3361 'D' +	Shot down in combat, buried at Den Haag, Westduein Cem, when body washed ashore on 17 August 1940.
213 Sqn	Hurricane I Sgt T Boyd	P3419 +	Shot down, buried St Joris, Belgium, aged 25. See 28 May 1940.
222 Sqn	Spitfire I P/O G G A Davies	N3295 'G' Safe	Force-landed on beach after hit by AA fire, returned by sea. See 31 August 1940.
229 Sqn	Hurricane I P/O V B S Verity	P3492 Safe	Baled out after combat with Me110s, picked up by paddle steamer. See 20 May 1940.
229 Sqn	Hurricane I Sgt D F Edgehill	P3553 Wounded	Wounded in combat with Me110s and crash on landing and SoC.
229 Sqn	Hurricane I P/O J E M Collins	L1982 +	Shot down over Dunkirk.
242 Sqn	Hurricane I P/O G M Stewart	P2732 +	Shot down by Me109.
245 Sqn	Hurricane I P/O K B McGlashan	N2702 Safe	Force-landed at Dunkirk and returned by sea.
264 Sqn	Defiant I F/L N G Cooke DFC Cpl A Lippett DFM	L6975 + +	Lost in combat with He111s and Me109s over Dunkirk. Cooke was aged 26.
264 Sqn	Defiant I P/O G L Hickman LAC A Fidler	L6968 + +	Shot down by Me109 off Belgian coast. Both buried Koksijde Military. Cemetery, aged 19 and 27.
264 Sqn	Defiant I P/O D Whitley LAC R C Turner	L6961 Safe Safe	Collided with L6980, force-landed on beach and returned by sea. See 28 August 1940.
264 Sqn	Defiant I P/O M H Young LAC S B Johnson	L6980 Safe +	Baled out after colliding with L6961, but gunner was lost.
609 Sqn	Spitfire I F/L D Persse-Joynt	N3202 +	Shot down in combat with He111s.
609 Sqn	Spitfire I F/O J C Gilbert	L1081 +	Shot down.
609 Sqn	Spitfire I Sgt G C Bennett	L1087 Wounded	Rescued from sea two miles from Dover. See 29 April 1941.
610 Sqn	Spitfire I F/O G L Chambers	N3274 +	Shot down by Me109.
610 Sqn	Spitfire I F/O G Keighley	L1013 'F' Safe	Baled out and rescued by trawler, then transferred to a RN pinnace. See 20 July 1940.

1 June 1940

17 Sqn	Hurricane I P/O K Manger	P3476 Safe	Baled out and returned by sea. See 11 August 1940.
19 Sqn	Spitfire I Sgt J A Potter	K9836 Safe	Ditched following combat with fighters and returned by sea. See 15 September 1940.
41 Sqn	Spitfire I P/O W Stapleton	N3107 PoW	Shot down in combat with He111s and Do17s. Stalag Luft III.

41 Sqn	Spitfire I F/O W E Legard	P9344 +	Ditto.
43 Sqn	Hurricane I P/O M K Cresswell	N2584 Injured	Rescued from sea by destroyer with burns. See 9 February and 2 September 1940.
43 Sqn	Hurricane I Sgt T A H Gough	L1758 +	Shot down by German fighters.
64 Sqn	Spitfire I P/O T C Hey	L1053 +	Missing from patrol.
145 Sqn	Hurricane I P/O H P Dixon	P2952 +	Shot down by enemy fighters.
222 Sqn	Spitfire I P/O R A L Morant	P9377 Safe	Force-landed on beach after fight with Me109s and Me110s. Returned by sea.
222 Sqn	Spitfire I P/O H E L Falkus	P9317 PoW	Shot down by enemy fighters. Stalag Luft III.
222 Sqn	Spitfire I P/O G Massey-Sharpe	P9339 +	Ditto. Buried Pihen-les-Guines War Cemetery, France. Aged 19.
222 Sqn	Spitfire I Sgt L J White	N3232 +	Ditto. Buried Koksijde Military Cemetery, Belgium. Aged 23.
242 Sqn	Hurricane I P/O G M Stewart	L2004 +	Shot down by Me109.
245 Sqn	Hurricane I P/O R A West	N2709 +	Shot down by Me109.
245 Sqn	Hurricane I P/O A L Treanor	N2658 +	Ditto.
609 Sqn	Spitfire I F/O I B N Russell DFC	L1058 +	Shot down by Me110. Australian, aged 29. See 15 May 1940.
609 Sqn	Spitfire I F/O J Dawson	N3222 +	Shot down in combat with He111 near Dunkirk.
616 Sqn	Spitfire I F/O J S Bell	K9948 Safe	Ditched after combat with Me109; strafed in the water but unharmed. Rescued by RN. See 26 and 30 August 1940.

2 June 1940

32 Sqn	Hurricane I Sgt D Flynn	P2727 PoW	Missing from patrol. Kopernikus.
66 Sqn	Spitfire I F/S M W Hayman	N3047 +	Missing from patrol.
66 Sqn	Spitfire I Sgt D A C Hunt	N3028 Safe	Baled out and returned.
66 Sqn	Spitfire I Sgt F N Robertson	N3033 Safe	Ditto.
72 Sqn	Spitfire I F/O O StJ Pigg	K9924 Wounded	Missing from patrol. See 1 September 1940.
111 Sqn	Hurricane I P/O R R Wilson	L1564 Safe	Baled out after fight with German fighters. Landed near Manston while Spitfire went into the sea. See 11 August 1940.
266 Sqn	Spitfire I	N3169	Shot down in combat with fighters.

	P/O J W B Stevenson	+	
266 Sqn	Spitfire I Sgt R T Kidman	N3092 +	Ditto. Buried Dunkirk, aged 26.
266 Sqn	Spitfire I F/O R K Compton	N3064 +	Ditto. Buried Etaples, aged 24.
266 Sqn	Spitfire I P/O N B Bowen	N3169 Safe	Ditto – damaged in combat and damaged further on landing – Cat 2. Repaired.
611 Sqn	Spitfire I F/O T D Little	N3055 +	Ditto. Buried Castricum, Netherlands, aged 23.

3 June 1940

17 Sqn	Hurricane I F/O R V Meredith	P3477 +	Missing on patrol. Buried at Malo-les-Baines, France.

F/L N G Cooke DFC (rear) and his gunner, Cpl A Lippert DFM, 264 Squadron, killed in action 31 May 1940. Defiants had some initial success in these actions but were quickly outclassed by Me109 pilots.

S/L P A Hunter DSO (rear) and Sgt F H King DFM of 264 Squadron survived Dunkirk, only to be shot down in the Battle of Britain on 24 August.

Chapter 4

Final Days over France – Post-Dunkirk

While the evacuation of Dunkirk was underway, the remnants of the RAF in France continued a fighting retreat towards the Cherbourg area from where they eventually returned to England, some via the Channel Islands. Casualty records are again fragmented due to records being lost by units based in France during the retreat period. When France finally capitulated, Britain stood alone. There followed a period between the fall of France and the commencement of the Battle of Britain while the RAF waited and watched for the impending assault.

24 May 1940

73 Sqn	Hurricane I F/O H B Bell-Syer	P2803 'L' Wounded	Patrol Amiens, pm. Baled out after combat with Me110. Pilot burned.
73 Sqn	Hurricane I P/O P E G Carter	'K' Safe	Ditto – crashed after combat with Me110s.

25 May 1940

1 Sqn	Hurricane I F/L D S Thom	P2880 PoW	Shot down by AA fire.

26 May 1940

1 Sqn	Hurricane I P/O R Dibnah	? Wounded	Wounded over Orchamps and force-landed near Nancy.
73 Sqn	Hurricane I P/O F Sydenham	P3274 'H' +	Patrol over Orchamps early am. Crashed after combat with Me109s. Buried at Chuffilly-Roche, France, aged 26.

1 June 1940

73 Sqn	Hurricane I P/O D S Scott	'D' Safe	Patrol Chalons late pm. Force-landed near Paris after a running fight with Me109s.
73 Sqn	Hurricane I P/O I G G Potts	P3543 'E' PoW	Ditto – shot down by Me109. Stalag Luft III.
73 Sqn	Hurricane I Sgt W Milner	P2700 'K' +	Ditto – buried at Terclincthun, France.

3 June 1940

73 Sqn	Hurricane I P/O I D Hawken	? +	Patrol over Aisne. Shot down by Me110 and buried Terclincthun.
501 Sqn	Hurricane I P/O P R Hairs	P2867 Safe	Shot down by Me109 and crash-landed Saint-Léger-des-Bois.

4 June 1940

616 Sqn	Spitfire I P/O E W S Scott	N3130 +	Crashed at Rochford in poor weather returning from patrol.

5 June 1940

1 Sqn	Hurricane I P/O N P W Hancock	P3590 Safe	Shot up in combat and crashed into a Blenheim at Rouen-Boos – SoC.

1 Sqn	Hurricane I P/O J A Shepherd	? +		Shot down over France.
501 Sqn	Hurricane I P/O A J Claydon	P3450 +		Shot down near Le Mans. Buried in St Sever Cemetery, Rouen. Aged 28.

6 June 1940

17 Sqn	Hurricane I Sgt S H Holman	P3360 +		Escort. Pilot seen heading for France early am, lost over Abbeville area.
111 Sqn	Hurricane I Sgt R J W Brown	P2885 Injured		Escort for Blenheims to Abbeville – fight with Me109s, baled out and returned to UK with slight injuries.

7 June 1940

17 Sqn	Hurricane I S/L G D Emms	P2905 +		Patrol over France; lost in combat with Do17 mid-afternoon.
17 Sqn	Hurricane I P/O R C Whittaker	P3472 +		Ditto – shot down by Me109.
43 Sqn	Hurricane I F/L T Rowland	L2116 Wounded		Patrol over Amiens late am. Shot down by Me109 and baled out north of Neufchâtel.
43 Sqn	Hurricane I F/O J D Edmonds	L1931 +		Ditto – over Puisenval. Buried St Valéry-en-Caux, France, aged 21.
43 Sqn	Hurricane I F/O W C Wilkinson	L1847 'J' +		Ditto – buried Bailleul Neuville, aged 26.
43 Sqn	Hurricane I Sgt H J L Hallowes	N2585 Safe		Ditto – baled out after aircraft set on fire by Me109.
43 Sqn	Hurricane I F/O C A Woods-Scawen	L1726 Safe		Ditto – shot down by Me109 and baled out. See 13, 16 August and 2 September 1940.
43 Sqn	Hurricane I Sgt P G Ottewill	L1608 Wounded		Ditto – badly burned after being shot down by Me109 over Wanchy-Capval.
43 Sqn	Hurricane I Sgt C A H Ayling	L1737 Safe		Ditto – shot down by Me109, crash-landed at Rouen-Boos. See 11 October 1940.
73 Sqn	Hurricane I F/O E J Kain DFC	L1826 +		Flying accident. Buried Choloy, France. New Zealander in RAF, aged 21. RAF's first ace in WW2. See 2 and 26 March 1940
151 Sqn	Hurricane I P/O J F Pettigrew	P3529 Wounded		Patrol over France. Shot down by Me109 near Le Tréport at 1930 hrs.
601 Sqn	Hurricane I F/O T E Hubbard	P3484 Safe		Patrol France. Shot down by Me109 near Abbeville, returned on foot. See 19 May 1940.
601 Sqn	Hurricane I F/O P B Robinson	P3490 Wounded		Ditto – hit in the leg, crash-landed and strafed on the ground.

8 June 1940

32 Sqn	Hurricane I P/O D H Grice	P3353 Safe		Patrol over Le Tréport early am. Crash-landed after combat with He111s near Rouen. See 15 August 1940.
32 Sqn	Hurricane I P/O G I Cherrington	N2582 +		Ditto – shot down, buried at St Marie, Le Havre.
32 Sqn	Hurricane I P/O K Kirkcaldie	N2406 +		Ditto – shot down, buried Houville-en-Vexin, aged 28. New Zealander.
151 Sqn	Hurricane I P/O D H Blomely	P3315 Safe		Patrol over France late am. Baled out after hit by AA fire.

501 Sqn	Hurricane I P/O R G Hulse	P3542 +	Shot down in combat over Bois Sentilie, Somme. Buried Somme. Buried Sentilie churchyard, aged 24.
501 Sqn	Hurricane I Sgt A A Lewis	P3347 'N' Missing	Ditto – near Boos. Reported KIA but not in CWGC records.

9 June 1940

17 Sqn	Hurricane I P/O D C Leary	? Safe	Patrol over France, late pm. Force-landed and returned by train on the 11 June. Hurricane assumed abandoned.
242 Sqn	Hurricane I P/O D G MacQueen	P2767 +	Patrol. Shot down over France by Me109.

10 June 1940

501 Sqn	Hurricane I P/O K N T Lee	L19__ Injured	Baled out as Hurricane exploded in attack on He111 near Le Mans. Evacuated. See 18 August 1940.

11 June 1940

32 Sqn	Hurricane I Sgt Jones	N2533 Missing	Patrol over Le Tréport pm. Missing after fight with Hs126.

18 June 1940

151 Sqn	Hurricane I P/O L Wright	P3313 +	Escort and patrol pm. Baled out during combat with He111s over French coast. Body washed up 16 August and buried Hook of Holland, aged 27.
151 Sqn	Hurricane I Sgt M R Aslin	P3324 +	Ditto. Shot down and buried at Westende, Belgium, aged 27.

18/19 June 1940

19 Sqn	Spitfire I F/O G W Petre	L1032 Wounded	Night patrol. Baled out during action – hit by rear gunner and burned.
23 Sqn	Blenheim If S/L J S O'Brien P/O C King-Clark Cpl D Little	L1458 'X' Safe + +	Same action as above. Baled out (see 7 September 1940) Baled out, struck propeller. Died in crash, 0125, near Newmarket.
23 Sqn	Blenheim If Sgt A C Close LAC J Angus	L8687 'S' + Safe	Night patrol. Shot down during combat early am. Angus baled out.
29 Sqn	Blenheim If P/O J S Barnwell Sgt K L Long	L6636 + +	Night patrol. Took off 0025 and failed to return from combat action. Pilot's body washed up 5 July 1940.

22 June 1940

615 Sqn	Hurricane I P/O J R Lloyd	P2764 +	Patrol over France early am. Shot down in combat with He111s and Me110s near Rouen.

27 June 1940

79 Sqn	Hurricane I F/L J W E Davies DFC	P3591 +	Escort to St Valéry am; shot down by fighters. American.
79 Sqn	Hurricane I Sgt R R McQueen	P3401 +	Ditto. Baled out and body found in sea off Rye.

28 June 1940

151 Sqn	Hurricane I F/O K E Newton	P3322 +	Escort, late pm. Baled out over sea after combat with Me109. London born but brought up in New Zealand and trained with RNZAF. Aged 24.

30 June 1940

151 Sqn	Hurricane I S/L E M Donaldson	P3787 Safe	Convoy patrol pm. Baled out and rescued.

Build up to the Battle of Britain

6 June 1940

152 Sqn	Spitfire I P/O B E Bell	K9896 DoI	Crash-landed at Catterick after a convoy patrol.

1 July 1940

29 Sqn	Blenheim If P/O P Sisman Sgt A Reed	L1376 + +	Night interception. Pilot apparently blinded by searchlights and crashed trying to land. EA bombed wreckage.

4 July 1940

79 Sqn	Hurricane I Sgt H Cartwright DFM	N2619 +	Patrol. Shot down by Me109 over St Margaret's Bay pm.

5 July 1940

64 Sqn	Spitfire I P/O D K Milne	P9507 +	Evening recce over France. Shot down by Me109 of JG51 near Rouen.

7 July 1940

54 Sqn	Spitfire I P/O A R McL Campbell	R6711 Wounded	Patrol pm. Shot down by Me109 off Deal; see 24 August 1940.
54 Sqn	Spitfire I P/O E J Coleman	P9390 Wounded	Ditto. A/c became instructional airframe, 2111M, October 1940.
65 Sqn	Spitfire I F/O G V Proudman	R6615 +	Convoy patrol evening; shot down by Me109 near Folkestone. See 27 May 1940.
65 Sqn	Spitfire I P/O N J Brisbane	R6609 +	Ditto.
65 Sqn	Spitfire I Sgt P S Hayes	N3129 +	Ditto.
79 Sqn	Hurricane I S/L J D C Joslin	P2756 +	Evening patrol. Shot down in flames by Spitfires over Chilverton Elms, near Dover.

8 July 1940

65 Sqn	Spitfire I S/L D Cooke	K9907 +	Afternoon patrol. Shot down by Me109 off Dover.
79 Sqn	Hurricane I P/O J E R Wood	N2384 +	Scramble 1515. Shot down off Dover by Me109; baled out wounded but died. See 14 May 1940.
79 Sqn	Hurricane I F/O E W Mitchell	P3461 +	Ditto – shot down over Kent.
610 Sqn	Spitfire I P/O A L B Raven	R6806 'N' +	Convoy patrol. Shot down in combat with Do17 off Dover. Pilot baled out over sea but was unable to be rescued – pm.

9 July 1940

43 Sqn	Hurricane I S/L G C Lott DSO DFC	P3464 Wounded	Patrol am. Shot down by Me110 and lost right eye; crashed near Fontwell racecourse.
43 Sqn	Hurricane I P/O J Cruttenden	L1824 'F' Safe	Late am patrol. Baled out following combat with Do17 near Beachy Head. See 8 August 1940.
54 Sqn	Spitfire I P/O A C Deere	N3183 Safe	Scramble. Collided with Me109 and force-landed near Manston; A/c lost. See 28 May, 15, 28 and 31 August 1940.
54 Sqn	Spitfire I P/O J W Garton	R6705 +	Scramble 1855. Shot down near Manston.
54 Sqn	Spitfire I P/O S J A Evershed	L1093 +	Ditto – off Dover.
151 Sqn	Hurricane I Mid. O M Wightman	P3806 Safe	Convoy patrol pm. Shot down over Thames Estuary and rescued by a trawler. FAA pilot: rejoined RN in February 1941. KIA on *Ark Royal* 30 June 1941.
151 Sqn	Hurricane I F/L H H A Ironside	P3309 Wounded	Ditto, am – wounded in the face but returned to base safely.
609 Sqn	Spitfire I F/O P Drummond-Hay	R6637 'Q' +	Patrol evening. Shot down by Me109 over Portland. Flown by Egon Meyer of I/JG2.

Sgt H Cartwright DFM, 79
Squadron, killed in action
on 4 July 1940. On the left
is Sgt A W Whitby DFM.

Chapter 5

The Battle of Britain

The Battle of Britain has been recorded in four phases for many years. First, there were the Channel battles, which tested Britain's defences while the Germans hoped that Britain might sue for peace following France's fall. The Luftwaffe then attacked Fighter Command's airfields in order to destroy its ability to fight prior to a planned invasion of southern England.The third phase began when German bombers were ordered to attack London following RAF Bomber Command's raid on Berlin. The fourth phase came as the summer began to fade and the bombers were withdrawn, replaced by fighter-bomber operations. The year ended with the final months of bitter fighting in the dangerous and cloudy skies of southern England.

Phase One – 10 July to 7 August 1940

10 July 1940

56 Sqn	Hurricane I F/L E J Gracie	P3554 Safe	Crash-landed after being damaged by Me109. A/c damaged but repairable.
111 Sqn	Hurricane I F/O T P K Higgs	P3671 +	Patrol. Baled out after collision with Do17 of 3/KG2 off Folkestone at 1300 hrs. Pilot drowned and was buried at Noordwijk, Holland, having been washed up on 15 August 1940.
253 Sqn	Hurricane I Sgt I C C Clenshaw	P3359 +	Patrol. Crashed in bad weather at Irby-on-Humber, Lincs.

11 July 1940

85 Sqn	Hurricane I S/L P W Townsend DFC	P2716 'F' Safe	Patrol. Shot down off Harwich. Baled out after attack on Do17 of II/KG2 at 1825. See 31 August 1940.
145 Sqn	Hurricane I S/L J R A Peel	P3400 Safe	Patrol. Ditched off Selsey Bill after combat at 1825. Rescued by Selsey Lifeboat. See 9 July 1941.
501 Sqn	Hurricane I Sgt F J P Dixon	N2485 +	Patrol. Shot down by Me109 of III/JG27 – baled out but drowned. Buried at Abbeville, France. Aged 21.
601 Sqn	Hurricane I Sgt A W Woolley	P3681 Wounded	Patrol. Crashed on Isle of Wight after attack on He111 off Selsey Bill 1820. Burnt and wounded, a/c written off. See 26 and 31 August 1940.
609 Sqn	Spitfire I P/O G T M Mitchell	L1095 +	Convoy patrol. Shot down by Me109 of JG27 off Portland 1810 hrs.
609 Sqn	Spitfire I F/L P H Barran	L1069 +	Ditto. Died of wounds. Buried Leeds cemetery. Aged 31.

12 July 1940

85 Sqn	Hurricane I Sgt L Jowitt	P2557 +	Convoy patrol. Crashed into sea after attack on He111 of II/KG53 at 0850 off Felixstowe.
145 Sqn	Hurricane I Sub-Lt(A) F A Smith	N2703 Safe	Patrol. Force-landed and over-turned near Ringwood with slight injuries. See 8 August 1940.
151 Sqn	Hurricane I F/O J H L Allen	P3275 +	Convoy patrol. Ditched after combat with Do17 of II/KG2 off Orfordness 0945. New Zealander with RAF. Aged 25.

501 Sqn	Hurricane I P/O D A Hewitt	P3084 +	Convoy patrol. Shot down after attacking a Do17 off Portland 1545. Canadian. NKG, aged 20.

13 July 1940

56 Sqn	Hurricane I Sgt J J Whitfield	P2922 +	Patrol. Shot down by Me109 of JG51 off Calais, 1645.
56 Sqn	Hurricane I Sgt J R Cowsill	N2432 +	Ditto. NKG, aged 20.
238 Sqn	Hurricane I F/L J C Kennedy	P2950 +	Patrol. Crashed at Southdown whilst avoiding HT cables returning from successful combat with Do17 of 2(F)/123 off Chesil Beach, 1520.
610 Sqn	Spitfire I Sgt P I Watson-Parker	R6807 +	Patrol. Crashed at Tatsfield near Biggin Hill, 1135, cause unknown. Cudham churchyard, Orpington, aged 22.

14 July 1940

615 Sqn	Hurricane I P/O M R Mudie	L1584 'G' DoI	Convoy patrol. Shot down by Me109 of JG51. Baled out and rescued but died next day. Aged 25.

15 July 1940

17 Sqn	Hurricane I P/O P L Dawburn	P3482 Safe	Patrol. Crashed and written off near Elsenham, Essex, after engine fire.
213 Sqn	Hurricane I Sub-Lt(A) H G K Bramah	N2541 Injured	Patrol. Baled out following attack on Do17 over Portland, 1320. A/c crashed off Dartmouth, Devon.

17 July 1940

64 Sqn	Spitfire I F/O D M Taylor	P9507 Wounded	Convoy patrol. Shot down by Me109 of JG2. Crash-landed at Hailsham at 1400 hrs. A/c became instructional airframe 2119M.

F/O G A Proudman, 65 Squadron, killed in action on 7 July 1940.

603 Sqn	Spitfire I	K9916	Missing from patrol. NKG, aged 21.
	F/O C D Peel	+	

18 July 1940

235 Sqn	Blenheim IV	N3541	Convoy patrol off East Anglia. Failed to return –
	P/O R L Patterson	+	mid-am. NKGs, aged 26, 18 and 26 respectively.
	Sgt R Y Tucker	+	
	Sgt L H M Reece	+	
236 Sqn	Blenheim I	L6779	Photo recce: shot down over Le Havre by
	P/O C R D Thomas	+	JG2 at 1215.
	Sgt H D B Elsdon	+	
236 Sqn	Blenheim I	L6639	Ditto.
	P/O R H Rigby	+	Buried Le Havre, aged 24.
	Sgt D D Mackinnon	+	Buried Villerville, aged 21.
609 Sqn	Spitfire I	R6636	Shot down by Ju88 off Swanage; crash-landed Studland
	F/O A R Edge	Safe	Beach at 1515 – damaged.
609 Sqn	Spitfire I	R6634	Baled out south of Poole after fight with Ju88 off
	F/L F J Howell	Safe	Swanage – rescued by the Royal Navy.
610 Sqn	Spitfire I	P9452 'T'	Patrol. Shot down by Me109 of JG51 north of Calais
	P/O P Litchfield	+	at 1000. NKG, aged 25.

19 July 1940

1 Sqn	Hurricane I	P3471	Patrol. Set on fire during attack on a He111; crash-landed
	P/O D O M Browne	Safe	near Brighton and burned out at 1815. See
			15 August 1940.
32 Sqn	Hurricane I	P3144	Patrol. Baled out over Dover in fight with Me109 at 1625.
	F/S G Turner	Wounded	Crashed at Hougham, pilot badly burned.
43 Sqn	Hurricane I	P3140	Patrol. Shot down by Me109 of JG27 and baled out
	F/L J W C Simpson	Wounded	slightly wounded near Selsey, 1715. See
			21 February 1940.
43 Sqn	Hurricane I	P3531	Patrol. Shot down by JG27, 1715. Baled out but drowned
	Sgt J A Buck	+	off Selsey. Buried Stretford, Lancs, aged 24.
141 Sqn	Defiant I	L7001	Convoy patrol. Crashed at Hawkinge after combat with
	F/L M J Louden	Wounded	JG51 over Channel at 1245. AG baled out and rescued.
	P/O E Farnes	Safe	A/C SoC.
141 Sqn	Defiant I	L7009	Convoy patrol. Shot down off Dover at 1245 by
	F/L I D G Donald	+	Me109 of JG51.
	P/O A C Hamilton	+	
141 Sqn	Defiant I	L6974	Ditto.
	P/O J R Kemp	+	New Zealand pilot, aged 25. NKG.
	Sgt R Crombie	+	NKG, aged 25.
141 Sqn	Defiant I	L6995	Ditto.
	P/O R A Howley	+	NKG, aged 20.
	Sgt A G Curley	+	NKG, aged 33.
141 Sqn	Defiant I	L7015	Ditto.
	P/O R Kidson	+	New Zealand pilot aged 26. NKG.
	Sgt F P J Atkins	+	AG buried Boulogne Eastern Cemetery.
141 Sqn	Defiant I	L7016	Ditto. Pilot baled out and rescued, 1245.
	P/O J R Gardner	Injured	
	P/O D M Slatter	+	
141 Sqn	Defiant I	L6983	Ditto. AG baled out and lost. A/C
	P/O I N MacDougall	Safe	returned and force-landed.
	Sgt J F Wise	+	NKG, aged 20.

48

20 July 1940

32 Sqn	Hurricane I Sub-Lt(A) G G R Bulmer	N2670 +	Patrol. Shot down by Me109 of JG51 off Dover at 1800. NKG, aged 20.
32 Sqn	Hurricane I S/L J Worrall	N2532 'H' Safe	Force-landed near Hawkinge after combat with Me109s of JG51 at 1820 and burned out.
43 Sqn	Hurricane I F/O J F J Haworth	P3964 +	Scramble. Baled out south of the Needles during combat at 1800.
152 Sqn	Spitfire I P/O F H Posener	K9880 +	Patrol. Shot down off Swanage by Me109 of JG27 at 1635.
236 Sqn	Blenheim I Sgt E E Lockton Sgt H Corcoran	L1300 'A' + +	Escort. Shot down off Cherbourg by Me109 of JG27 at 1820.
238 Sqn	Hurricane I Sgt C Parkinson	P3766 DoW	Shot down by JG27 S of Swanage at 1315. Rescued but died on 21 July.
501 Sqn	Hurricane I P/O E J H Sylvester	P3082 +	Shot down in Lyme Bay by JG27 at 1630. NKG, aged 26.
610 Sqn	Spitfire I P/O G Keighley	N3201 'S' Wounded	Baled out after combat with JG51 at 1830. See 31 May 1940.

21 July 1940

43 Sqn	Hurricane I P/O R A de Mancha	P3973 +	Patrol. Collided with Me109 of JG27 S of Needles at 1515. NKG, aged 23.
54 Sqn	Spitfire I P/O J L Kemp	N3184 Safe	Convoy patrol. Baled out after engine failure off Clacton. Rescued by RN destroyer.

24 July 1940

54 Sqn	Spitfire I F/O J L Allen DFC	R6812 +	Convoy patrol. Damaged by Me109 of JG26 over Margate at 1230; stalled and crashed at Cliftonville. Also see 26 May 1940.
54 Sqn	Spitfire I Sgt G R Collett	N3192 Injured	Ran out of fuel on convoy patrol chasing EA. Force- landed Dunwich Beach, Suffolk, 1215, and SoC.
66 Sqn	Spitfire I Sgt A D Smith	N3041 Safe	Crashed into sea on convoy patrol and rescued. See 4 September 1940.

25 July 1940

54 Sqn	Spitfire I F/L B H Way	R6707 +	Shot down by Me109 over convoy off Dover 1500. Aged 22, buried at Oostdienkerke, Belgium.
54 Sqn	Spitfire I P/O D R Turley-George	P9387 Safe	Crash-landed at Dover after action; A/c later returned to service.
54 Sqn	Spitfire I P/O A Finnie	R6816 +	Ditto – crashed Kingsdown, 1810. Buried Margate, aged 24.
64 Sqn	Spitfire I F/O A J O Jeffrey DFC	P9421 +	Shot down over convoy off Dover at 1455. Body washed up 21 August and buried Vlissingen, Holland.
64 Sqn	Spitfire I Sub-Lt(A) F D Paul	L1035 DoW	Shot down in action with Me109s off Folkestone. Badly wounded, he was rescued by Germans but died 30 July 1940. Aged 24.
152 Sqn	Spitfire I F/L E C Deansely	K9901 Safe	Shot down in combat with Ju87s over convoy S of Portland, 1050. Rescued by ship. See 26 September 1940.
610 Sqn	Spitfire I S/L A T Smith	R6693 'A' +	Convoy patrol. Stalled and crashed at Hawkinge following combat with Me109s over the Channel at 1540. Buried, Delemere, Cheshire. Aged 34.

| 610 Sqn | Spitfire I | R6595 'O' | Hit in the arm during action at 1540. A/c damaged |
| | P/O F T Gardiner | Wounded | but returned to service. See 12 and 26 August 1940. |

26 July 1940

| 601 Sqn | Hurricane I | P2753 'T' | Patrol. Shot down by Me109 of JG27 two miles off St |
| | P/O P Challoner Lindsey | + | Catharine's Point at 1000. Buried Wimereux, France, aged 20. |

27 July 1940

501 Sqn	Hurricane I	P3808	Shot down over Dover by Me109 of JG52 at 1745.
	F/O P A N Cox	+	
609 Sqn	Spitfire I	N3023	Shot down off Weymouth on convoy patrol by Oblt Gert
	P/O J R Buchanan	+	Framm of JG27, at 1020. NKG, aged 25.

27/28 July 1940

| 92 Sqn | Spitfire I | N3287 | Night patrol. Baled out in bad weather over Exeter while |
| | P/O T S Wade | Safe | patrolling Swansea Bay at 0350. See 19 August 1940 and 25 June 1941. |

28 July 1940

41 Sqn	Spitfire I	P9429	Patrol. Wounded in combat with Me109s of JG51
	F/O A D J Lovell	Wounded	over Dover, 1435. Crash-landed at Hornchurch. See 5 September 1940. A/c repaired.
74 Sqn	Spitfire I	P9336	Shot down by Me109s of JG26 off Dover and baled out.
	Sgt E A Mould	Wounded	See 25 May 1940 and 20 January 1943.

P/O J L Allen DFC, 54 Squadron, killed in a forced landing after combat with Me109s on 24 July 1940.

P/O J R Buchanan of 609 Squadron, killed in action off Weymouth on 27 July 1940.

74 Sqn	Spitfire I P/O J H R Young	P9547 +	Shot down near Goodwin Sands by of JG26 1420. Buried Pihen-lès-Guînes, France. Aged 22.
257 Sqn	Hurricane I Sgt R V Forward	P3622 Injured	Damaged in combat with JG26 over convoy off Dover. Landed at RAF Hawkinge but SoC.

29 July 1940

41 Sqn	Spitfire I F/O D R Gamblen	N3038 +	Patrol. In combat with Ju87s and Me109s off Dover, 0745.
41 Sqn	Spitfire I F/O W J Scott	N3100 Safe	Patrol. written off after wheels-up landing after combat over Dover at 0750. A/c repaired. See 8 September 1940.
41 Sqn	Spitfire I P/O G H Bennions	N3113 Safe	Patrol. Crashed on landing due to battle damage over Dover, 0800. See 1st October 1940.
56 Sqn	Hurricane I F/S C J Cooney	P3879 +	Convoy patrol. Shot down over the Channel off Dover by Me109, 0745.
66 Sqn	Spitfire I P/O L W Collingridge	N3042 Injured	Patrol. Crashed on the beach at Orford Ness after combat with He111 at 1450. A/c SoC.

30/31 July 1940

234 Sqn	Spitfire I Sgt W W Thompson	P9365 Safe	Night patrol. Written off after crash at St Eval at 0128 am.

31 July 1940

74 Sqn	Spitfire I Sgt F W Eley	P9398 +	Patrol. Shot down off Folkestone by Me109 of JG51, 1600.
74 Sqn	Spitfire I P/O H R Gunn	P9379 +	Ditto. Buried Oostende, Belgium, aged 27.
74 Sqn	Spitfire I F/L D P D G Kelly	R6983 Safe	Ditto. A/c Cat 2 damage but pilot managed to land at base. Repaired.
501 Sqn	Hurricane I P/O R S Don	P3646 Injured	Patrol. Baled out after combat with Ju87s and Me109s over Dover, 1715.

1 August 1940

145 Sqn	Hurricane I Sub-Lt(A) I H Kestin	P3155 +	Patrol. Shot down in combat with Hs126 south of Hastings, 1500.
236 Sqn	Blenheim IV S/L P E Drew F/O B Nokes-Cooper	N3601 'K' + +	Bomber escort. Shot down during attack on Querqueville, France, 1715. Aged 30 and 32 respectively.
236 Sqn	Blenheim IV P/O B M McDonough Sgt F A P Head	R2774 'N' + +	Ditto. Flak or Me109 of III/JG27. NKGs.

1/2 August 1940

65 Sqn	Spitfire I S/L H C Sawyer	R6799 +	Night patrol. Crashed on take-off from Rochford and burned out, 2335.

5 August 1940

64 Sqn	Spitfire I Sgt L R Isaac	L1029 +	Patrol. Shot down by Me109 off Folkestone, 0850. NKG, aged 24.
64 Sqn	Spitfire I P/O A G Donahue	K9991 Safe	Ditto – force-landed at Hawkinge and repaired. American pilot. See 12 August 1940 and 11 September 1942.

6 August 1940

72 Sqn	Spitfire I Sgt R C J Staples	L1078 Safe	Patrol. Crashed landing at Acklington and wrecked, 1240.
234 Sqn	Spitfire I F/O P W Horton	P9366 Safe	Crashed landing from night patrol at St Eval, 2305. See 6 September 1940.

Phase Two – 8 August to 6 September 1940

8 August 1940

23 Sqn	Blenheim If P/O C F Cardnell Sgt C Stephens	L1448 'K' + +	Night patrol. Crashed 2348/nr Peterborough. Aged 22. Aged 24.
43 Sqn	Hurricane I P/O J Cruttenden	P3781 +	Patrol. Shot down in combat south of Isle of Wight, 1645. See 9 July 1940.
43 Sqn	Hurricane I P/O J R S Oelofse	P3468 +	Ditto. South African, aged 23.
64 Sqn	Spitfire I Sgt J W C Squier	P9369 Injured	Patrol. Force-landed at Gt Couldham after attack by Me109 of JG51, 1110.
64 Sqn	Spitfire I P/O P F Kennard-Davis	L1039 DoW	Ditto: baled out at 1205 over West Langdon, Kent. Died on 10 August 1940. Aged 19, buried at Brookwood Cemetery.
65 Sqn	Spitfire I Sgt D I Kirton	K9911 +	Patrol. Shot down over Manston by Me109 of JG26, 1140. Aged 21.
65 Sqn	Spitfire I F/S N T Phillips	K9905 +	Ditto. Aged 30.
145 Sqn	Hurricane I P/O L A Sears	P2955 +	Patrol. Shot down by Me109 off Isle of Wight, 0905. NKG, aged 19.
145 Sqn	Hurricane I Sgt E D Baker	P3381 +	Ditto. NKG, aged 28.
145 Sqn	Hurricane I P/O E C Wakeham	P2957 +	Patrol. Shot down in fight with Ju87s and Me110s over convoy off Isle of Wight, 1640. See 27 May 1940.
145 Sqn	Hurricane I Sub-Lt(A) F A Smith RN	P3545 +	Ditto. See 12 July 1940. NKG, aged 20.
145 Sqn	Hurricane I F/O Lord R U P Key-Shuttleworth +	P3163	Ditto. Aged 26. NKG.
152 Sqn	Spitfire I P/O W Beaumont	R6811 +	Shot down by Me109 of II/JG53 off Swanage, 1620.
152 Sqn	Spitfire I Sgt D N Robinson	K9894 'N' Safe	Crash-landed at Bestwall after action, 1615.
234 Sqn	Spitfire I Sgt J Szlagowski	N3278 Safe	Patrol. Ran out of fuel and crashed at Pensilva, 1015. A/c repaired and lost 8 January 1943. Polish pilot.
238 Sqn	Hurricane I F/L D E Turner	P3823 +	Convoy patrol. Shot down by Me109 south of the Isle of Wight, 1245.
238 Sqn	Hurricane I F/O D C MacCaw	P3617 +	Ditto. Buried Somerville-sur-Fécamp, France, aged 24.
238 Sqn	Hurricane I S/L H A Fenton	P2947 Injured	Convoy patrol. Ditched after combat with He59 off Isle of Wight, 1340, and rescued by the RN.
257 Sqn	Hurricane I F/L N M Hall	P2981 +	Patrol. Shot down over Channel, 1200, by JG27. Aged 24. Criel Cemetery, France.

257 Sqn	Hurricane I Sgt K B Smith	R4094 +	Ditto. NKG, aged 21.
257 Sqn	Hurricane I F/O B W J D'Arcy-Irvine	P3058 +	Ditto. NKG, aged 22.
600 Sqn	Blenheim If F/O D N Grice Sgt F J Keast AC1 J B W Warren	L8665 'A' + + +	Patrol. Shot down by Me109 of JG26 over Ramsgate, 1155. Grice stayed at the control of his burning aircraft to clear houses and crashed into the sea. Ages 32, 28 and 19 respectively.

9 August 1940

600 Sqn	Blenheim If F/O S P le Rougetel Sgt E C Smith	L8679 'O' Safe Safe	Night patrol. Baled out off Ramsgate after engine failed. Pilot rescued while observer swam ashore. 1100.
605 Sqn	Hurricane I Sgt R D Ritchie	L2103 +	Patrol. Crashed into the sea off Dunbar due to glycol fumes leak. Picked up by boat but neck broken. Lesley Cemetery, Fife, aged 24.

11 August 1940

1 Sqn	Hurricane I P/O J A J Davey	P3172 +	Patrol. Crashed and burnt out attempting to force-land on Sandown golf course after combat with Me110, 1120.
17 Sqn	Hurricane I P/O K Manger	P3760 +	Patrol. Shot down off east coast by Me110, 1150. See 1 June 1940.
56 Sqn	Hurricane I Sgt R D Baker	N2667 +	Convoy patrol. Crashed into the sea during combat. Baled out but died.

Spitfire K9894 of 152 Squadron, wrecked in crash-landing at Bestwall, east of Wareham, shot down by JG53 on 8 August 1940. P/O D N Robinson survived unhurt.

74 Sqn	Spitfire I P/O P C F Stevenson	P9393 Safe	Patrol. Baled out near Dover at 0810 after combat with Me109. Rescued by MTB. See 27 May 1940.
74 Sqn	Spitfire I P/O D G Cobden	R6757 +	Patrol. Combat with Me110s east of Harwich. New Zealander. Killed on his 26th birthday. Buried Oostende.
74 Sqn	Spitfire I P/O D N E Smith	R6962 +	Patrol. Ditto. Aged 26.
87 Sqn	Hurricane I F/L R Voase Jeff DFC CdG	V7231 +	Patrol. Lost in combat over Portland Bill, 1045. Aged 27. NKG.
87 Sqn	Hurricane I P/O J R Cock	V7233 Sl/WIA	Ditto – baled out and swam ashore slightly wounded. Australian. A/c salvaged from the sea in 1983.
111 Sqn	Hurricane I P/O J H H Copeman	P3105 +	Patrol. Shot down off Margate, 1420. Buried Middlekerke, Belgium. Aged 27.
111 Sqn	Hurricane I P/O J W McKenzie	P3922 +	Ditto. NKG.
111 Sqn	Hurricane I P/O R R Wilson	P3595 +	Ditto. See 2 June 1940. Canadian, aged 20. NKG.
111 Sqn	Hurricane I Sgt R B Sim	P3942 +	Ditto. NKG, aged 23.
111 Sqn	Hurricane I Sgt H S Newton	P3548 Safe	Patrol. Ran out of fuel after combat 1450 and crash-landed near Boyton, Oxford and SoC. See 18 August 1940.
145 Sqn	Hurricane I F/O G R Branch GC	P2951 +	Patrol. Crashed into the sea off Swanage after combat with Me109s at 1030. Buried Quiberville, France, aged 26. GC (EGM) won in 1937.
145 Sqn	Hurricane I F/O A Ostowicz	V7294 +	Ditto. Polish pilot, aged 29.
152 Sqn	Spitfire I P/O J S B Jones	R6614 +	Patrol. Shot down over Channel by Me109, 1100. Buried St Marie, Le Havre, France. Aged 21.
213 Sqn	Hurricane I F/L R D G Wight DFC	N2650 'O' +	Patrol. Shot down off Portland, 1100. Buried Cayeux-sur-Mer, France. 24.
213 Sqn	Hurricane I Sgt S L Butterfield DFM	P3789 'P' +	Ditto – buried Boulogne, aged 27. See 28 May 1940.
238 Sqn	Hurricane I Sgt G Gledhill	P2978 +	Patrol. Shot down off Weymouth at 1040. Buried Criquebeuf-en-Caux, France.
238 Sqn	Hurricane I F/L S C Walch	R4097 +	Ditto. Australian pilot. NKG, aged 23.
238 Sqn	Hurricane I F/O M J Stęborowski	P3819 +	Ditto. Polish pilot. NKG, aged 31.
238 Sqn	Hurricane I P/O F N Cawse	P3222 +	Ditto. Buried Cayeux-sur-Mer, France. Aged 25.
601 Sqn	Hurricane I P/O J L Smithers	P3885 +	Patrol. Shot down by Me109s off Portland, 1045. Buried Le Havre.
601 Sqn	Hurricane I F/O R S Demetriadi	R4092 +	Ditto. Buried Cayeux-sur-Mer, France, aged 21.
601 Sqn	Hurricane I F/O J Gillan	P3783 +	Ditto. NKG, aged 26.
601 Sqn	Hurricane I P/O W G Dickie	L2057 +	Ditto. NKG, aged 24.

610 Sqn	Spitfire I F/S J H Tanner	R6918 'D' +	Patrol. Shot down off Calais, 1130. Buried Calais Southern, France, aged 25.
610 Sqn	Spitfire I Sgt W J Neville	R6630 +	Ditto. NKG, aged 26.

12 August 1940

32 Sqn	Hurricane I P/O A R H Barton	N2596 Safe	Patrol. Shot down over Dover, 1700. Crashed near Hawkinge. See 20 September 1940.
56 Sqn	Hurricane I P/O A G Page	P2970 'X' Wounded	Patrol. Shot down attacking a Do17 and baled out badly burned north of Margate. Rescued by tender and the Margate lifeboat, 1750.
64 Sqn	Spitfire I P/O A G Donahue	X4018 Wounded	Patrol. Shot down 1230 by Me109 over south coast. Baled out, A/C fell at Sellindge. See 5 August 1940 and 11 September 1942. American.
145 Sqn	Hurricane I P/O J H Harrison	R4180 +	Patrol. Shot down by German fighter 1230, south of the Isle of Wight. NKG, aged 22.
145 Sqn	Hurricane I Sgt J Kwieciński	P3391 +	Ditto. Polish pilot. NKG, aged 23.
145 Sqn	Hurricane I F/L W Pankratz	R4176 +	Ditto. Polish, NKG, aged 36.
151 Sqn	Hurricane I F/O A B Tucker	P3302 Wounded	Patrol. Shot down off north Foreland with back wounds, 1100. Rescued by launch.
151 Sqn	Hurricane I P/O R W G Beley	P3304 DoW	Shot down by Me109 off Ramsgate, 1100. Rescued but died later. Canadian, aged 20.
152 Sqn	Spitfire I F/L L C Withall	P9456 +	Patrol. Shot down off Isle of Wight by Ju88, 1220. Australian. NKG, 29.
152 Sqn	Spitfire I P/O D C Shepley	K9999 +	Patrol. Shot down in combat with Ju88s south of the the Isle of Wight, 1220. NKG, aged 22.
213 Sqn	Hurricane I Sgt G N Wilkes	P2854 'M' +	Patrol. Shot down off Bognor by fighters, 1245. NKG, aged 21.
213 Sqn	Hurricane I Sgt S G Stuckey	P2802 'R' +	Ditto. NKG, aged 26.
257 Sqn	Hurricane I P/O J A G Chomley	P3662 +	Patrol. Shot down off Portsmouth by fighter, 1300. Rhodesian. NGK, aged 20.
257 Sqn	Hurricane I F/O The Hon D A Coke	P3776 Wounded	Ditto, A/c damaged but repaired.
266 Sqn	Spitfire I P/O W S Williams	N3175 Safe	Patrol. Force-landed and burned after combat with Ju88 over the Isle of Wight, 1220.
266 Sqn	Spitfire I P/O D G Ashton	P9333 +	Ditto. Body recovered by HMS *Cedar* (minesweeper) and buried at sea. Aged 20.
501 Sqn	Hurricane I F/O K Łukaszewicz	P3803 'Z' +	Patrol. Shot down off Ramsgate by fighters at 1255. Polish pilot. Aged 27.
610 Sqn	Spitfire I P/O E B B Smith	K9818 'H' Sl/WIA	Shot down in flames by Me109 over New Romney, 0800. Baled out with slight burns.
610 Sqn	Spitfire I ?	P9495 'K' Safe	Severely damaged in combat over Dover, 0805, and SoC.
610 Sqn	Spitfire I F/O F T Gardiner	R6806 Sl/WIA	Ditto. Also damaged in heavy landing landing at base. Pilot wounded in left leg. A/c repaired. See 25 July and 25 August 1940.

13 August 1940

Squadron	Aircraft / Pilot	Serial / Status	Notes
43 Sqn	Hurricane I F/L T F Dalton Morgan	P3972 Sl/WIA	Patrol. Baled out after combat with He111 near Cocking Down, 0650. See 6 September 1940.
43 Sqn	Hurricane I P/O C A Woods-Scawen	R4102 Safe	Crash-landed and burned at 0730, near Midhurst, Sussex, after combat with He111. See 7 June, 16 August and 2 September 1940.
56 Sqn	Hurricane I P/O C C O Joubert	P3479 Safe	Patrol. Baled out after attack by Me110 near Rochford, 1615. Pilot slightly injured.
56 Sqn	Hurricane I F/O P F McD Davies	P2692 'T' Wounded	Ditto. Pilot badly burned.
56 Sqn	Hurricane I Sgt P Hillwood	R4093 'P' Safe	Patrol. Baled out after combat with Me110s over Sheppey 1620. Swam ashore. See 17 May 1940.
56 Sqn	Hurricane I F/O R E P Brooker	P3587 Safe	Patrol. Force-landed at Hawkinge after combat with Me110s over Sheppey 1630; A/c written off. See 21 and 30 August 1940 and 16 April 1945.
74 Sqn	Spitfire I F/L S Brzezina	N3091 Safe	Patrol. Baled out after combat with Do17 over Thames Estuary, 0705. Polish pilot.
74 Sqn	Spitfire I P/O H Szcznśny	K9871 'O' Safe	Patrol. Crash-landed and tipped up and damaged; repaired.
87 Sqn	Hurricane I F/O R L Glyde DFC	P3387 +	Patrol. Shot down in combat with Ju88 off Selsey Bill, 0800. See 14 November 1939. Australian.
213 Sqn	Hurricane I Sgt P P Norris	P3348 'B' +	Patrol. Shot down off Portland, 1650. Buried Etaples, France. Aged 22.
238 Sqn	Hurricane I Sgt E W Seabourne	P3764 Wounded	Patrol. Shot down by Me109 off Isle of Wight, 0730 and baled out badly burned. Rescued by destroyer.
238 Sqn	Hurricane I Sgt H J Marsh	P3177 +	Patrol. Shot down off Portland at 1630 by Me109. NKG, aged 27.
238 Sqn	Hurricane I Sgt R Little	P3805 Safe	Crashed unhurt at Burton Bradstock at 1630 after combat over Portland. A/c repaired. See 28 September 1940.
601 Sqn	Hurricane I P/O H C Mayers	P2690 Safe	Patrol. Shot down over Portland at 1215 and baled out; rescued by MTB with slight shrapnel wounds. See 7 October 1940 and 4 May 1941.

14 August 1940

Squadron	Aircraft / Pilot	Serial / Status	Notes
32 Sqn	Hurricane I P/O R F Smythe	P3171 Safe	Patrol. written off after battle damage by Me109s over Dover, 1315. See 24 August 1940.
43 Sqn	Hurricane I Sgt H F Montgomery	L1739 +	Patrol. Crashed 40 miles south of Beachy Head, 1915, after combat with He111. Buried Senneville-sur-Fécamp, France. Aged 26.
151 Sqn	Hurricane I Sgt G Atkinson	P3310 Safe	Patrol. Baled out over Christchurch in combat with Do17s at 0700.
609 Sqn	Spitfire I F/O H MacD Goodwin	N3024 'H' +	Patrol. Shot down over Bournemouth at 1730. Body later washed up on Isle of Wight. Aged 25.
615 Sqn	Hurricane I F/O P Collard	P3109 +	Patrol. Shot down of Dover 1245. Buried Oye-Plage, France. Aged 24.
615 Sqn	Hurricane I P/O C R Montgomery	P3160 +	Ditto. Aged 26.

15 August 1940

1 Sqn	Hurricane I F/L M H Brown DFC	P3047 'E' Safe	Patrol. Shot down off Harwich 1500. Baled out with slight injuries and rescued by trawler.
1 Sqn	Hurricane I P/O D O M Browne	R4075 +	Ditto. See 19 July 1940. NKG, aged 22.
1 Sqn	Hurricane I Sgt M M Shanahan	P3043 'G' +	Ditto. NKG, aged 25.
32 Sqn	Hurricane I P/O D H Grice	N2459 'C' Wounded	Patrol. Baled out after combat with Me109s south of Harwich, 1525. Burned but rescued by MTB. See 8 June 1940.
54 Sqn	Spitfire I Sgt N A Lawrence	N3097 Safe	Patrol. Shot down by Me109. Crashed in sea off Dover, 1145. Rescued by the RN.
54 Sqn	Spitfire I Sgt W Kloziński	R7015 WIA	Patrol. Crashed near Hythe after fight over Dover, 1145. A/C SoC. Polish.
54 Sqn	Spitfire I F/L A C Deere DFC	R6981 Safe	Baled out after combat with Me109s, near Ashford. See 28 May, 9 July and 28 and 31 August 1940.
64 Sqn	Spitfire I F/O C J D Andreae	R6990 +	Patrol. Shot down by Me109 near Dungeness, 1520. NKG, aged 23.
64 Sqn	Spitfire I P/O R Roberts	K9964 'W' PoW	Force-landed Calais-Marck after combat with Me109s at 1525. Stalag Luft III Camp.
87 Sqn	Hurricane I S/L T G Lovell-Gregg	P3215 +	Patrol. Shot down by fighters at 1800 over Portland. Buried Holy Trinity Church, Warmwell. New Zealander.
87 Sqn	Hurricane I Sgt J Cowley	P3465 Sl/inj	Ditto. Force-landed near Bridport with slight injuries. A/c SoC but later became an instructional airframe.
87 Sqn	Hurricane I P/O P W Comely	P2872 +	Ditto – shot down by Me109, 1908, off Portland. NKG.
111 Sqn	Hurricane I P/O A G McIntyre	P3595 Sl/WIA	Landed Hawkinge badly damaged in combat over Thorney Island, 1800. A/c SoC. New Zealander.
111 Sqn	Hurricane I F/O B M Fisher	P3944 +	Shot down in combat with Ju88 over Selsey Bill, 1750. Baled out but he did not survive. Aged 23.
151 Sqn	Hurricane I P/O J T Johnston	P3941 +	Patrol. Shot down by Me109, 1915, off Dymchurch. Buried Folkestone. Canadian, aged 26.
151 Sqn	Hurricane I Sub-Lt(A) H W Beggs	P3065 'G' Wounded	Ditto. Came down at Shorncliffe. A/c repaired.
151 Sqn	Hurricane I P/O M Rozwadowski	V7410 +	Ditto. Polish pilot. NKG, aged 25.
151 Sqn	Hurricane I S/L J A G Gordon	P3940 Sl/WIA	Wounded in combat with Me109 over Dover but landed safely at North Weald. Canadian. See 18 August 1940 and 1 June 1942.
152 Sqn	Spitfire I F/L B P A Boitel-Gill	K9954 Safe	Patrol. Severely damaged by Me109 over Portland and SoC.
213 Sqn	Hurricane I P/O M S H C Buchin	V7227 'C' +	Patrol. Lost over Portland, 1745. Belgian pilot. NKG, aged 34.
234 Sqn	Spitfire I P/O C H Hight	R6988 +	Patrol. Baled out over Bournemouth after fight with Me109s, 1815. Parachute failed. New Zealander.
234 Sqn	Spitfire I P/O R Hardy	N3277 'H' PoW	Ditto. Force-landed near Cherbourg after combat with Me109. Stalag Luft III Camp.

234 Sqn	Spitfire I P/O V Parker	R6985 PoW	Patrol. Missing 1615 after combat off Swanage; rescued by the Germans. Stalag Luft III Camp.
234 Sqn	Spitfire I Sgt Z Klein	P9363 Safe	Patrol. Badly damaged in combat and crashed at Twyford. Polish pilot.
257 Sqn	Hurricane I P/O C G Frizell	L1703 Safe	Patrol. Baled out following a fire. Crashed near Edgware.
266 Sqn	Spitfire I Sgt F B Hawley	N3189 +	Patrol. Combat with He115 off Dunkirk; crashed off Deal, Kent. NKG, aged 23.
266 Sqn	Spitfire I P/O F W Cale	N3168 +	Patrol. Shot down near Maidstone 1850; baled out into the River Medway and drowned. Buried at Ealing, aged 25. Australian.
501 Sqn	Hurricane I F/L J A A Gibson	P3582 Safe	Patrol. Baled out after combat with Ju87 over Hawkinge, 1130. See 29 August 1940.
501 Sqn	Hurricane I F/L A R Putt	P3040 Safe	Patrol. Baled out after engagement with Ju87s, 1130.
601 Sqn	Hurricane I F/O G N S Cleaver	P3232 Wounded	Patrol. Baled out over Winchester at 1750. See 19 May 1940.
604 Sqn	Blenheim I Sgt C Haigh Sgt G J Evans	L6610 Safe Safe	Written off after crash following attack by Spitfires of 609 Sqn. See 25 August 1940.
605 Sqn	Hurricane I F/O C W Passy	P3827 Safe	Scramble. Crash-landed near Usworth after combat with He111s of KG26 off Newcastle, 1410. Repaired. See 26 October and 1 December 1940.

F/O P Collard (DFC) of 615 Squadron, killed in action over the Channel on 14 August 1940.

Sgt P K Walley of 615 Squadron remained with his damaged Hurricane to avoid houses and died in attempting to land on Morden Park, Surrey, on 18 August 1940.

605 Sqn	Hurricane I P/O K Schadtler-Law	P2717 Injured	Scramble. Hit by return fire from a He111 of KG26 off Newcastle and force-landed on Hartlepool golf course. A/c repaired.
615 Sqn	Hurricane I Sgt D W Halton	P2801 +	Shot down by Me109 at 1205. NKG, aged 21.
615 Sqn	Hurricane I P/O A J J Truran	P2581 Sl/WIA	Patrol. Damaged by Me109 near Folkestone. SoC.

16 August 1940

1 Sqn	Hurricane I P/O J F D Elkington	P3173 Wounded	Patrol. Shot down over Thorney Island, 1305, and written off.
43 Sqn	Hurricane I P/O C A Woods-Scawen	P3216 Wounded	Patrol. Crashed after combat with Ju87s over Sussex coast. Repaired. See 7 June, 13 August and 2 September 1940.
43 Sqn	Hurricane I Sgt J L Crisp	L1736 'H' Injured	Baled out near Portsmouth after being hit by Me109, 1800. Pilot broke thigh.
56 Sqn	Hurricane I P/O L W Graham	V7368 Injured	Patrol. Baled out near Manston, 1205, after attack by EA. South African pilot.
56 Sqn	Hurricane I F/S F W Higginson DFM	P3547 'A' Injured	Patrol. Force-landed after combat with Do17 off Whitstable, 1715. SoC. See 17 June 1941.
64 Sqn	Spitfire I S/L A R D MacDonnell	P9554 Safe	Patrol. Shot down by Me109 near Uckfield, 1715, and baled out. See 13 March 1941.
65 Sqn	Spitfire I P/O L L Pyman	K9915 +	Patrol. Shot down over Channel, near Deal. Buried Calais, aged 23.
111 Sqn	Hurricane I F/L H M Ferris	R4193 +	Patrol. Collided with Do17 of KG76 over Marden, Kent, during head-on attack, 1245. Aged 23.
111 Sqn	Hurricane I Sgt R Carnall	P3029 Injured	Patrol. Shot down in combat near Paddock Wood, 1230. Pilot was badly burned.
213 Sqn	Hurricane I P/O J E P Laricheliere	?'U' +	Patrol. Shot down off Portland in combat, 1300. Canadian, aged 27.
234 Sqn	Spitfire I F/O K S Dewhurst	R6967 Safe	Patrol. Baled out near Southampton after combat with Me109, 1300.
234 Sqn	Spitfire I F/O F H P Connor	X4016 Safe	Ditto – over Portsmouth. Rescued by RN launch.
249 Sqn	Hurricane I F/L J B E Nicholson	P3576 'A' Wounded	Patrol. Baled out after combat with Ju88 and Me110 over Southampton, 1350. Awarded VC 15 November 1940.
249 Sqn	Hurricane I P/O M A King	P3616 +	Ditto – 1355. Baled out but parachute collapsed.
266 Sqn	Spitfire I S/L R L Wilkinson	R6768 +	Patrol. Shot down by Me109 near Deal at 1235.
266 Sqn	Spitfire I P/O N G Bowen	N3095 +	Patrol. Shot down by Me109 over Adisham, Kent, 1245.
266 Sqn	Spitfire I F/L S H Bazley	P9312 Injured	Patrol. Baled out after combat with Me109 over Canterbury, 1245.
266 Sqn	Spitfire I Sub-Lt(A) H L Greenshields	N3240 +	Patrol. Crashed near Calais after combat with Me109, 1240. RNVR. Buried Calais Southern, aged 22.
266 Sqn	Spitfire I P/O J F Soden	K9864 Sl/WIA	Patrol. Written off after force-landing following combat with Me109 over Canterbury. A/c repaired. See 25 October 1940.

601 Sqn	Hurricane I	P3358	Patrol. Landed on fire at Tangmere. Badly burned after
	P/O W M L Fiske	DoW	combat with Ju87s over Bognor, 1300. Died 17 August. American.
610 Sqn	Spitfire I	R6802 'Z'	Patrol. Shot down by Me109, 1715, off Dungeness. NKG,
	F/L W H C Warner	+	aged 21.
610 Sqn	Spitfire I	P2963	Patrol. Force-landed after attack on He111 and engaged
	P/O P H Hugo	Wounded	by Me110, 1730. A/c repaired.

17 August 1940

235 Sqn	Blenheim I	N3540	Night patrol. Overshot on landing at Thorney Island
	Sgt S J Hobbs	Safe	and crashed. SoC.
	Sgt H W Ricketts	Safe	
	Sgt T A Maslen	Safe	

18 August 1940

17 Sqn	Hurricane I	L1921	Patrol. Shot down by Me109, 1305, off Dover. Buried
	P/O N D Soloman	+	Pihen-les-Guines, France. Aged 26.
32 Sqn	Hurricane I	P3147	Patrol. Baled out seriously wounded during combat over
	P/O J F Pain	Wounded	Biggin Hill, 1345. A/c crashed near Herne Bay. Australian.
32 Sqn	Hurricane I	V7363	Baled out seriously wounded after combat over Biggin
	F/L H a'B Russell	Wounded	Hill, 1345. See 28 May 1944.
32 Sqn	Hurricane I	N2461 'F'	Patrol. Baled out over Gillingham after combat with
	S/L M N Crossley DFC	Safe	Me109, 1730. See 24 August 1940.
32 Sqn	Hurricane I	V6535	Ditto – baled out badly burned near Biggin Hill, 1735.
	P/O R G C deH de Grunne	Wounded	See 21 May 1941. Belgian pilot.
32 Sqn	Hurricane I	R4106	Baled out slightly wounded after combat near
	Sgt L H B Pearce	Wounded	Canterbury with Me109, 1730.
43 Sqn	Hurricane I	R4109	Scramble. Wounded in combat near Tangmere; crash-
	F/L F R Carey DFC DFM	Wounded	landed at 1426 in a field at Pulborough. Repaired. See 14 May 1940.
65 Sqn	Spitfire I	R6713	Patrol. Shot down near Canterbury at 1330. Polish pilot,
	F/O F Gruszka	+	aged 30. His aircraft and body were excavated in 1976. He was buried at Northwood.
85 Sqn	Hurricane I	P2923 'R'	Patrol. Lost chasing EA off east coast at 1750.
	F/O R H A Lee DSO DFC	+	See 11 and 27 May 1940. NKG, aged 23.
85 Sqn	Hurricane I	V7249	Baled out after combat with He111 over Thames
	P/O J A Hemingway	Safe	Estuary, 1745. See 11 May and 26 August 1940.
92 Sqn	Spitfire I	N3040	Patrol. Baled out after combat with a Ju88, 1415. A/c
	F/L R R S Tuck DFC	Safe	crashed near Horsmonden, Kent. See 25 August 1940, 21 June 1941 and 28 January 1942.
111 Sqn	Hurricane I	P3943	Patrol. Baled out during attack on Do17 near Kenley,
	Sgt H S Newton	Wounded	suffering burns. See 11 August 1940.
111 Sqn	Hurricane I	N2340	Hit by ground fire at 1320 on returning from combat.
	Sgt A H Deacon	Wounded	Baled out with wounds to legs. A/c crashed at Oxted.
111 Sqn	Hurricane I	R4187	Hit by AA fire while attacking Do17 at 1320, near
	F/L S D P Connors DFC	+	Wallington. Aged 28.
151 Sqn	Hurricane I	P3940	Patrol. Baled out badly burned after combat with Me110
	S/L J A C Gordon	Wounded	over Rochford, 1730. Canadian pilot. See 15 August 1940 and 1 June 1942.

151 Sqn	Hurricane I P/O J B Ramsey	R4181 +	Crashed near Burnham-on-Crouch after combat, 1730. Body discovered during excavation in 1983 and buried at Brookwood cemetery. Aged 21.
257 Sqn	Hurricane I Sgt A G Girdwood	P3708 Wounded	Patrol. Baled out after combat with Me110 over Thames Estuary, 1800. See 29 October 1940.
501 Sqn	Hurricane I F/O R C Dafforn	R4219 Safe	Patrol. Baled out after combat over Biggin Hill, 1205. See 2 December 1940.
501 Sqn	Hurricane I P/O K N T Lee	P3059 'D' Wounded	Patrol. Shot down by Me109 of JG26 over Canterbury at 1330. Baled out with bullet wound to one leg. See 10 June 1940.
501 Sqn	Hurricane I P/O F Kozlowski	P3815 Wounded	Shot down over Canterbury by Me109 of JG26, 1330. See also 13 March Polish pilot.
501 Sqn	Hurricane I Sgt D A S McKay	N2617 Injured	Ditto. Slightly burned during bale out.
501 Sqn	Hurricane I P/O J W Bland	P3208 'T' +	Ditto. Aged 26.
501 Sqn	Hurricane I F/L G E B Stoney	P2549 +	Patrol. Shot down by Me110 over Thames Estuary by JG51, 1745. Aged 29.
601 Sqn	Hurricane I Sgt L N Guy	R4191 +	Patrol. Shot down by Me109 off Sussex coast, 1415. NKG, aged 25.
601 Sqn	Hurricane I Sgt R P Hawkings	L1990 +	Ditto – shot down by JG27, 1450. Buried Filton, Gloucestershire. Aged 22.
602 Sqn	Spitfire I F/L J D Urie	X4110 Wounded	Patrol. Badly damaged by cannon shell near Tangmere and SoC. Pilot wounded in both legs.
602 Sqn	Spitfire I Sgt B E P Whall	L1019 'G' Safe	Patrol. Ditched after fight with Ju87 at 1445 at Middleton-on-Sea, Sussex. See 22 May (Norway) and 7 October 1940.

F/Lt C R Davis DFC, 601 Squadron, killed in action on 6 September 1940.

615 Sqn	Hurricane I F/L L M Gaunce	P2966 Wounded	Patrol. Baled out after combat with Me109 near Sevenoaks, 1315. See 26 August 1940 and 19 November 1941. Canadian pilot.
615 Sqn	Hurricane I P/O P H Hugo	R4221 Wounded	Crash-landed near Orpington after fight with Me109, 1315. See 16 August 1940 and 27 April 1942. South African pilot.
615 Sqn	Hurricane I Sgt P K Walley	P2768 +	Crashed in Morden Park after combat with Me109 of JG3, 1330, staying with his aircraft to avoid nearby houses. Buried Kenley, aged 20.
615 Sqn	Hurricane I P/O D J Looker	L1592 'Z' Wounded	Shot up by Me109 over Sevenoaks and by airfield defences at Croydon. A/c repaired. Now on display at the Science Museum, London. See 15 May 1940.

19 August 1940

1 Sqn	Hurricane I P/O C N Birch	P3684 Safe	Night patrol. Crashed near Finsbury Park, 2330. Baled out after hitting a balloon cable.
66 Sqn	Spitfire I P/O J A P Studd	N3182 +	Patrol. Hit by return fire from He111. Baled out into the sea. Rescued but died later. Aged 22.
92 Sqn	Spitfire I P/O T S Wade	R6703 Safe	Patrol. Crash-landed near Lewes after combat with Ju88 over the Solent. See 28 July 1940 and 25 June 1941.
248 Sqn	Blenheim IVf Sgt J H Round Sgt W H Want Sgt M P Digby-Worsley	L9457 'S' + + +	Recce. FTR from Norwegian coast early am. NKG, aged 27. NKG, aged 28. NKG, aged 18.
602 Sqn	Spitfire I P/O H W Moody	P9423 Sl/inj	Patrol. Baled out 1450 near North Berstead after being hit from a Ju88 off Bognor. Slight burns to hands. See 7 September 1940.

20 August 1940

65 Sqn	Spitfire I P/O K G Hart	R6818 Safe	Patrol. written off after damage by Me109 over Thames Estuary, 1530. See 22 and 26 May 1940.
242 Sqn	Hurricane I Mid. P J Patterson	P2976 +	Patrol. Crashed into the sea at 1345, off Winterton. Cause unknown. FAA pilot, aged 29.

21 August 1940

56 Sqn	Hurricane I F/O R E P Brooker	P3153 Safe	Patrol. Shot down by rear gunner of Do17 over East Anglia at 1815. Slightly injured in forced landing. Written off. See 13 August and 30 August 1940 and 16 April 1945.

22 August 1940

54 Sqn	Spitfire I Sgt G R Collett	R6708 +	Patrol. Shot down into the sea by Me109, 1315. Buried Bergen op Zoom, Holland, aged 24. See 25 July 1940.
65 Sqn	Spitfire I Sgt M Keymer	K9909 'O' +	Patrol. Shot down by Me109 of JG26 off Dover, 1935. Buried Bazinghem, France, aged 24.
610 Sqn	Spitfire I Sgt D F Corfe	R6695 'O' Safe	Patrol. Written off after combat with Me109, 1415, and crashed at RAF Hawkinge. See 18 September 1940.
616 Sqn	Spitfire I F/O H S L Dundas	R6926 Wounded	Patrol. Baled out after combat with Me109 at 1930. Wounded in leg and arm.

23 August 1940

1 Sqn	Hurricane I Sgt H J Merchant	P2980 Safe	Night patrol. Force-landed, 0409, having run out of fuel at Withyham, Kent, and hit trees. See 31 August 1940.

24 August 1940

Sqn	Aircraft / Pilot	Serial / Status	Remarks
32 Sqn	Hurricane I P/O K Pniak	V6572 Sl/WIA	Patrol. Shot down over Folkestone by Me109, 1615. Baled out with slight wounds. Polish pilot. See 23 July 1941.
32 Sqn	Hurricane I P/O R F Smythe	V6568 Wounded	Written off after combat with Me109 over Folkestone, 1615. See 14 August 1940.
32 Sqn	Hurricane I P/O E G A Seghers	V6567 Safe	Shot down by Me109 near Elham and baled out, 1630. Belgian pilot. See 26 July 1944.
32 Sqn	Hurricane I S/L M N Crossley DFC	P3481 Safe	Ditto – Folkestone. A/C written off in crash. See 18 August 1940.
54 Sqn	Spitfire I P/O A R McL Campbell	X4019 Injured	Patrol. Combat with Me109 over RAF Manston 1040. A/c damaged and pilot slightly injured. Canadian pilot. See 7 July 1940. A/C repaired.
65 Sqn	Spitfire I Sgt G Hill	R6884 Safe	Patrol. Damaged in combat at 1535 off Margate. Repaired and lost on 27 September 1940 with 41 Sqn.
151 Sqn	Hurricane I P/O K B L Debenham	R4183 Wounded	Patrol. Shot down by Me109, crashed and SoC. Pilot badly burned. A/C repaired.
151 Sqn	Hurricane I Sgt G T Clarke	P3273 Wounded	Damaged in combat at 1555 over Ramsgate. A/c repaired.
234 Sqn	Spitfire I P/O J Zurakowski	N3239 Safe	Patrol. Shot down by Me109 and crashed on the Isle of Wight, 1640. Polish pilot. See 6 September 1940.
235 Sqn	Blenheim IVf P/O D N Woodger Sgt D L Wright	T1804 'E' + +	Patrol. Shot down in error by 1 RCAF Sqn, 1645. Crashed Bracklesham Bay. NKG, aged 20. Wright was aged 18 and buried in St Anne's Churchyard, Chasetown, Burntwood, Staffs.
264 Sqn	Defiant I S/L P A Hunter DSO Sgt F H King DFM	N1535 'A' +	Patrol. Missing after chasing a Ju88 out to sea. NKGs, aged 27 and 25 respectively.
264 Sqn	Defiant I P/O J T Jones P/O W A Ponting	L6966 + +	Shot down by Me109 of JG3 off Ramsgate, 1240. NKGs, aged 21 and 30 respectively.
264 Sqn	Defiant I F/O I G Shaw Sgt A Berry	L7027 + +	Ditto. NKGs.
264 Sqn	Defiant I P/O R S Gaskell Sgt W H Machin	L6965 Sl/WIA DoW	Written off after combat with Me109s of JG51 over Hornchurch, 1600. Buried Handsworth Cemetery, aged 20.
501 Sqn	Hurricane I P/O P Zenker	P3141 'W' +	Patrol. Lost during combat with Do17 NW of Dover, 1015. NGK aged 25. Polish pilot.
501 Sqn	Hurricane I P/O K R Aldridge	L1865 'R' Injured	Baled out and broke an arm in fight with Me109s over West Kingsdown at 1635. Possible AA hit too.
610 Sqn	Spitfire I Sgt S J Arnfield	R6686 Injured	Patrol. Baled out and broke ankle after combat with JG51 off Ramsgate at 0850.
610 Sqn	Spitfire I P/O D McI Gray	X4102 'K' Wounded	Written off after shot down by Me109 over Dover, c.1130.
610 Sqn	Spitfire I P/O C Merrick	L1037 'D' Wounded	Written off after combat with Me109. Crash-landed at Fyfield, 1630.
615 Sqn	Hurricane I P/O D H Hone	V7318 Safe	Glycol tank pierced attacking Do17 and force-landed near Meopham at 1603. Cat B damage. See 26 August 1940 and 26 February 1941.

25 August 1940

17 Sqn	Hurricane I S/L C W Williams	R4199 +	Patrol. Shot down in head-on attack against Me110s off Portland, 1745. NKG, aged 30.
17 Sqn	Hurricane I F/L A W A Bayne	V7407 Safe	Baled out in combat with Me110s and Me109s off Portland, 1750.
29 Sqn	Blenheim If P/O R A Rhodes Sgt R J Gouldstone AC2 N Jacobson	L1330 + + +	Night Patrol. Shot down into the sea by EA, 2200, off Wainfleet, Lincs. Pilot NKG, aged 19. Gouldstone aged 19, body washed ashore at Skegness and buried St Martin's churchyard, Ryarsh. Jacobson's body recovered and buried at sea, aged 18.
32 Sqn	Hurricane I P/O J Rose	V6547 Safe	Patrol. Baled out over Channel during combat with Me109, 1900. Rescued.
32 Sqn	Hurricane I P/O K R Gillman	P2755 +	Shot down by Me109 off Dover, 1900. NKG, aged 19. His portrait was used on many RAF posters.
54 Sqn	Spitfire I P/O M M Shand	R6969 Wounded	Damaged by Me109 over Dover at 1920. Force-landed near Manston. A/c repaired. New Zealander. See 28 November 1942.
73 Sqn	Hurricane I Sgt M E Leng	P3758 Safe	Night patrol. Brought down by British AA fire near Beverley at 0130 and baled out. See 23 September 1940.
87 Sqn	Hurricane I Sgt S R E Wakeling	V7250 +	Patrol. Shot down in combat near Portland, 1805. Buried Holy Trinity churchyard, Warmwell, aged 21.
92 Sqn	Hurricane I F/L R R S Tuck DFC	N3268 Wounded	Written off after forced landing after combat with Do215 over St Gowan's Head, Pembroke, at 1820. Slight leg wound. See 18 August 1940, 21 June 1941 and 28 January 1942.
152 Sqn	Spitfire I P/O R M Hogg	R6810 +	Patrol. Shot down by fighters off Portland at 1730. NGK, aged 21.
152 Sqn	Spitfire I P/O T S Wildblood	R6994 +	Ditto. Mentioned in Dispatches: it brings the men's name to the attention of 'higher authority' and sometimes led to a decoration, 17 March 1941. NKG, aged 20.
213 Sqn	Hurricane I P/O H D Atkinson DFC	P3200 +	Patrol. Shot down off Portland, 1800. Buried Market Weighton Cemetery, Yorks. Aged 22.
213 Sqn	Hurricane I P/O J A L Philippart	V7226 +	Shot down off Portland by JG53 at 1730. Baled out but drowned. Belgian pilot. Aged 31.
213 Sqn	Hurricane I Sgt E G Snowden	N2646 Safe	Damaged by Me109 over Portland and force-landed at Burton Bradstock, Dorset. SoC.
213 Sqn	Hurricane I F/L J M Strickland	P2766 Safe	Shot down near Portland.
602 Sqn	Spitfire I Sgt M H Sprague	N3226 Safe	Patrol. Baled out after combat with Me109s off Portland, 1745, and rescued. See 11 September 1940.
602 Sqn	Spitfire I F/O W H Coverley	P9381 Safe	Ditto. See 7 September 1940.
604 Sqn	Blenheim If Sgt C Haigh Sgt J G B Fletcher LAC A L Austin	L6782 + + DoI	Patrol, late pm. Crashed near Exeter. Buried Swinton, Yorks, aged 23 Buried Forest Row, aged 20. Buried Northwood Cemetery, aged 25. See 15 August 1940.
609 Sqn	Spitfire I P/O P Ostaszewski-Ostoja	R6986 Wounded	Crashed Warmwell due to battle damage by Me109 over Swanage, 1730, with wound to arm. Polish pilot.

610 Sqn	Spitfire I F/O F T Gardiner	K9931 'P' Sl/WIA	Patrol. Baled out after combat with Me109 over Dover, 1920. See 25 July and 12 August 1940.
616 Sqn	Spitfire I Sgt T E Westmoreland	R6966 +	FTR from patrol after combat with Me109 over Canterbury at 1900. NKG, aged 27.
616 Sqn	Spitfire I Sgt P T Wareing	K9819 PoW	Ditto – over the Channel, crashed near Calais. Stalag Luft III camp; escaped while at Oflag XXIB and awarded DCM. Arrived England January 1943.

26 August 1940

1 Sqn (RCAF)	Hurricane I F/O R L Edwards	P3874 +	Patrol. Shot down by Do17, 1540. Crashed at Little Bardfield, Essex.
43 Sqn	Hurricane I P/O R Lane	P3220 Wounded	Patrol. Crashed after combat with He111s over Portsmouth, 1645. Pilot badly burned.
43 Sqn	Hurricane I P/O C K Gray	P3202 Wounded	Ditto – baled out, wounded in the arm.
43 Sqn	Hurricane I P/O H L North	V7259 Wounded	Ditto – wounded head and shoulders and baled out. New Zealander. See 1 May 1942.
43 Sqn	Hurricane I P/O G C Brunner	V7308 Wounded	Ditto – bellied in at Tangmere after combat. A/c repaired.
56 Sqn	Hurricane I P/O B J Wicks	V7340 Safe	Patrol. Baled out over River Stour after combat with Me109 at 1230. See 22 May 1940.
56 Sqn	Hurricane I Sgt G Smythe	P3473 Safe	Written off after combat (as above), crash-landing near Foulness. See 28 August 1940.
85 Sqn	Hurricane I P/O J A Hemingway	P3966 Safe	Baled out over Eastchurch after combat with Me109, 1600. See 11 and 18 May 1940. Irish pilot.
264 Sqn	Defiant I Sgt E R Thorn DFM Sgt F J Barker DFM	L7005 Injured Injured	Written off after combat with Me109 and crash-landing near Chislet, 1210.
264 Sqn	Defiant I F/L A J Banham Sgt B Baker	L6985 Safe +	Ditto – off Herne Bay; pilot rescued. See 15 October 1940. NKG, aged 27.
264 Sqn	Defiant I F/O I R Stephenson Sgt W Maxwell	L7025 Injured +	Ditto. Baled out 1230. Pilot rescued from sea. NKG, aged 23.
310 Sqn	Hurricane I S/L G D M Blackwood	P3887 'P' Safe	Patrol. Baled out after return fire from Do17 over Clacton, 1540.
310 Sqn	Hurricane I P/O V Bergman	P3960 Sl/WIA	Patrol. Baled out slightly wounded during attack on a Do17 over Clacton at 1540.
601 Sqn	Hurricane I Sgt A W Woolley	V7238 Safe	Patrol. Burnt out after crashing at Great Totham, Essex. See 11 July and 31 August 1940.
602 qn	Spitfire I F/O C H Maclean	X4187 Wounded	Aircraft damaged and pilot badly injured. Crash-landed at Tangmere after combat with Me109 of JG53 at 1635. Lost right leg. A/c repaired.
602 Sqn	Spitfire I Sgt C F Babbage	X4188 Safe	Ditto – baled out south of Selsey and rescued by lifeboat.
610 Sqn	Spitfire I F/O F K Webster	R6595 'O' +	Patrol. Crashed and destroyed while attempting to land at Hawkinge after combat with Me109 over Folkestone at 1240. See 25 July 1940. Buried Sandown, Isle of Wight, aged 26.
610 Sqn	Spitfire I Sgt P Else	P9496 'L' Wounded	Ditto. Baled out badly wounded. Lost left arm and suffered burns.

615 Sqn	Hurricane I P/O J A P McClintock	R4121 Safe	Patrol. Baled out off Sheerness 1510, and rescued.
615 Sqn	Hurricane I F/L L M Gaunce DFC	R4111 Safe	Ditto. Baled out off Herne Bay and rescued. See also 18 August 1940 and 19 November 1941.
615 Sqn	Hurricane I P/O D H Hone	V6564 Wounded	Ditto. Crash-landed at Rochford. Wounded in leg and thigh. See also 24 August 1940 and 26 February 1941. A/c repaired.
615 Sqn	Hurricane I F/O J R H Gayner	P2878 Wounded	Written off in crash-landing after combat over Portsmouth, 1650.
616 Sqn	Spitfire I P/O W L B Walker	R6701 Wounded	Patrol. Baled out off Dover, 1200, and rescued. Wounded in the foot.
616 Sqn	Spitfire I F/O J S Bell	R6632 Safe	Force-landed after combat with Me109 over Dungeness, 1200. A/c repaired. See also 1 June and 30 August 1940.
616 Sqn	Spitfire I F/O E F StAubyn	R7018 Wounded	Burned after crash-landing at RAF Eastchurch, after combat with Me109. Pilot suffered burns. A/c repaired.
616 Sqn	Spitfire I Sgt M Ridley	R6633 +	Shot down by Me109s of JG51 over Dover, 1215. Buried Folkestone, aged 24. See also 29 May 1940.
616 Sqn	Spitfire I F/O G E Moberly	N3275 +	Ditto. Crashed into the Channel; body picked up, buried Caterham, aged 25.
616 Sqn	Spitfire I Sgt P Copeland	K9827 Wounded	Ditto. Shot down by Me109 near Wye at 1315, and burnt out.
616 Sqn	Spitfire I P/O R Marples	R6758 Wounded	Ditto. Force-landed at Adisham 1320; written off. Pilot wounded in the leg.

27 August 1940

1 Sqn	Hurricane I P/O C A G Chetham	P3897 Safe	Night Patrol. Caught in searchlights over Buckinghamshire and baled out at 0100 after losing control.
152 Sqn	Spitfire I P/O W Beaumont	R6831 Safe	Patrol. Baled out during combat with Ju88 off Portland, 1230. See also 23 September 1940.
213 Sqn	Hurricane I Sub-Lt(A) W J M Moss	N2336 'G' +	Flew into the sea during a patrol over the Channel. NKG, aged 22. FAA.
248 Sqn	Blenheim IVf P/O C J Arthur Sgt E A Ringwood Sgt R C R Cox	L9449 + + +	Recce. Lost off Norwegian coast, NKG, aged 22. NKG, aged 20. Buried Sweden, aged 30.

28 August 1940

54 Sqn	Spitfire I F/L A C Deere DFC	R6832 Safe	Patrol. Baled out, shot down by a Spitfire over Detling, 1300. See also 28 May, 9 July, 15 and 31 August 1940.
54 Sqn	Spitfire I S/L D O Finlay	X4053 Wounded	Baled out wounded over Ramsgate, hit by a Me109, 1715.
56 Sqn	Hurricane I P/O M H C Maxwell	R4117 Safe	Patrol. Written off in crash-landing near Herne Bay after combat with Me109 at 1310. See also 27 May and 30 September 1940.
56 Sqn	Hurricane I P/O F B Sutton	R4198 Wounded	Baled out badly burned, possibly by a Spitfire, over Thames Estuary at 1700.
56 Sqn	Hurricane I Sgt G Smythe	N2523 Safe	Ditto. Baled out in combat with Me109 over Hawkinge 1710. See also 26 August 1940.
151 Sqn	Hurricane I P/O J W E Alexander	L2005 Injured	Patrol. Baled out and badly burned in combat over Thames Estuary, 1730.

264 Sqn	Defiant I	N1574	Patrol. Shot down by Me109 of JG26 over Thanet, 0855.
	P/O D Whitley	+	See also 31 May. Aged 21 and 25 respectively.
	Sgt R C Turner	+	
264 Sqn	Defiant I	L7026 'V'	Ditto.
	P/O P L Kenner	+	Buried Brentwood, aged 21.
	P/O C E Johnson	+	Aged 35.
264 Sqn	Defiant I	L7021	Ditto.
	S/L G D Garvin	Injured	Baled out.
	F/L R C V Ash	+	Baled out but killed, aged 31.
603 Sqn	Spitfire I	R6751 'U'	Patrol. Lost in combat with Me109s over Dover, 1645.
	F/L J L G Cunningham	+	NKG, aged 23.
603 Sqn	Spitfire I	L1046	Ditto. NKG, aged 22.
	P/O D K MacDonald	+	
603 Sqn	Spitfire I	R6989 'X'	Ditto. Pilot wounded and A/c later repaired.
	F/O I S Ritchie	Wounded	
603 Sqn	Spitfire I	N3105 'P'	Ditto – over Tenterden. Buried Gt Ouseburn, Yorks,
	P/O N J V Benson	+	aged 21.
610 Sqn	Spitfire I	P9511	Patrol. Shot down by Me109 over Dover, 1700.
	P/O K H Cox	+	Aged 24.
610 Sqn	Spitfire I	R4116	Patrol. Written off in forced-landing after combat with
	P/O S J Madle	Injured	Do17 at 0915, over Sandwich.

The burnt-out remains of Carl Davis's Hurricane P3363.

29 August 1940

85 Sqn	Hurricane I Sgt J H M Ellis	L1915 'B' Safe	Patrol. Baled out after combat with Me109 1600. See also 1 September 1940.
85 Sqn	Hurricane I Sgt F R Walker-Smith	V7350 Wounded	Ditto. Wounded in foot.
85 Sqn	Hurricane I F/L H R Hamilton	V6623 'L' +	Shot down near Rye by Me109 at 1815. Canadian, aged 23.
151 Sqn	Hurricane I P/O A G Wainwright	P3882 Injured	Night (dusk) patrol. Baled out near Basildon, Essex, 1940 hrs.
501 Sqn	Hurricane I Sgt W J Green	R4223 'L' Safe	Patrol. Baled out and rescued after combat with Me109 off Folkestone, See also 22 February 1945.
501 Sqn	Hurricane I F/L J A A Gibson	P3102 Injured	Ditto – over Hawkinge – 1930, and rescued by motor launch. See also 15 August 1940. New Zealander.
603 Sqn	Spitfire I P/O D J C Pinckney	R6753 'G' Wounded	Patrol. Baled out and slightly burned in combat with Me109 at 1840 near Dymchurch.
603 Sqn	Spitfire I P/O R Hillary	L1021 Safe	Shot down by Me109, crash-landing at Lympne, 1900. A/c repaired. See also 3 September 1940.
610 Sqn	Spitfire I Sgt A C Baker	X4011 'O' Safe	Patrol. Crash-landed at Gatwick at 1600 after combat. A/c repaired.
610 Sqn	Spitfire I Sgt E Manton	R6695 'E' +	Patrol. Shot down over Mayfield at 1600 (serial according to AM Form 1582, but see 22 August 1940). Aged 25.

30 August 1940

43 Sqn	Hurricane I Sgt D Noble	P3179 +	Patrol. Shot down by Me109 over Sussex coast, near Hove, 1150. Aged 20. Remains excavated in 1966 and buried in an original grave at East Retford, Notts.
43 Sqn	Hurricane I S/L J V C Badger DFC	V6548 Injured	Shot down and baled out in combat with Me109 at 1735. Badly injured falling in trees and died on 30 June 1941. Aged 28.
56 Sqn	Hurricane I F/O R E P Brooker	N2668 Safe	Written off in crash-landing after fight with Me109s over Essex, 1645. See also 13 and 21 August 1940, and 16 April 1945.
56 Sqn	Hurricane I F/L J E Gracie	R2689 Injured	Crashed and burned near Halstead after combat with He111, 1645. Pilot suffered a broken neck but recovered.
66 Sqn	Spitfire I P/O J H T Pickering	R6715 Safe	Patrol. Shot down into the sea off Aldeburgh, 1700, attacking a Do17. Rescued. See also 11 October 1940.
74 Sqn	Spitfire I Sgt W M Skinner	X4022 Safe	Patrol. Baled out after collision at 1100. See also 6 July 1941.
79 Sqn	Hurricane I P/O E J Morris	P3203 Safe	Pilot rammed a He111 of 10/KG1, over Reigate, 1112, and baled out. South African. See also 31 August 1940.
85 Sqn	Hurricane I P/O J E Marshall	V6624 Safe	Patrol. Baled out 1140 after attack on He111 over Smarden, Kent.
151 Sqn	Hurricane I S/L E B King	V7369 +	Patrol. Shot down by Me110s at 1150 near Strood, Kent. Irish, aged 29.
151 Sqn	Hurricane I Sgt F Gmur	R4213 +	Shot down over Thames Estuary at 1600. Polish pilot, aged 25.
222 Sqn	Spitfire I Sgt S Baxter	P9325 Safe	Patrol. Force-landed at Eastchurch, damaged in action over Canterbury, 1600. A/c repaired. See also 14 September 1940.

222 Sqn	Spitfire I P/O J M V Carpenter	P9375 Safe	Ditto. Baled out 1630. See also 4 September 1940.
222 Sqn	Spitfire I P/O H P M Edridge	K9826 'X' Wounded	Baled out with slight burns, shot up by Me109 over Barham, Kent, 1800. See also 30 October 1940.
222 Sqn	Spitfire I Sgt J I Johnson	R6628 +	Ditto. Buried Towcester Cem, Northamptonshire, aged 26.
222 Sqn	Spitfire I F/L G C Matheson	P9443 Wounded	Damaged in above action, with pilot seriously wounded, 1810. See also 23/24 August 1943.
222 Sqn	Spitfire I Sgt A W P Spears	P9323 'F' Safe	Ditto. Baled out over Sheppey, 1830 See also 4 April 1941.
222 Sqn	Spitfire I P/O W R Assheton	R6720 Safe	Crash-landed at Bekesbourne after combat over Canterbury. A/c repaired. See also 11 and 20 September 1940.
253 Sqn	Hurricane I F/L G A Brown	P3802 Wounded	Patrol. Written off after forced-landing near Maidstone after combat at 1115 with Me109s. Wounds to shoulder and legs.
253 Sqn	Hurricane I P/O C D Francis	L1965 +	Shot down by Me109 at Wrotham at 1115. Remains discovered during an excavation of his a/c in 1981 and interred at Brookwood. Aged 19.
253 Sqn	Hurricane I P/O D N O Jenkins	P3921 +	Ditto – over Redhill. Buried at Bagendon, Glos, aged 21.
253 Sqn	Hurricane I Sgt J H Dickinson	P3213 +	Ditto. Baled out 1715 but killed, near Woodchurch, by JG26. Aged 21.
253 Sqn	Hurricane I Sgt S F Cooper	P2631 'X' Safe	Ditto. Written off in crash at 1720 near Biddenden.
603 Sqn	Spitfire I S/L G L Denholm	L1067 'D' Safe	Patrol. Baled out after combat with Me110s over Snargate, Kent, 1655. See also 15 September 1940.
603 Sqn	Spitfire I Sgt A R Sarre	R7021 'X' Safe	Ditto. See also 7 September 1940.
616 Sqn	Spitfire I F/O J S Bell	X4248 +	Patrol. Crashed approaching West Malling after combat with Me109 at 1200. Buried Eastgate, Lincoln. 23. See also 1 June and 26 August 1940.

31 August 1940

1 Sqn	Hurricane I Sgt H J Merchant	V7375 Wounded	Patrol. Baled out and burned after combat with Me110 over Halstead, 0845. See also 23 August 1940.
1 Sqn (RCAF)	Hurricane I F/O G G Hyde	P2971 Wounded	Patrol. Baled out and burned after combat with Me109 over Channel 0915.
1 Sqn (RCAF)	Hurricane I F/L V B Corbett	P3869 Wounded	Ditto – 0920.
1 Sqn (RCAF)	Hurricane I F/O W Sprenger	P3858 Safe	Ditto – baled out near Dover.
1 Sqn (RCAF)	Hurricane I P/O J P J Desloges	N2530 Wounded	Baled out 1700 over Gravesend in combat with Do215.
19 Sqn	Spitfire I F/O J B Coward	X4231 Wounded	Patrol. Baled out with serious leg injury (later amputated) near Duxford after combat with Do17, 0830.
19 Sqn	Spitfire I F/O F N Brinsden	R6958 Safe	Baled out over Thames Estuary at 0845.
19 Sqn	Spitfire I P/O R C Aeberhardt	R6912 +	Crashed on landing with combat damage, Fowlmere, 0850. Aged 19.

54 Sqn	Spitfire I F/L A C Deere DFC	R6895 Safe	Bombed on take-off from Hornchurch at 1315. Slightly injured. See also 28 May, 9 July, 15 and 28 August 28 1940.
54 Sqn	Spitfire I P/O E F Edsall	X4236 'L' Injured	Ditto. See also 20 September and 27 October 1940. Hip injury.
54 Sqn	Spitfire I Sgt D G Gibbons	X4054 Safe	Patrol. Baled out after attack by RAF Hurricane, 1930.
56 Sqn	Hurricane I P/O M H Mounsdon	R4197 Injured	Patrol. Written off after being shot up by Me109 over Colchester, 0840, and badly burned.
56 Sqn	Hurricane I Sgt C Whitehead DFM	V6628 Safe	Baled out after combat with fighters over Colchester, 0840.
56 Sqn	Hurricane I F/L P S Weaver DFC	V7378 +	Shot down over Colchester by Me109s. NKG, aged 25.
56 Sqn	Hurricane I F/O I B Westmacott	V7341 Safe	Shot down by Me110 over Colchester at 0905 and baled out.
72 Sqn	Spitfire I F/L F M Smith	P9438 Wounded	Patrol. Baled out over Dungeness at 1835 following combat. Badly burnt. Canadian.
72 Sqn	Spitfire I F/O E J Wilcox	P9457 +	Ditto – 1910. Buried Staplehurst, aged 25.
79 Sqn	Hurricane I P/O G H Nelson-Edwards	N2345 Safe	Patrol. Written off in crash following combat at 0930 near Biggin Hill. See also 29 September 1940.
79 Sqn	Hurricane I Sgt H A Bolton	V7200 +	Crashed attempting to land after combat at Kenley, 1600. A/C repaired. Buried Hartlepool, aged 21.
79 Sqn	Hurricane I P/O W H Millington	P3050 Wounded	Patrol. Crash-landed on fire following combat with Me109 over Romney, at 1800. Wounded and burned. See also 30 October 1940. Australian.
79 Sqn	Hurricane I P/O E J Morris	P3877 Wounded	Damaged in combat with Do17 and crashed at 1850. A/c repaired. See also 30 August 1940. South African.
85 Sqn	Hurricane I S/L P W Townsend DFC	P3166 'Q' Wounded	Patrol. Shot down by Me110 over Tunbridge at 1300. Baled out with wound in the foot. See also 11 July 1940.
85 Sqn	Hurricane I P/O P A Worrall	V6581 Wounded	Baled out 1330 slightly wounded after combat with Me110 over Tunbridge.
111 Sqn	Hurricane I Sgt J T Craig	P2888 Injured	Patrol. Baled out after combat with Me110 over Felixstowe, 0920. See also 18 May 1940.
151 Sqn	Hurricane I P/O F Czajkowski	P3301 Wounded	Patrol. Shot down by Me109, force-landed at Foulness, 1025. Pole.
151 Sqn	Hurricane I P/O J L W Ellecombe	P3312 Injured	Patrol. Baled out with burns after attack on Ju88 near Southend as glycol tank exploded. See also 19 August 1942.
222 Sqn	Spitfire I P/O G G A Davies	P9337 Wounded	Patrol. Shot down by Me109, 1815, near Tenterden and burned about the face and neck. A/c SoC. See also 31 May 1940.
253 Sqn	Hurricane I S/L H M Starr	L1830 +	Patrol. Shot down by fighter near Grove Ferry, Kent. Baled out but machine-gunned during descent. Aged 25, buried Swindon, Wilts.
253 Sqn	Hurricane I S/L T P Gleave	P3115 Wounded	Patrol. Baled out and badly burned during attack on Ju88 over Cudham, Kent at 1305.
257 Sqn	Hurricane I P/O G H Maffett	P3175 'S' +	Patrol. Shot down over Clacton by Me110 at 0855. Wreckage is on display in the RAF Museum, Hendon. Aged 24.

257 Sqn	Hurricane I P/O J A MacD Henderson	V6601 'E' Wounded	Baled out and burned in combat with Me110 over Clacton 0900.
310 Sqn	Hurricane I P/O J Štěrbaček	P3159 +	Patrol. Shot down over the Thames Estuary by Me109, 1330. NKG, aged 27.
310 Sqn	Hurricane I P/O M Kredba	P8814 'Y' Safe	Patrol. Baled out after combat with Me109 over Thames Estuary, 1330.
501 Sqn	Hurricane I Sgt A Glowacki	V6540 Injured	Patrol. Baled out after combat with Me109 over Gravesend, 1315. Pole.
601 Sqn	Hurricane I Sgt N Taylor	P3735 Safe	Patrol. Baled out after combat with Me109 over Gravesend, 1330.
601 Sqn	Hurricane I F/O M D Doulton	R4215 +	Ditto. Remains found in excavation in 1984 and ashes interred in Salehurst Churchyard, East Sussex. Aged 31.
601 Sqn	Hurricane I F/O H T Gilbert	V7260 Safe	Baled out over Thames Estuary at 1340. See also 6 September 1940.
601 Sqn	Hurricane I Sgt A W Woolley	N2602 Injured	Shot down off Gravesend by Me109 and baled out with burns. See also 11 July and 26 August 1040.
603 Sqn	Spitfire I F/O R McG Waterston	X4273 'K' +	Patrol. Shot down by Me109 of JG3 over London, 1830. Aged 23.
603 Sqn	Spitfire I P/O G K Gilroy	X4271 'N' Injured	Patrol. Baled out over Wanstead after combat; injured by civilians who attacked him. 1820 hrs.

1 September 1940

1 Sqn	Hurricane I F/Sgt F G Berry DFM	P3276 +	Patrol. Shot down by Me109 over Tonbridge, 1130. Buried Pinner, Middx, aged 26.
1 Sqn (RCAF)	Hurricane I F/O B V Kerwin	P3963 Wounded	Patrol. Baled out over Shipbourne, Kent, 1425, in combat with Do216 and Me110s. Pilot suffered burns.
1 Sqn (RCAF)	Hurricane I F/O A McL Yuile	R4171 Safe	Baled out 1430 near West Malling, Kent. See also 15 September 1940.
72 Sqn	Spitfire I F/O R A Thomson	P9448 Wounded	Crash-landed near Leeds Castle, after combat with Me109 at 1130. Several splinter wounds. New Zealander. A/c repaired.
72 Sqn	Spitfire I F/O O StJ Pigg	P9458 +	Shot down by Me109 over Pluckley, Kent, 1115. See also 2 June 1940. Buried Durham, aged 22.
72 Sqn	Spitfire I Sgt M H Pocock	L1056 Wounded	Damaged by Me109 over Beachy Head, and wounded in leg and arm. Belly landed at West Malling, 1140. A/c repaired.
72 Sqn	Spitfire I F/O D F B Sheen DFC	X4109 Sl/WIA	Baled out after combat with fighters at Ham Street, Kent, 1150. See also 5 September 1940. Australian.
85 Sqn	Hurricane I F/O A V Gowers	V7343 Wounded	Patrol. Baled out wounded and burnt after combat with Me109 over Oxted, Kent, 1415. See also 24 October 1943.
85 Sqn	Hurricane I Sgt G B Booth	L2071 '0' DoI	Baled out and fell with parachute on fire at 1415, and severely injured – died of these injuries 7 February 1941. Buried Crystal Palace, aged 20.
85 Sqn	Hurricane I F/O P P Woods-Scawen DFC	P3150 +	Baled out during combat with Me109 near Kenley, 1415 but parachute failed. Body not located till 6 September. Age 24. See also 17 and 19 May 1940. Brother C A W-S died 2 September 1940.
85 Sqn	Hurricane I Sgt J H M Ellis	P2673 'E' +	Shot down in combat over Kenley, at 1415. Body finally identified in 1993 in an unmarked grave and re-interred in Brookwood Cem. He was 21. See 29 August 1940.

253 Sqn	Hurricane X P/O J K G Clifton	P5185 +	Shot down over Dungeness at 1400. Aged 21.
603 Sqn	Spitfire I P/O P M Cardell	L1020 'L' Safe	Written off after forced landing at Ilford, Essex, 1645. See also 27 September 1940.
610 Sqn	Spitfire I P/O L H Casson	R6778 Safe	Written off after damage by Do215 at 1420 over Kenley. See also 5 May and 9 August 1941.

2 September 1940

43 Sqn	Hurricane I P/O D A R G LeR DuVivier	P3903 Wounded	Patrol. Written off after crash-landing near Old Romney, 1320, after fight with Me109. Wounds to leg. Belgian pilot.
43 Sqn	Hurricane I P/O M K Carswell	P3786 Wounded	Baled out injured following combat with Me109 near Ashford, 1330. See also 9 February and 1 June 1940.
43 Sqn	Hurricane I F/O C A Woods-Scawen	V7420 +	Baled out too low after aircraft set on fire in combat with Me109, 1330, near Ivychurch, Kent. See also 2 and 13 June and 16 August 1940. Aged 22.
46 Sqn	Hurricane I P/O J C L D Bailey	P3067 +	Patrol. Shot down by Me109 over Thames Estuary, 1730; crashed near Biggin Hill. Aged 20.
72 Sqn	Spitfire I Sgt N R Norfolk	K9938 Safe	Patrol. Written off in crash-landing over Herne Bay, 1300.
72 Sqn	Spitfire I F/L E Graham	X4262 Safe	Shot down over Lympne, 1610, making forced-landing.
72 Sqn	Spitfire I W/C R B Lees	K9840 Wounded	Damaged in combat over Lympne at 1615 and crash- landed. A/c repaired. Australian.
72 Sqn	Spitfire I S/L A R Collins	? Wounded	Believed written off after combat over Thames Estuary, 1730, with Me110s.
111 Sqn	Hurricane I Sgt W L Dymond DFM	P3875 +	Patrol. Shot down in combat with Me109 over Thames Estuary, 1250. NKG, aged 22.
222 Sqn	Spitfire I F/L A I Robinson	X4280 Wounded	Patrol. Damaged by Me110, 1745; pilot hit in the leg. A/c repaired.

F/Lt W Rhodes-Moorhouse DFC, **son of a First World War** VC **winner, was killed in action with 601 Squadron on 6 September 1940.**

249 Sqn	Hurricane I P/O R E N E Wynn	V7352 Wounded	Patrol. Damaged in crash-landing after combat over Rochester, 2000. A/c repaired. See also 7 April 1941.
249 Sqn	Hurricane I P/O H J S Beazley	P2988 Safe	Baled out over Rochester in combat with Me110, 0800. See also 27 September 1940.
253 Sqn	Hurricane I Sgt J Metham	P2946 Injured	Patrol. Shot down over Thanet by Me109, 0815, baled out and burned.
253 Sqn	Hurricane I F/O D B Bell-Salter	V6640 Wounded	Baled out near Rye after combat at 1300. See also 18 May 1940.
501 Sqn	Hurricane I F/O A T Rose-Price	L1578 +	Patrol. Shot down over Dungeness, 0630. First patrol and first day on the squadron. NKG, aged 21.
501 Sqn	Hurricane I P/O H C Adams	V7234 'A' Safe	Cat B damage in combat with EA over Gravesend. Repaired. See also 6 September 1940.
501 Sqn	Hurricane I P/O S Skalski	V7230 Safe	Crash-landed after combat. Pole. See also 5 September 1940.
603 Sqn	Spitfire I Sgt J Stokoe	N3056 'B' Wounded	Patrol. Baled out wounded after combat with fighters at 1725. See also 20 April 1941.
616 Sqn	Spitfire I F/L D E Gillam AFC	X4181 Safe	Patrol. Baled out after combat with Me110 at 1635 over Tunbridge Wells, Kent. See also 17 October and 23 November 1941.

3 September 1940

1 Sqn	Hurricane I P/O R H Shaw	P3782 +	Patrol. Lost in action 1130, south of Maidstone. NKG, aged 24. He is possibly buried in unmarked grave at Sittingbourne Cemetery.
1 Sqn	Hurricane I F/L H B L Hillcoat	P3044 +	Ditto. NKG, aged 23.
17 Sqn	Hurricane I Sgt D Fopp	P3672 'E' Wounded	Patrol. Baled out and burned after combat with Me110 over Essex, 1030. Australian.
17 Sqn	Hurricane I F/O D H W Hanson	R4174 +	Baled out too low 1055, after attack on Do17 over Foulness. Buried at Mappleton, Yorks, aged 22.
25 Sqn	Blenheim If P/O D W Hogg Sgt W Powell	L1512 + Safe	Patrol. Shot down by RAF Hurricane over North Weald, 1055. Buried at Eastwood, Glasgow, aged 23. AG baled out.
46 Sqn	Hurricane I P/O H Morgan-Gray	P3024 Wounded	Patrol. Baled out wounded after hits by Me109 over Rochford, 1030.
46 Sqn	Hurricane I Sgt G H Edworthy	P3064 +	Shot down over Essex coast at 1035. NKG, aged 25.
46 Sqn	Hurricane I Sgt E Bloor	P3063 Injured	Baled out slightly burned at 1045 over Canewdon, nr Foulness. Buried Stamford, Lincs, aged 27.
222 Sqn	Spitfire I Sgt R B Johnson	L1010 Injured	Patrol. Baled out slightly injured after glycol leak over Burnham on Crouch, 0730. See also 14 September 1940.
253 Sqn	Hurricane I P/O L C Murch	P3610 Safe	Patrol. Crashed at Nonnington, Kent 0700, engine cut during a forced-landing near Ingatestone, Essex. See also 11 October 1940.
257 Sqn	Hurricane I P/O C R Bonsigneur	P3518 +	Patrol. Baled out but killed, following combat with Me109 over Ingatestone, at 1045. Buried Saffron Walden, aged 22. Canadian.
257 Sqn	Hurricane I P/O D W Hunt	L1585 Wounded	Baled out severely burned after being shot down by a Me109 at 1045, over Margaretting, Essex.

310 Sqn	Hurricane I Sgt J Kopřiva	P8811 'F' Safe	Patrol. Written off after being brought down by Me110 at 1000.
603 Sqn	Spitfire I P/O R H Hillary	X4277 'M' Wounded	Patrol. Baled out severely burned being shot down by JG26 off Margate at 1004. Rescued. See also 29 August 1940.
603 Sqn	Spitfire I P/O D Stewart-Clarke	X4185 'Z' Wounded	Ditto. Wounded and baled out. See also 21 June and 19 September 1941.

4 September 1940

46 Sqn	Hurricane I F/O R P Plummer	P3052 DoW	Patrol. Shot down by fighters and baled out badly burned, 1315, near Stambridge. Died 14 Sep 1940. Buried Haywards Heath, aged 28.
46 Sqn	Hurricane I P/O C F Ambrose	P3066 Safe	Baled out over Rochford, 1315, after combat with Me109. See also 30 Nov 1940.
66 Sqn	Spitfire I P/O A N R L Appleford	P9316 Sl/WIA	Patrol. Baled out slightly wounded after combat with Me109 over the Thames Estuary, 0950.
66 Sqn	Spitfire I Sgt A D Smith	N3048 DoW	Shot down by Me109, baled out badly wounded near Purleigh, Essex at 1000. Died 6 September 1940, aged 22. See also 24 July 1940.
66 Sqn	Spitfire I P/O C A Cooke	R6689 Sl/WIA	Baled out slightly wounded over Ashford, 1340, after attack by Me109.
72 Sqn	Spitfire I P/O E E Males	R6971 Safe	Patrol. Baled out after combat with Me110 over Hartfield, Sussex, 1340. See also 10 and 27 September 1940.
72 Sqn	Spitfire I P/O R D Elliott	P9460 Safe	Patrol. Baled out over Kent after combat with Me110, 1320. See also 6 September 1940.
79 Sqn	Hurricane I Sgt J Wright	P3676 +	Patrol. Crashed, wounded, 1340, after combat with Me110s. Died the next day. Aged 24.
111 Sqn	Hurricane I F/L D C Bruce	R4172 +	Patrol. Lost off Folkestone following combat with Me109 at 0915. Aged 22.
111 Sqn	Hurricane IIa P/O J Macinski	Z2309 +	Ditto. NKG, aged 24. Polish pilot.
152 Sqn	Spitfire I Sgt K J Barker	R6909* +	Patrol. Shot down by Do17 off Bognor Regis, baled out but not recovered. Body washed up on French coast and buried at Etaples. Aged 23. (*According to AM Form 1582.)
222 Sqn	Spitfire I P/O J M Carpenter	P9378 Safe	Patrol. Shot down by British AA fire at 1320 and blown from cockpit with slight injuries. See also 30 August 1940.
222 Sqn	Spitfire I F/O J W Cutts	X4278 'D' +	Shot down by Me109 over Maidstone at 1330. NKG, aged 20.
222 Sqn	Spitfire I Sgt J W Ramshaw	K9962 +	Crashed near Yalding, nr Maidstone at 1335. See also 22 February 1940.
253 Sqn	Hurricane I F/O A A G Trueman	V6638 +	Patrol. Shot down over Kenley, 1000. Canadian, aged 26.
601 Sqn	Hurricane I F/O J S Jankiewicz	R4214 Wounded	Patrol. Damaged in combat at 1345 with Me110. A/c repaired. Polish pilot. See also 25 May 1942.

5 September 1940

19 Sqn	Spitfire I S/L P C Pinkham	P9422 +	Patrol. Shot down by Me109 over Thames Estuary, 1015. Aged 25.
41 Sqn	Spitfire I F/L J T Webster DFC	R6635 +	Patrol. Crashed at Laindon, Essex, at 1525, after mid-air collision with P9428 during combat. Aged 24.

41 Sqn	Spitfire I S/L H R L Hood	P9428 +	Ditto. NKG, aged 32.
41 Sqn	Spitfire I P/O R W Wallens	X4021 Wounded	Badly wounded in the leg after attack by Me109 at 1530. Crash-landed, a/c repaired to MkVa, then MkXIII.
41 Sqn	Spitfire I F/O A D J Lovell	R6885 Safe	Baled out 1530 after combat at 1530, south Benfleet. See also 28 July 1940.
66 Sqn	Spitfire I F/O P J C King	N3060 +	Patrol. Baled out after combat with Me109 over Medway, but parachute failed to open. Aged 19.
66 Sqn	Spitfire I F/L G P Christie DFC	K9944 Wounded	Written off after combat with Me109s at 1605 over Kent. Canadian.
72 Sqn	Spitfire I P/O D C Winter	X4013 +	Patrol. Baled out too low and killed, 1424, near Elham, Kent. Me109 combat. Buried South Shields, 26.
72 Sqn	Spitfire I Sgt M Gray	N3093 +	Shot down in above action. Buried Fulford, N Yorks, aged 20.
72 Sqn	Spitfire I F/O D F B Sheen DFC	X4034 Wounded	Baled out near Hawkinge in above action. See also 1 September 1940.
73 Sqn	Hurricane I S/L M W S Robinson	P2815 Safe	Patrol. Damaged and force-landed at Wallasea, after action with He111s. A/c repaired but lost with 229 Sqn on 30 September 1940.
73 Sqn	Hurricane I P/O R D Rutter	P3110 'G' Wounded	Patrol. Baled out after engagement with Ju88 near Billericay, Essex, at 1525, being shot down by a Me109.
73 Sqn	Hurricane I Sgt A L McNay	P3224 'L' +	Shot down over Burnham, Essex, 1530. NKG, aged 22.

Pilots of 43 Squadron on 7 September 1940. Shortly after this picture was taken, two of them were killed in action. F/L C B Hull DFC, third from the left, and F/Lt R C Reynall, sixth from left. Others are from left: P/O H C Upton (DFC), Marshall, W/C G Lott DSO DFC, who lost his right eye in combat on 9 July, F/L F R Carey DFC DFM (wounded 18 August), P/O D G Gorrie, W/C J Boret (Stn Cdr), F/L I G Kilmartin (DFC) and an army liaison officer.

73 Sqn	Hurricane I F/L R E Lovett	P3204 'H' Safe	Baled out during above action. See also 10 May and 7 September 1940.
222 Sqn	Spitfire I Sgt D J Chipping	X4057 Wounded	Patrol. Baled out after hit by AA fire over Dover, while in combat with a Me109 at 1500.
249 Sqn	Hurricane I F/L R A Barton	V6625 Safe	Patrol. Baled out after combat with Me109 over Shell Haven, Essex, 1530. Canadian.
303 Sqn	Hurricane I P/O W Łapkowski	P2985 Wounded	Patrol. Baled out after combat with Me109 over Gillingham, Kent. See also 2 July 1941.
501 Sqn	Hurricane I P/O S Skalski	V6644 Injured	Patrol. Shot down by Me109 over Canterbury at 1000. Polish pilot. See also 2 September 1940.
603 Sqn	Spitfire I F/L R W Rushmer	X4261 +	Patrol. Shot down over Biggin Hill at 1000. Buried at Staplehurst, aged 30.
603 Sqn	Spitfire I P/O W P H Rafter	X4264 Wounded	Written off after combat with Me109 over Biggin Hill, 1000.

6 September 1940

1 Sqn	Hurricane I P/O G E Goodman	P2686 Safe	Patrol. Baled out after combat with Me110 at 0930, south of Penshurst.
43 Sqn	Hurricane I F/L T F D Morgan DFC	V6542 Wounded	Crash-landed at Tangmere, after combat with Me109s over Dungeness and wounded in the knee. Aircraft repaired. See also 13 August 1940.
64 Sqn	Spitfire I Sgt H W Charnock	K9903 Safe	Patrol. Crashed 0830 near Ternhill and written off.
72 Sqn	Spitfire I P/O R D Elliott	N3070 Safe	Patrol. Baled out after combat with Me109 over Maidstone, 1315. See also 4 September 1940.
73 Sqn	Hurricane I P/O H W Eliot	P2875 'X' Wounded	Patrol. Baled out after combat above Thames Estuary, 0920. Burn injuries.
111 Sqn	Hurricane I Sgt L J Tweed	L1892 Wounded	Hit by fire from Ju88 and baled out near Kenley 0910.
234 Sqn	Spitfire I P/O W H G Gordon	X4035 'G' +	Patrol. Shot down by Me109 over Hadlow Down, Sussex, at 0910. Aged 20.
234 Sqn	Spitfire I Sgt W H Hornby	X4183 Wounded	Ditto. Baled out over Northiam, 0920.
234 Sqn	Spitfire I P/O J Zurakowski	N3279 Safe	Damaged by Me109 over Beachy Head and crash-landed West Malling. A/c repaired. See also 24 August 1940.
234 Sqn	Spitfire I P/O P W Horton	N3061 Injured	Baled out and rescued off Portland at 1315 after combat with Ju88. See 6 August 1940.
249 Sqn	Hurricane I S/L J Grandy	R4229 'J' Wounded	Patrol. Baled out after combat with Me109 over Maidstone, 0845.
253 Sqn	Hurricane I S/L W P Cambridge	P3032 +	Patrol. Baled out over Kingsnorth, Kent, at 0945, but killed. Aged 28.
303 Sqn	Hurricane I Sgt S Karubin	V7290 'H' Injured	Patrol. Written off in crash-landing at 0915 near Pembury, after combat with He111. A/c repaired.
303 Sqn	Hurricane I S/L Z Krasnodębski	P3974 'J' Wounded	Baled out badly burned after combat with Me109 south of Bexley, 0920.
303 Sqn	Hurricane I S/L R G Kellett	V7284 'A' Safe	Crash-landed at Biggin Hill and SoC.
303 Sqn	Hurricane I F/L J A Kent	R2685 'G' Safe	Crash-landed, repaired.

303 Sqn	Hurricane I Sgt J Rogowski	V7243 'P' Wounded	Crash-landed Biggin Hill following damage from Do17. SoC.
501 Sqn	Hurricane I P/O H C Adams	V6612 +	Patrol. Shot down over Ashford at 0900. Buried Tandridge, Surrey, aged 22. See also 2 September 1940.
501 Sqn	Hurricane I Sgt O V Houghton	V6646 +	Shot down over Ashford, 0900. Buried Allesley, Coventry, aged 19.
501 Sqn	Hurricane I Sgt G W Pearson	P3516 +	Ditto. Buried as unknown airman at Lympne, his identity finally confirmed in 1982 and a headstone erected. He was 21.
601 Sqn	Hurricane I P/O H T Gilbert	V6647 Wounded	Patrol. Baled out over Mayfield after combat with Me109 at 0930. See also 31 August 1940.
601 Sqn	Hurricane I F/O J Topolnicki	P3382 Wounded	Ditto. Polish pilot.
601 Sqn	Hurricane I F/L C R Davis	P3363 'W' +	Ditto, over Tunbridge Wells. American, aged 29.
601 Sqn	Hurricane I F/L W H Rhodes-Moorhouse DFC	P8818 +	Ditto. Son of WW1 VC airman. Buried Parnham, Beaminster, Dorset, Aged 26.
602 Sqn	Spitfire I Sgt G A Whipps	N3227 Safe	Patrol. Baled out after combat with Me109 over Hailsham, 1330.
603 Sqn	Spitfire I P/O J R Caister DFM	X4260 'D' PoW	Shot down over the Channel off Calais, by Me109 of JG54, 1330. Force-landed in France. Stalag Luft III camp.

* From 19 June 1940, Fighter Command had two No. 1 Squadrons, the second being No. 1 Squadron RCAF. From 16 August, it was at Northolt and then rested to Prestwick on 10 October. To avoid confusion, the squadron was renumbered to 401 Squadron RCAF from 1 March 1941.

**Another 43 Squadron casualty on 7 September was
Sgt A I M Deller who baled out near Ashford.**

Phase Three – 7 September to 30 September 1940

7 September 1940

41 Sqn	Spitfire I Sgt J McAdam	P9340 Safe	Patrol. Written off after crashing at Raleigh, Essex, 1800. See also 24 September 1940 and 20 February 1941.
43 Sqn	Hurricane I Sgt A L M Deller	V7309 Safe	Patrol. Baled out in combat over Ashford area at 1645.
43 Sqn	Hurricane I S/L C B Hull DFC	V6641 +	Shot down by Me109 over Purley, Surrey, at 1645. Buried Tangmere, aged 27. See also 27 May 1940 (Norway).
43 Sqn	Hurricane I F/L R C Reynell	V7257 +	Shot down by Me109, South London, 1645. Buried Brookwood, aged 28.
54 Sqn	Spitfire I P/O W Krepski	R6901 +	Patrol. Lost off Flamborough Head at 1430. NKG, aged 23.
66 Sqn	Spitfire I P/O C A W Bodie	X4321 'F' Safe	Patrol. Force-landed near Hawkinge after combat at 1230. A/c repaired.
72 Sqn	Spitfire I F/O T A F Elsdon	X4254 Wounded	Patrol. Badly damaged by Me109 over Thames Estuary at 1820. Crash landed at Biggin Hill. A/c repaired.
72 Sqn	Spitfire I Sgt J White	R7022 Sl/WIA	Ditto. Damaged. Force-landed at Eynsford, with slight injuries to forehead and one leg.
73 Sqn	Hurricane I F/L R E Lovett	P3234 'E' +	Patrol. Shot down over Billericay at 1700. See also 10 May and 5 September 1940.
111 Sqn	Hurricane I Sgt T Y Wallace	P3025 Wounded	Patrol. Baled out after combat with Me109 at 1830, near Ashford, Kent. See also 11 November 1944. South African.
234 Sqn	Spitfire I S/L J S O'Brien DFC	P9466 +	Patrol. Shot down attacking a Do17 over Kent at 1825. See also 18/19 June 1940.
234 Sqn	Spitfire I F/L P C Hughes DFC	X4009 +	Ditto. Collided with EA and crashed. Australian, aged 22.
242 Sqn	Hurricane I P/O J Benzie	P2962 +	Patrol. Lost in combat over Thames Estuary at 1700. See 23 May 1940. NKG, aged 25. Canadian.
249 Sqn	Hurricane I P/O R D S Fleming	R4114 +	Patrol. Shot down by Me109 over Maidstone at 1700. Aged 20.
249 Sqn	Hurricane I Sgt R Smithson	V6574 Wounded	Damaged by Me109 in above action. Wounded in one arm. A/c repaired.
249 Sqn	Hurricane I Sgt F W G Killingback	R4230 Wounded	Ditto. Baled out over Maidstone.
249 Sqn	Hurricane I F/O P H V Wells	P3594 Wounded	Ditto. Hit by return fire from He111 over Faversham, and baled out with wounds to head, hand, legs and arms. See also 28 November 1940.
249 Sqn	Hurricane I Sgt J M B Beard	N2440 'N' Safe	Baled out in above action at 1800, hit by AA fire. See 25 October 1940.
249 Sqn	Hurricane I F/L R G A Barclay	V6610 Safe	Ditto. Wheels-up landing 4 miles from North Weald after combat. A/c repaired. See also 29 November 1940.

257 Sqn	Hurricane I F/L H R A Beresford	P3049 'D' +	Patrol. Shot down over Thames Estuary, 1730. Remains found in 1979 and buried in Brookwood Cemetery aged 25.
257 Sqn	Hurricane I F/O L R G Mitchell	V7254 +	Ditto. NKG, aged 24.
303 Sqn	Hurricane I P/O J K M Daszewski	P3890 'N' Wounded	Patrol. Baled out severely wounded in combat with Me109 of Estuary at 1700. See also 4 April 1942.
303 Sqn	Hurricane I F/O M Pisarek	R4173 'T' Safe	Baled out in above action. See also 29 April 1942.
310 Sqn	Hurricane I Sgt J Koukal	V7437 Wounded	Patrol. Baled out badly burned in combat over Thames Estuary, 1810.
504 Sqn	Hurricane I F/O K V Wendel	L1615 +	Patrol. Crashed near Faversham after combat and died of his injuries. New Zealander, aged 24.
602 Sqn	Spitfire I F/O W H Coverley	N3198 +	Patrol. Baled out over Biggin Hill in combat and died of his wounds. Body not found till 16 September. Aged 23. See also 25 August 1940.
602 Sqn	Spitfire I P/O H W Moody	X4256 +	Ditto, 1730. NKG, aged 30. See also 19 August 1940.
603 Sqn	Spitfire I Sgt A R Sarre	P9467 Wounded	Patrol. Baled out over the Thames Estuary at 1739. See also 30 August 1940.

8 September 1940

41 Sqn	Spitfire I F/O W J Scott	R6756 +	Patrol. Shot down by Me109 at 1215 off Dover. See also 29 July 1940. Buried Dundee Western Cemetery, aged 25.
46 Sqn	Hurricane I P/O P R McGregor	P3053 Safe	Patrol. Shot down near Maidstone at 1235, crash-landed at Meopham Green, Kent. See also 11 September 1940.
46 Sqn	Hurricane I Sub-Lt(A) J C Carpenter	P3201 +	Shot down off Sheppey, baled out but killed, 1230. Buried at sea on the 16th. Aged 21.
46 Sqn	Hurricane I F/L N W Burnett	V6631 Wounded	Crashed following combat at 1230 over Sheppey; written off.
600 Sqn	Blenheim If P/O H B L Hough Sgt E C Barnard LAC A Smith	L1111 Safe Safe Safe	Night Patrol. Crew baled out at 2130 out of fuel and with radio failure.
605 Sqn	Hurricane I P/O J Fleming	L2061 Wounded	Patrol. Shot down by Me109 at 1230 near Tunbridge Wells, and baled out, badly burned. New Zealander.

9 September 1940

1 Sqn (RCAF)	Hurricane I F/O W B MacD Millar	P3081 Wounded	Patrol – 'tail-end charlie'. Baled out burned during combat near Loxwood, Sussex.
66 Sqn	Spitfire I P/O G H Corbett	N3049 Wounded	Patrol. Baled out over East Grinstead after combat with Me109 at 1800. See also 27 September and 8 October 1940.
92 Sqn	Spitfire I P/O C H Saunders	L1077 Wounded	Patrol. Damaged by Me109 near Rye at 1730. Crash-landed and written off. Shrapnel wounds to leg. See also 1 November 1940.
92 Sqn	Spitfire I P/O W C Watling	P9372 Wounded	Baled out into the sea off Rye at 1730 and suffered burn injuries.
242 Sqn	Hurricane I P/O K MacL Sclanders	P3087 +	Patrol. Shot down 1745 over Thames Haven. Buried Whyteleafe, Surrey, aged 24. Canadian.

242 Sqn	Hurricane I Sgt R H Lonsdale	P2831 'K' Safe	Baled out after attack on Do17 over Thames Estuary at 1745.
303 Sqn	Hurricane I F/S K Wünsche	P3700 'E' Wounded	Patrol. Baled out slightly burned in combat with Me109 over Beachy Head at 1755.
303 Sqn	Hurricane I Sgt J Frantisek	P3975 'U' Safe	Shot-up, crash-landed; repaired.
310 Sqn	Hurricane I F/O J E Boulton	V7412 'P' +	Patrol. Collided with R4084 in combat over Croydon, 1735, then crashed into a Me110. Buried Beddington, aged 20.
310 Sqn	Hurricane I F/L G L Sinclair DFC	R4084 Safe	Baled out after above collision. See 27 September 1940.
602 Sqn	Spitfire I F/O P C Webb	K9910 Injured	Patrol. Crash-landed at Boxgrove, Sussex, after combat with Me109 at 1800. SoC.
605 Sqn	Hurricane I P/O J S Humphreys	P2765 Wounded	Patrol. Baled out during attack on He111s over Farnborough, Kent at 1730. Shot at and robbed by Canadian soldiers upon landing. New Zealander.
605 Sqn	Hurricane I P/O G M Forrester	L2059 +	Caught in cross-fire he collided with He111 of KG53 over Farnborough at 1730. Buried Odiham, aged 26.
607 Sqn	Hurricane I P/O S B Parnell	P3574 +	Patrol. Crashed and written off after combat over Goudhurst at 1730. Aged 30. His brother, S/L J B Parnell, OC 504 Sqn, KIA in France 14 May 1940.
607 Sqn	Hurricane I P/O J D Lenahan	P3117 +	Shot down in combat over Mayfield at 1735. Buried Cranbrook, aged 20.
607 Sqn	Hurricane I P/O G J Drake	P2728 +	Shot down over Goudhurst at 1730. Remains found excavating aircraft in 1972 and buried at Brookwood Cemetery, aged 20. South African.
607 Sqn	Hurricane I Sgt R A Spyer	P2680 Wounded	Crashed and written off after combat over Mayfield at 1730.

10 September 1940

72 Sqn	Spitfire I P/O E E Males	K9841 Safe	Patrol. Damaged in combat and was written off in forced-landing near Etchingham, Sussex at 1739. See 4 and 27 September 1940.
312 Sqn	Hurricane I Sgt J Keprt	L1644 Safe	Patrol. Baled out when aircraft caught fire south of Cambridge.

11 September 1940

1 Sqn (RCAF)	Hurricane I F/O T B Little	P3534 Wounded	Patrol. Baled out during attack on a He111 over Tunbridge at 1615. Wounds and burn injuries. See 27 August 1941.
1 Sqn (RCAF)	Hurricane I F/O P W Lochnan	V6670 Safe	Crashed and burnt out near Romney after combat with He111s at 1620.
41 Sqn	Spitfire I P/O G A Langley	X4325 Safe	Patrol. Baled out after attack on Ju88 over Sevenoaks, 1635. See 15 September 1940.
46 Sqn	Hurricane I Sgt S Andrew	P3525 +	Patrol. Crashed at 1100, spun into the ground near Stapleford, Essex. Buried North Ferriby, Yorkshire, aged 21.
46 Sqn	Hurricane I Sgt R E deCannert-d'Hamale	V6549 Safe	Baled out after combat near Bodiam, Kent, 1530. Belgian. See also 1 November 1940.

Squadron	Aircraft / Pilot	Serial	Status	Details
46 Sqn	Hurricane I Sgt W A Peacock	V7232 +		Shot down over Thames Estuary at 1530. NKG, aged 20.
46 Sqn	Hurricane I P/O P R McGregor	P3094 Injured		Written off in crash-landing at 1540, near Staple Cross, Kent.
72 Sqn	Spitfire I P/O B Douthwaite	R6710 Wounded		Patrol. Force-landed through battle damage and wounds, after combat over Gravesend, 1600. SoC.
73 Sqn	Hurricane I Sgt H G Webster	P2796 Safe		Patrol. Baled out after combat with Me110 over Sheppey, 1610. Aircraft excavated in 1976, Detling village.
92 Sqn	Spitfire I P/O F N Hargreaves	K9793 +		Patrol. Shot down off Dungeness, 1615. NKG, aged 21.
92 Sqn	Spitfire I F/L J A Paterson	R6613 Injured		Patrol. Written off after crash-landing 1850, after combat with Me109 over Folkestone. Facial burn injuries. See 27 September 1940. New Zealander.
92 Sqn	Spitfire I P/O H D Edwards	P9464 +		Crashed near Smeeth, Kent following combat with Me109 at 1900. Aircraft not discovered till 7 October. Aged 24. Buried Folkestone Cemetery. Canadian.
213 Sqn	Hurricane I Sgt A Wójcicki	W6667 'P' +		Patrol. Shot down off Selsey Bill at 1600. Polish. NKG, aged 26.
213 Sqn	Hurricane I F/L J E Sing	P3780 'A' Safe		Baled out over Selsey Bill 1600, in combat with Me110s.
222 Sqn	Spitfire I P/O W R Assheton	R6638 Safe		Patrol. Damaged in combat over Maidstone and crash-landed on a farm at Fletching, Cat B. See also 30 August and 20 September 1940.
229 Sqn	Hurricane I P/O M Ravenhill	P3038 Safe		Patrol. Baled out over Biggin Hill at 1600. See also 30 September 1940.
229 Sqn	Hurricane I P/O K M Carver	N2466 Wounded		Baled out during attack on He111 at 1620 over Maidstone. Burn injuries.
235 Sqn	Blenheim IVf P/O P C Wickings-Smith P/O A W V Green Sgt R D H Watts	Z5725 'E' + + +		Shot down by Me109 escorting FAA Albacores raiding Calais, 1730. NKGs, aged 22, 21 and 35.
235 Sqn	Blenheim IVf F/L F W Flood P/O N B Shorrocks Sgt B R Sharp	L9396 'G' + + +		Ditto. NKGs. Aged 25, Australian. Aged 29. Aged 27.
238 Sqn	Hurricane I P/O W Towers-Perkins	P3096 Wounded		Patrol. Baled out with burns after fight with Ju88 south of Tunbridge Wells, 1615.
238 Sqn	Hurricane I F/L D P Hughes	V7240 +		Ditto. NKG, aged 22.
238 Sqn	Hurricane I Sgt S Duszyński	R2682 +		Ditto, near Romney Marsh. Polish pilot, aged 24.
249 Sqn	Hurricane I Sgt W L Davis	V6682 Wounded		Patrol. Baled out over Benenden, Kent, after combat with He111. See 10 February 1941.
266 Sqn	Spitfire II P/O R J B Roach	P7313 Safe		Patrol. Baled out, hit by return fire from He111 over Billericay, 1620.
303 Sqn	Hurricane I F/O A Cebrzyński	V6667 'K' DoW		Patrol. Shot down Pembury following combat south of London at 1620 and died on 19 September. Buried Northwood Cemetery, aged 28.
303 Sqn	Hurricane I F/L A S Forbes	V7465 'V' Wounded		Ditto. A/c damaged but repaired.

303 Sqn	Hurricane I Sgt S Wójtowicz	V7242 'B' +	Shot down by Me109, 1625, near Westerham. Buried Northwood, aged 24. See also 2 August 1940.
501 Sqn	Hurricane X Sgt T P Pickering	P5200 Safe	Patrol. Shot down by Me109, 1545, over Maidstone, and baled out.
504 Sqn	Hurricane I P/O A W Clarke	P3770 +	Patrol. Shot down over Romney at 1600. Aged 20.
602 Sqn	Spitfire I Sgt M H Sprague	N3282 +	Patrol. Shot down by Me110 at 1620, near Selsey. Body washed ashore at Brighton on 10 October and buried at Tangmere, aged 30. See also 25 August.
611 Sqn	Spitfire II Sgt F E R Shepherd	P7298 +	Patrol. Baled out over Croydon 1600, but parachute burned. Buried at Whyteleafe, Surrey, aged 22.

12 September 1940

213 Sqn	Hurricane I W/C J S Dewar DSO DFC	V7306 +	Patrol. Lost over coast on flight from Exeter to Tangmere. Believed shot down into the sea, body washed up on on 30 September. Aged 33.

13 September 1940

248 Sqn	Blenheim IVf Sgt W J Garfield Sgt B W Mesner Sgt A Kay	L9451 'V' + + +	Recce. Missing off Norwegian coast, 1900. Buried Bergen, Norway, aged 25. NKG, aged 29. NKG, aged 24.
501 Sqn	Hurricane I Sgt J H Lacey DFM CdG	P2793 Safe	Patrol. Baled out during attack on He111 over Maidstone, 1345. See 7 September 1940.
FIU	Blenheim IVf F/L R G Ker-Ramsey W/O G Dixon W/O E L Byrne	Z5721 PoW PoW PoW	Night Patrol. Baled out off French coast near Calais. Stalag Luft I and III. Stalag Luft 6. Stalag Luft III.

14 September 1940

19 Sqn	Spitfire I Sgt F Marek	R6625 +	Patrol. Crashed near Orsett, Essex, possibly due to oygen failure at 1620. Czech, aged 27.
41 Sqn	Spitfire I S/L R C F Lister DFC	R6605 Wounded	Patrol. Baled out after attack by a Me109, wounded in the arm. See 24 September 1940.
66 Sqn	Spitfire I P/O R H Robbins	X4327 Wounded	Patrol. Shot down by Me109 over Maidstone at 1900.
72 Sqn	Spitfire I Sgt H J Bell-Walker	K9960 Safe	Patrol. Baled out over Ashford at 1830. See 18 September 1940 and 12 August 1941.
73 Sqn	Hurricane I S/L M W S Robinson	L2039 'F' Wounded	Patrol. Baled out over Tonbridge at 1600. See also 28 May and 5 September 1940.
73 Sqn	Hurricane I Sgt J J Griffin	L2118 'L' Wounded	Baled out over Maidstone, 1605. Leg wounds and dislocated shoulder.
73 Sqn	Hurricane I Sgt J J Brimble	P2542 'D' +	Shot down over Maidstone, 1605. Aircraft excavated in 1980 and his body found. Buried Brookwood, aged 23.
92 Sqn	Spitfire I P/O R H McGowan	R6624 Wounded	Patrol. Baled out after combat with Me109 over Faversham, 1900. See also *Bomber Command Losses, 1944*, 22 December 1944 (189 Sqn).
222 Sqn	Spitfire I Sgt S Baxter	X4275 +	Patrol. Written off in crash-landing after combat with Me109 at 1615, at Rochford. Aged 23. See 20 August 1940.
222 Sqn	Spitfire I Sgt R B Johnson	X4249 Safe	Ditto. Baled out over Aveley, Essex. See 3 September 1940.

253 Sqn	Hurricane I Sgt J A Anderson	P3804 Wounded	Patrol. Baled out badly burned after combat with Me109 near Faversham, at 1810.
253 Sqn	Hurricane X Sgt W B Higgins	P5184 +	Shot down over Faversham at 1800 by Me109. Buried Whitwell, aged 26.

15 September 1940

1 Sqn (RCAF)	Hurricane I F/O A D Nesbitt	P3080 Wounded	Patrol. Baled out over Tunbridge after combat with Me109 at 1210.
1 Sqn (RCAF)	Hurricane I F/O R Smither	P3876 +	Shot down by Me109 in above action. Buried Brookwood Cemetery, aged 27.
1 Sqn (RCAF)	Hurricane I F/O A McL Yuile	L1973 Wounded	Damaged in combat with He111 at 1445, south of London. Repaired. See 1 September 1940.
19 Sqn	Spitfire I Sgt J A Potter	X4070 PoW	Patrol. Shot down chasing Me109 to French coast, 1505, and wounded. Stalags Luft I, III, 6 and 3A.
19 Sqn	Spitfire I Sgt H A C Roden	P9431 Injured	Written off after crash-landing, hit by Me109 at 1510. See 15 November 1940.
25 Sqn	Beaufighter If P/O H M S Lambert F/O M J Miley LAC J P Wyatt	R2067 + + +	Night Patrol. Crashed near Biggin Hill, 1820. Aged 21. Aged 22. Aged 32.
41 Sqn	Spitfire I P/O G A Langley	P9324 +	Patrol. Shot down by Me109 at 1230, near Thurrock. Aged 24. See also 11 September 1940.
73 Sqn	Hurricane I P/O R A Marchand	P3865 +	Patrol. Shot down by Me109 at 1220 over Maidstone. Aged 22. See 13 May 1940.
92 Sqn	Spitfire I P/O R H Holland	R6606 Safe	Patrol. Baled out west of Ashford at 1450. Slightly injured on landing.
213 Sqn	Hurricane I Sgt R T Llewellyn	P3113 'F' Wounded	Patrol. Baled out severely wounded after combat with Me110 at 1500, over Hawkhurst.
229 Sqn	Hurricane I P/O G L J Doutrepont	N2537 +	Patrol. Shot down over Sevenoaks, at 1150. Aged 27. Belgian.
229 Sqn	Hurricane I P/O R R Smith	V6616 Wounded	Ditto. Baled out with leg wounds. Canadian.
238 Sqn	Hurricane I Sgt L Pidd	P2836 +	Patrol. Baled out too low after hitting a tree during combat over Kenley. Aged 22.
242 Sqn	Hurricane I F/L G ff Powell-Sheddon	P2884 Injured	Patrol. Baled out after combat with Do17, hit by Me109, over Udimore, 1640. Suffered dislocated shoulder.
249 Sqn	Hurricane I P/O K T Lofts	V6566 Safe	Patrol. Crash-landed at West Malling at 1435 after combat with He111. A/c repaired. See 16 October 1940.
302 Sqn	Hurricane I F/L T P Chlopik	P2954 'E' +	Patrol. Baled out over North Weald at 1445 but he was dead on landing. Buried Southend, aged 32.
303 Sqn	Hurricane I P/O W Łokuciewski	P2903 Wounded	Patrol. Aircraft damaged in combat with Me109 over Kent, 1245, wounded in the leg. Repaired but see 25 October 1940 (501 Sqn). See 13 March 1942.
303 Sqn	Hurricane I Sgt T Andruszkow	P3939 Safe	Baled out over Dartford after combat with Me109. See 27 September 1940.
303 Sqn	Hurricane I Sgt M Brzezowski	P3577 +	Shot down off Gravesend, 1505, by Me109. NKG, aged 20.
310 Sqn	Hurricane I S/L A Hess	R4085 'A' Safe	Patrol. Baled out over Thames at 1445.

310 Sqn	Hurricane I Sgt J Hubácek	R4087 'X' Injured	Ditto. Injuries to one foot.
501 Sqn	Hurricane I P/O A E A D G J van den Hove d'Ertsenrijck	P2760 +	Patrol. Aircraft exploded in combat at 1245, and fell into the River Stour. Buried Lympne, aged 32. Belgian.
504 Sqn	Hurricane I Sgt R T Holmes	P2725 Safe	Patrol. Baled out after combat with Do17 over Chelsea, London, 1215.
504 Sqn	Hurricane I P/O J V Gurteen	N2481 +	Shot down over south London at 1300. Aged 24.
504 Sqn	Hurricane I F/O M Jebb	N2705 DoW	Shot down near Dartford, 1445. Died 19 September. See 20 May 1940.
603 Sqn	Spitfire I F/O A P Pease	X4324 +	Patrol. Shot down by Me109 at 1505, over Kingswood, Kent. Aged 22.
603 Sqn	Spitfire I S/L G L Denholm	R7019 Safe	Ditto. Baled out after attack on Do17.
605 Sqn	Hurricane I P/O T P M Cooper-Slipper	L2012 Safe	Baled out in combat at 1140 over Kent, having rammed a Do17 from KG3. See 15 November 1940.
605 Sqn	Hurricane I P/O R E Jones	L2122 Injured	Baled out in combat over Kent at 1140. See 15 November 1940.
607 Sqn	Hurricane I P/O P J T Stephenson	V6688 Wounded	Patrol. Baled out slightly wounded after attacking a Do17 of KG3 over Appledore.
609 Sqn	Hurricane I P/O G N Gaunt	R6690 'A' +	Patrol. Shot down near Kenley at 1230. Buried Huddersfield, aged 24.

16 September 1940

616 Sqn	Spitfire I Sgt T C Iveson	L1036 Safe	Patrol. Went into the sea having run short of fuel chasing Ju88 north of Cromer at 1030. Rescued by MTB.

17 September 1940

41 Sqn	Spitfire I P/O J N Mackenzie	R6887 Safe	Patrol. Crash-landed after combat with Me109 over Dover, 1540. A/c repaired and converted to MkVa.
151 Sqn	Hurricane I Sgt J Winstanley	R4185 Injured	Patrol. Hit the ground chasing He111 through low cloud, 1730. Crashed at Biscathorpe, Lincs. SoC.
501 Sqn	Hurricane I Sgt J H Lacey DFM CdG	V7357 Safe	Patrol. Baled out after combat with Me109 over Ashford at 1540. See 13 September 1940.
501 Sqn	Hurricane I Sgt E J Egan	P3820 +	Shot down in above action, 1540. Interred Brookwood in 1970s, aged 19.
504 Sqn	Hurricane I Sgt D A Helcke	V7529 +	Patrol. Baled out after losing control after dummy attack on his aircraft by RAF fighters over Faversham, 1600. Hit aircraft and fell dead. Aged 24.
607 Sqn	Hurricane I Sgt J Lansdell	P3860 +	Patrol. Shot down by JG27, 1540. Buried Hempnall, Norfolk, aged 23.

18 September 1940

1 Sqn (RCAF)	Hurricane I P/O E W B Beardmore	P3859 Sl/WIA	Patrol. Baled out slightly wounded after combat over the Thames at 1030.
46 Sqn	Hurricane I Sgt G W Jefferys	V7442 +	Patrol. Baled out in combat at 1230 over Chatham, but parachute failed. Buried Winterbourne, Wilts, aged 20.
46 Sqn	Hurricane I P/O P W LeFevre	V6554 Injured	Baled out in above action. See also 16 April 1943 and 6 February 1944.

46 Sqn	Hurricane I Sgt C A L Hurry	P3816 Wounded	Baled out and burned and wounded in above fight.
66 Sqn	Spitfire I Sgt D F Corfe	R6603 Injured	Patrol. Written off in crash following combat over Canterbury, 1030. See 22 August 1940.
66 Sqn	Spitfire I P/O J R Mather	R6925 Safe	Baled out in combat over the Thames Estuary at 1700. See 27 October 1940.
72 Sqn	Spitfire I Sgt H J Bell-Walker	R6704 Wounded	Patrol. Aircraft damaged and pilot badly wounded by Me109 over Gravesend at 1030. See also 14 September 1940 and 12 August 1941. A/c repaired.
72 Sqn	Spitfire I P/O J P Lloyd	P9368 Wounded	Seriously wounded and force-landed in above action. A/c repaired.
92 Sqn	Spitfire I P/O R Mottram	N3193 Wounded	Patrol. Crashed and burned after fight with Me109 over Hollingbourne, Kent, at 0955. See also 31 August 1941.
222 Sqn	Spitfire I Sgt I Hutchinson	R6772 Wounded	Patrol. Baled out over Canterbury in combat with Me109, 1355. See also 30 September 1940.
249 Sqn	Hurricane I F/L D G Parnell	V6685 +	Patrol. Shot down over Gravesend at 1325. Buried St Gennys, Cornwall. Aged 25.
501 Sqn	Hurricane I Sgt C J Saward	V6600 Safe	Patrol. Shot down by Me109 at 0935 and baled out over Tonbridge.
501 Sqn	Hurricane I S/L H A V Hogan	V6620 Safe	Baled out following combat over West Malling at 1230.

Two pilots of 19 Squadron. On the left is F/S G C Unwin DFM and Sergeant J A Potter, who became a prisoner of war on 15 September 1940.

603 Sqn	Spitfire I P/O P Howes	X4323 +	Patrol. Shot down over Ashford at 0950 by Me109. Aged 21.

20 September 1940

72 Sqn	Spitfire I P/O D F Holland	X4410 +	Patrol. Baled out badly wounded after combat over Canterbury at 1210 and died of his wounds. Aged 23.
92 Sqn	Spitfire I P/O H P Hill	X4417 +	Patrol. Shot down by Me109 of JG51 (Oberst Werner Mölders) at 1135, over Dungeness. New Zealander, aged 20.
92 Sqn	Spitfire I Sgt P R Eyles	N3248 +	Ditto. Mölders second victory in this action. NKG, aged 24.
222 Sqn	Spitfire I P/O H L Whitbread	N3203 +	Patrol. Shot down by Me109 at 1115, over Rochester. Aged 26.
222 Sqn	Spitfire I P/O W R Assheton	K9993 Wounded	Ditto, over Thames Estuary, 1135 and baled out with burns. See 30 August and 11 September 1940.
222 Sqn	Spitfire I P/O E F Edsall	R6840 Safe	Damaged by Me109, crash-landed at base, going through a fence. Cat B damage. See also 31 August and 27 October 1940.
253 Sqn	Hurricane I P/O A R H Barton	R2686 Wounded	Patrol. Crashed and burned out at 1130 after attack by Me109 over Kent. See 12 August 1940.

23 September 1940

72 Sqn	Spitfire I P/O B W Brown	X4063 Safe	Patrol. Shot down, crashed and burnt out at 1030 after combat with Me109 over Gravesend. Baled out wounded. New Zealander.
73 Sqn	Hurricane I Sgt M E Leng	P8812 Injured	Patrol. Baled out 1055 after combat with Me109 near Faversham, Kent.
73 Sqn	Hurricane I Sgt F S Perkin	V7445 'A' Safe	Ditto over Sheppey.
73 Sqn	Hurricane I P/O D S Kinder	P3226 Wounded	Ditto over Thames Estuary. Burned but rescued from the sea.
73 Sqn	Hurricane I P/O N C Langham-Hobart	L2036 Wounded	Ditto.
74 Sqn	Spitfire II Sgt D H Ayres	P7362 +	Patrol. Baled out off Southwald, due to unknown cause, 1130. Body later recovered on 4 October. Aged 26.
92 Sqn	Spitfire I P/O A J S Pattinson	P9371 Wounded	Patrol. Crashed attempting to land after combat over Gravesend with Me109 at 1000. A/c repaired. See 12 October 1940.
152 Sqn	Spitfire I P/O W Beaumont DFC	R7016 +	Patrol. Lost over the Channel, cause unknown. See also 27 August 1940. NKG, aged 26.
229 Sqn	Hurricane I P/O P O D Allcock	P2879 Wounded	Patrol. Baled out over Hoo, Kent, at 1050, after attack by enemy fighter.
234 Sqn	Spitfire I F/O T M Kane	R6896 PoW	Patrol. Baled out after combat off the French coast, 1100. Rescued. Stalag Luft III camp.
257 Sqn	Hurricane I Sgt D J Aslin	P2960 Wounded	Patrol. Baled out and burned after combat with Me109 over Thames Estuary at 0950.

24 September 1940

17 Sqn	Hurricane I P/O H A C Bird-Wilson DFC	P3878 'W' Wounded	Patrol. Baled out after combat with Me109 flown by Adolf Galland of JG26. Chatham, 0955.
17 Sqn	Hurricane I P/O D H Wissler	P3168 Wounded	Crash-landed after combat 0915. A/c repaired. See 11 November 1940.

41 Sqn	Spitfire I Sgt J McAdam	N3118 Safe	Patrol. Baled out off Dover and rescued, 1345. See 7 September and 20 February 1941.
41 Sqn	Spitfire I Sgt E V Darling	R6604 Safe	Crash-landed near Dover after hits by Me109. Aircraft repaired. See also 27 September 1940 and 2 June 1942.
92 Sqn	Spitfire I P/O J S Bryson	X4037 +	Patrol. Shot down by Me109 at 0900, near North Weald. Canadian, aged 27.
92 Sqn	Spitfire I S/L R C F Lister	X4427 Wounded	Wounded in combat with Me109 at 0915. See 14 September 1940.
605 Sqn	Hurricane I P/O W J Glowacki	P3832 'P' +	Shot down by Me109 while chasing Do17 towards France at 1630. Force landed but died from allergic reaction to anti-tetanus injection. Buried by pilots of LG2 at Guines. Polish pilot, aged 26. (It has been suggested he was shot by the Germans.)

25 September 1940

152 Sqn	Spitfire I Sgt W G Silver	P9463 +	Patrol. Shot down off Portsmouth at 1155.
152 Sqn	Spitfire I Sgt K C Holland	N3173 +	Shot down attacking He111 west of Bristol at 1200. Australian aged 20.
234 Sqn	Spitfire I P/O R MacKay	X4182 Wounded	Patrol. Baled out near St Mawgan, Cornwall, at 1845. Badly wounded.
238 Sqn	Hurricane I Sgt F A Sibley	N2597 Safe	Patrol. Force-landed at Glastonbury after combat, 1540. Aircraft repaired. See 1 October 1940.

26 September 1940

152 Sqn	Spitfire I F/L E C Deanesly	K9982 Wounded	Patrol. Baled out 10 miles off Swanage after combat, 1640. Rescued from sea by the RN. See also 15 July 1940.
152 Sqn	Spitfire I Sgt J McB Christie	K9882 +	Shot down off Swanage by Me109 at 1650. Picked up dead. Aged 22.
229 Sqn	Hurricane I Sgt S W Merryweather	V6745 'Y' Wounded	Patrol. Written off after force-landing at Hambleton, Surrey, after combat with Me110 at 1650.
238 Sqn	Hurricane I Sgt V Horsky	P3098 +	Patrol. Shot down by Me110 over the Solent at 1630. Czech, 26, NKG.
238 Sqn	Hurricane I P/O R A Kings	P3830 Safe	Ditto. See 13 September 1940.
253 Sqn	Hurricane I F/L G R Edge DFC	P2958 Safe	Patrol. Baled out after combat at 1100 over the Channel – rescued.
253 Sqn	Hurricane I P/O W M C Samoliński	V7470 +	Ditto. Polish pilot; NKG, aged 23.
607 Sqn	Hurricane I F/L C E Bowen	P5205 Safe	Patrol. Baled out over Isle of Wight at 1620. See 1 October 1940.

27 September 1940

1 Sqn (RCAF)	Hurricane I F/O O J Peterson	P3647 +	Patrol. Combat with Ju88 and fighter escort. Shot down near Hever, Kent, at 0915. American in RCAF, age 25.
19 Sqn	Spitfire I P/O E Burgoyne	X4352 +	Patrol. Shot down over Canterbury by Me109 at 1230. Aged 25.
19 Sqn	Spitfire I Sgt D G S R Cox	X4237 Wounded	Written off in crash-landing near Wye following combat with Me109 at 1230.

41 Sqn	Spitfire I Sgt F Usmer	R6884 'S' Wounded	Patrol. Baled out after combat with Me109 over West Malling at 1215. Leg wound and burn injuries.
41 Sqn	Spitfire I Sgt E V Darling	X4409 Wounded	Baled out over West Malling, 1215. See also 24 September 1940 and 2 June 1942.
41 Sqn	Spitfire I F/L E N Ryder DFC	R6755 Safe	Baled out over Malling, shot down by Me109, 1545. See 3 April 1940 and 31 October 1941.
64 Sqn	Spitfire I Sgt L A Dyke	X4032 +	Missing from Patrol at 1030. NKG, aged 22.
66 Sqn	Spitfire I P/O G H Corbett	P9519 Safe	Shot down by AA fire while attacking Ju88, crash-landed near Orpington. Aircraft repaired. See 9 September 1940 and 8 October 1940.
72 Sqn	Spitfire I P/O E E Males	X4340 +	Patrol. Shot down over Sevenoaks by Me109, 0940. See also 4 and 10 September 1940.
72 Sqn	Spitfire I F/O P J Davies-Cooke	N3068 +	Baled out but fell dead after combat with Me109 in above action. Age 23.
92 Sqn	Spitfire I F/L J A Paterson	X4422 +	Patrol. Shot down by Me109 at 0920 over Sevenoaks. See 11 September 1940. Aged 20. New Zealander.
92 Sqn	Spitfire I F/S C Sydney	R6767 +	Shot down over Kingston, crashing at Esher, 0940. Buried Orpington. Aged 25.
92 Sqn	Spitfire I Sgt T G Oldfield	R6622 +	Shot down over Dartford, 1520. Buried Chertsey, Surrey. Aged 21.
213 Sqn	Hurricane I F/L L H Schwind	N2401 'Q' +	Patrol. Shot down over Gatwick by Me110 at 0925. Aged 27.
222 Sqn	Spitfire I Sgt R H Gretton	R6720 Wounded	Patrol. Damaged and crash-landed at Rainham, Essex, after combat with Me109, 1200. Badly wounded; A/c repaired.
222 Sqn	Spitfire I Sgt E Scott	P9364 +	Failed to return, 1600, crashed at Hollingbourne, and finally excavated in 1990. His remains buried Margate the following February. Aged 22.
229 Sqn	Hurricane I F/L R F Rimmer	V6782 'T' +	Patrol. Shot down by Me109 at 1530 over Burwash, Sussex. Aged 21.
229 Sqn	Hurricane I F/L W A Smith	P3603 'X' Safe	Written off after forced landing at Lingfield following above action.
242 Sqn	Hurricane I F/O M G Homer DFC	P2967 +	Patrol. Shot down by Me109 at 1225 over Sittingbourne, Kent. Aged 21.
249 Sqn	Hurricane I F/O P R-F Burton	V6683 +	Patrol. Rammed Me110 of V/LG1 at 0950 over Hailsham, Sussex. South African aged 23.
249 Sqn	Hurricane I P/O J R B Meaker DFC	P3834 +	Patrol. Baled out but hit tailplane after attack on Ju88 over Sussex, at 1520. Buried West Dean, Sussex, aged 21.
249 Sqn	Hurricane I P/O H J S Beazley	V6559 Wounded	Wounded in the foot during combat. See 2 September 1940.
303 Sqn	Hurricane I F/O W Zak	V7289 'S' Wounded	Patrol. Baled out with burns at 0935, over Horsham.
303 Sqn	Hurricane I F/O L W Paszkiewicz	L1696 'T' +	Shot down over Kent, 0935. Buried Brookwood, aged 32.
303 Sqn	Hurricane I Sgt T Andruszków	V6665 'J' +	Ditto. See also 15 September 1940.

310 Sqn	Hurricane I F/O G L Sinclair DFC	V6608 'B' Safe	Patrol. Baled out in combat at 1220 with Me109 over Thanet. See 9 September 1940.
501 Sqn	Hurricane I Sgt V H Ekins	V6672 Sl/WIA	Patrol. Baled out after an attack on a Me110 over Godstone, Surrey, at 1225. Slightly wounded.
501 Sqn	Hurricane I P/O E M Gunter	V6645 +	Baled out in above combat but his parachute failed. Buried Aldeby, Norfolk, aged 20.
603 Sqn	Spitfire I P/O P M Cardell	N3244 +	Patrol. Baled out over Channel at 1245 but parachute failed. See 1 September 1940. Buried Great Paxton, Hunts, aged 23.
609 Sqn	Spitfire I P/O R F G Miller	X4107 +	Patrol. Collided with Me110 of ZG76 at 1145, near Kingcome, Dorset. Buried Radford Semele, Warks, aged 20.
616 Sq	Spitfire I P/O D S Smith	R6702 DoW	Patrol. Shot down near Faversham at 1220, by Me109 and died on the 28th. Buried Highley, Shropshire, aged 26.
616 Sqn	Spitfire I ?	X4328 Safe	Listed as a loss this date – no details found.

28 September 1940

41 Sqn	Spitfire I P/O H H Chalder	X4409 DoW	Patrol. Baled out in combat at 1030, Chilham, Kent. Died 10 November.Buried Newcastle-upon-Tyne, aged 25.
41 Sqn	Spitfire I F/O J G Boyle	X4426 +	Ditto. Canadian, aged 26.
41 Sqn	Spitfire I P/O E S Aldous	X4345 Injured	Written off after forced landing after above action. See 16 October 1941.
66 Sqn	Spitfire I P/O A B Watkinson	X4322 Wounded	Patrol. Baled out over Mayfield, Sussex. Hit in shoulder and leg. South African.
213 Sqn	Hurricane I P/O J M Talman	L1770? Safe	Patrol. Baled out during combat with Me110 over Isle of Wight at 1510.
238 Sqn	Hurricane I Sgt R Little	N2400 +	Patrol. Shot down over Channel by Me109, 1445. NKG, aged 23. See 13 August 1940.
238 Sqn	Hurricane I Sgt S E Bann	V6776 +	Baled out over Fareham at 1550 but parachute failed. Aged 26.
238 Sqn	Hurricane I P/O D S Harrison	P3836 +	Shot down by Me109 over the Solent at 1450. Body washed ashore on 9 October. Buried Tangmere, aged 29.
249 Sqn	Hurricane I P/O A G Lewis	V6617 'R' Wounded	Patrol. Baled out and badly burned at 1420 over Faversham.
501 Sqn	Hurricane I P/O E B Rogers	V7497 Safe	Patrol. Baled out in combat with Me109s over Deal at 1010.
501 Sqn	Hurricane I P/O F C Harrold	P3417 'W' +	Ditto. Buried Cherry Hinton, Cambs, aged 23.
603 Sqn	Spitfire I F/L H K MacDonald	L1076 +	Patrol. Shot down over Gillingham at 1020 by Me109 of JG26. Brother D K MacDonald KIA 28 August. Aged 28.
605 Sqn	Hurricane I F/O P G Crofts	V6699 +	Patrol. Shot down by Me109 at 1355, over Dallington, Sussex. Baled out but parachute failed. Buried Tilford, Surrey, aged 22.
605 Sqn	Hurricane I F/O R Hope	P3828 Safe	Ditto at 1420 but baled out safely. See 14 October 1940.
607 Sqn	Hurricane I F/L W E Gore	P3108 +	Patrol. Shot down over the sea at 1550, off Selsey. NKG, aged 25. See 12 May 1940.

| 607 Sqn | Hurricane I | R4189 | Ditto. NKG, aged 29. |
| | F/L M M Irving | + | |

29 September 1940

79 Sqn	Hurricane I	P3203	Patrol. Baled out after combat at 1830, with He111
	P/O G H Nelson-Edwards	Safe	off Welsh coast, pilot rescued. See 31 August 1940.
79 Sqn	Hurricane X	P5177	Shot down during engagement with He111 off Cork,
	F/O G C B Peters	+	1830. NKG, age 27.
79 Sqn	Hurricane X	P5178 'G'	Force-landed in Ireland after above action. Aircraft
	P/O P F Mayhew	Safe	impounded and became Irish Air Corps, No. 93. Pilot escaped in June 1941. (KIFA February 1942.)
253 Sqn	Hurricane I	P2677	Patrol. Baled out after encounter with Me109 over
	Sgt A Edgeley	Wounded	Newhaven, 1625. Shoulder wound.
253 Sqn	Hurricane I	V6621	Baled out with burns after combat at 1635 over
	P/O R C Graves	Wounded	Weymouth with Me109.
504 Sqn	Hurricane I	L1913	Night patrol. Baled out after being hit by AA fire over
	?	Safe	Nuneaton, Warks.

30 September 1940

46 Sqn	Hurricane I	V6748	Patrol. Shot down by Me109, 1330, over Forest Row,
	P/O J D Crossman	+	Sussex. Aged 21, Australian.
56 Sqn	Hurricane I	P2866	Patrol. Shot down by fighters over Bournemouth, 1130.
	F/O K J Marston	Safe	Crash-landed with slight injuries. A/c SoC.
56 Sqn	Hurricane I	L1764 'M'	Written off after crash-landing at 1700 on Chesil Beach
	P/O M H C Maxwell	Safe	after combat with Me109. See also 27 May and 28 August 1940.
56 Sqn	Hurricane I	P3088 'N'	Baled out in the above action. Irish.
	F/L R S J Edwards	Safe	
56 Sqn	Hurricane I	N2434 'H'	Ditto. Leg wound. See also 20 October 1941.
	Sgt P H Fox	Wounded	
56 Sqn	Hurricane I	P3655 'R'	Shot down near Portland at 1130, by fighters. Suffered
	Sgt R W Ray	Wounded	wounds and a broken arm. A/c SoC.
64 Sqn	Spitfire I	P9564	Patrol. Killed in collision with another Spitfire. Aged 28.
	P/O A F Laws DFM	+	
87 Sqn	Hurricane I	V7307	Convoy Patrol. Baled out after shot down by Me110 at
	Sgt H Walton	Wounded	1649, with slight wounds.
92 Sqn	Spitfire I	X4069	Patrol. Written off in forced-landing near Shoreham after
	P/O A R Wright	Wounded	attack by Me109 at 1700. Slight shrapnel wounds.
151 Sqn	Hurricane X	P5182	Patrol. Battle damage by Ju88 over North Sea at 0730.
	Sgt D B F Nicholls	Safe	A/c repaired.
152 Sqn	Spitfire I	L1072	Patrol. Shot down off Portland, 1645. NKG, aged 26.
	Sgt L A E Reddington	+	
222 Sqn	Spitfire I	P9492	Patrol. Written off after forced-landing after combat at
	Sgt I Hutchinson	Wounded	1345. See 18 September 1940.
229 Sqn	Hurricane I	P2815	Patrol. Shot down over Ightham, Kent at 1040. Buried
	F/O M Ravenhill	+	Sheffield, aged 27. See 11 September 1940.
229 Sqn	Hurricane I	N2652	Baled out – shot down by Me109 in above action.
	P/O N K Stansfeld	Wounded	Canadian.

229 Sqn	Hurricane I P/O L B R Way	P3037 Safe	Baled out after combat at 1645.
238 Sqn	Hurricane I P/O R A Kings	L1702 Injured	Patrol. Baled out after colliding with N2474 near Shaftesbury, 1400. See 26 September 1940.
238 Sqn	Hurricane I P/O V C Simmonds	N2474 Safe	See above.
303 Sqn	Hurricane I P/O J Radomski	P3663 Safe	Crash-landed near Lydd after attack by Me109. Repaired.
504 Sqn	Hurricane I F/O J R Hardacre	P3414 'K' +	Patrol. Shot down in combat at 1700 over Weymouth. Body washed up on 10 October, buried Fawley, Hamps, aged 24.
504 Sqn	Hurricane I Sgt B M Bush	P3021 Safe	Crash-landed Yeovil after above fight with battle damage, but repaired.

F/O W McKnight DFC, 242 Squadron, killed in action 12 January 1941 on a rhubarb mission.

Sgt J McAdam, 41 Squadron, one of two pilots Werner Mölders shot down on 20 February 1941.

Phase Four – 1 to 31 October 1940

1 October 1940

41 Sqn	Spitfire I P/O G H Bennions DFC	X4559 Wounded	Patrol. Baled out badly wounded in combat with Me109 over Henfield, Sussex, 1455. See 29 July 1940.
238 Sqn	Hurricane I Sgt F A Sibley	P3599 +	Patrol. Shot down at 1110 over Poole Harbour. NKG, aged 26.
238 Sqn	Hurricane I P/O A R Covington	R4099 Safe	Baled out near Poole after fight with Me109 at 1110. See 7 October 1940.
248 Sqn	Blenheim IVf P/O C C Bennett Sgt G S Clarke Sgt G B Brash	R3626 + + +	Failed to return from recce sortie to Norwegian coast. Pilot was a 23-year-old Australian. All have NKGs.
607 Sqn	Hurricane I F/L C E Bowen	P2900 +	Patrol. Shot down by Me110 over the Isle of Wight, 1050. NKG, aged 24. See 26 September 1940.
607 Sqn	Hurricane I Sgt N Brumby	V6686 +	Ditto. Buried Hull, Yorkshire, aged 22.

2 October 1940

603 Sqn	Spitfire I P/O P G Dexter	P9553 Wounded	Patrol. Baled out after combat with Me109 of JG53 over Croydon, 1030. See 14 July 1940.

2/3 October 1940

600 Sqn	Blenheim IVf P/O C A Hobson Sgt D E Hughes AC2 C F Cooper	L4905 'M' + + +	Night patrol. Engine trouble, crashed near Forest Row, Sussex. Ages 21, 27 and 20 respectively. Hughes was from New Zealand.

4 October 1940

66 Sqn	Spitfire I F/L K McL Gillies	X4320 +	Failed to return from interception of a He111 off Dungeness, 1600. Body washed up at Covehithe, Suffolk, on 21 October. Aged 27.

5 October 1940

1 Sqn (RCAF)	Hurricane I F/O H De M Molson	P3873 Wounded	Patrol. Baled out after combat with fighters over Canterbury.
238 Sqn	Hurricane I S/L J R MacLachlan	P3611 Wounded	Patrol. Baled out with burns after fight with Me109 over Shaftesbury, 1420. First day as CO.
303 Sqn	Hurricane I F/O W Januszewicz	P3892 'T' +	Patrol. Shot down by Me109 at 1200, Stowting, Kent. Buried Northwood, aged 29.
603 Sqn	Spitfire I P/O J S Morton	K9807 Wounded	Patrol. Baled out and burned after fight with Me109s of JG53 over Dover at 1155. See 14 March 1943.
607 Sqn	Hurricane I P/O D Evans	P3554 Safe	Patrol. Baled out over Swanage after combat with Me109, 1400.
609 Sqn	Spitfire I F/O T Nowierski	N3223 'M' Safe	Patrol. Baled out over Salisbury Plain at 1815, due to undercarriage failure.

6 October 1940

64 Sqn	Spitfire I Sgt F F Vinyard	R6683 +	Patrol. Crashed into the sea at 1420, off Flamborough Head, Yorks, due to unknown cause. NKG, aged 24.
303 Sqn	Hurricane I Sgt A Siudak	P3120 'A' +	Bombed on the ground at Northolt at 1205. Buried Northwood, aged 31.

7 October 1940

41 Sqn	Spitfire I P/O D A Adams	N3267 Safe	Patrol. Baled out during attack on a Do17 over Folkestone, 1045.
56 Sqn	Hurricane I Sgt D H Nicholls	P3154 Injured	Patrol. Baled out during combat over Yeovil at 1600. Parachute failed to open properly and he broke his back on landing.
152 Sqn	Spitfire I P/O H J Akroyd	N3039 DoI	Patrol. Shot down and crashed near Lyme Regis, 1640. Died next day; buried Warmwell, aged 27.
222 Sqn	Spitfire I P/O J W Broadhurst	P9469 +	Patrol. Baled out but killed, during an attack on bombers over Salehurst, Sussex, at 1650. Aged 23.
238 Sqn	Hurricane I P/O A R Covington	V6777 Injured	Patrol. Baled out after combat with Me109 over Blandford at 1620. See 1 October 1940.
501 Sqn	Hurricane I F/O N J M Barry	V6800 +	Patrol. Shot down by Me109 at 1040 over Wrotham, Kent. Baled out but landed dead. Aged 22.
501 Sqn	Hurricane I F/O K W MacKenzie	V6799 Injured	Rammed Me109 with right wing, then force-landed minus most of this wing near Folkestone. Aircraft repaired. See 25 October 1940 and 29 September 1941.
601 Sqn	Hurricane I P/O H C Mayers DFC	R4218 Injured	Patrol. Force-landing after combat at 1405 with Me110 over Portland. Aircraft rebuilt as MkII BV155. See 13 August 1940 and 4 May 1941.
602 Sqn	Spitfire I Sgt B E P Whall DFM	X4160 DoW	Patrol. Crash-landed after combat at 1750, with Ju88 over Somerset. See 22 May and 18 August 1940.
603 Sqn	Spitfire I F/O H K F Matthews	N3109 +	Patrol. Shot down by Me109 of JG26, at 1045 over Godmersham Park, Kent. Buried Crystal Palace, aged 28.
603 Sqn	Spitfire I P/O J M Strawson	? Sl/inj	Ditto: ditched in Thames Estuary. SoC.
605 Sqn	Hurricane I P/O I J Muirhead DFC	V7305 Safe	Patrol. Baled out after combat over Bexley with Me109 at 1145. See 26 May and 15 October 1940.
605 Sqn	Hurricane I P/O C E English	P3677 +	Patrol. Shot down over Westerham at 1400 in fight with Me109. Parachute caught on tailplane. Aged 28: buried in Newcastle. His brother was KIA in 1941 as a Sergeant Pilot.
607 Sqn	Hurricane I F/O I B Difford	L1728 +	Patrol. Collided with P3860, crashing at Slindon, Sussex. South African, aged 30. He is buried at Tangmere.
607 Sqn	Hurricane I P/O A M W Scott	P3860 Safe	See above. Baled out.
609 Sqn	Spitfire I Sgt A N Feary	N3238 +	Patrol. Baled out too low after combat with Me109 over Yeovil, 1630. Buried Warmwell, aged 28. Brother H P-D Morgan, KIA 41 Sqn, 27 August 1941.
609 Sqn	Spitfire I P/O M E Staples	N3231 Wounded	Patrol. Baled out in above action.
609 Sqn	Spitfire I F/O J C Dundas DFC	R6915 '0' Sl/WIA	Patrol. Crash-landed at Warmwell, after combat with Me110s. A/c repaired and is now in Imperial War Museum, London.

8 October 1940

66 Sqn	Spitfire I	R6779	Patrol. Shot down by Me109, 0930, near Chatham.
	P/O G H Corbett	+	Canadian, aged 20. See 9 and 27 September 1940.
66 Sqn	Spitfire I	N3043 'K'	Shot down by Me109 near Rochester at 1155. Buried
	Sgt R A Ward	+	Croydon, aged 23.
72 Sqn	Spitfire I	K9847	Hit in the engine during combat, and crash-landed near
	Sgt N V Glew	Safe	Halstead, Kent. A/c repaired.
264 Sqn	Defiant I	N1627	Night patrol. Crashed near Marlow, Bucks, 2140.
	P/O H L Goodall	+	Buried Poole, aged 25.
	Sgt R B M Young	+	New Zealander, aged 22.
303 Sqn	Hurricane I	R4175 'R'	Patrol. Crashed at Ewell, Surrey, at 0940, cause unknown.
	Sgt J Frantisek DFM*	+	Aged 27. Buried at Northwood Cemetery. Czech pilot
			with Polish squadron.

9 October 1940

92 Sqn	Spitfire I	X4597	Patrol. Baled out badly burned after fight with Me109s
	Sgt E T G Frith	DoW	near Ashford at 1250. Died on the 17 October, aged 26.
235 Sqn	Blenheim IVf	N3530 'S'	Patrol – aerodrome protection, south of Thorney Island.
	P/O J C Kirkpatrick	+	Shot down over the Channel at 1730. Ages 25, unknown,
	P/O R C Thomas	+	unknown and 20 respectively.
	Sgt G E Keel	+	

10 October 1940

56 Sqn	Hurricane I	P3421	Patrol. Shot down by Me109 over Wareham, 1220.
	Sgt J Hlavac	+	Czech pilot, 26, buried at Warmwell.
92 Sqn	Spitfire I	X4038	Patrol. Collided with R6616 during attack on Do17 over
	P/O D G Williams	+	Tangmere at 0815. Buried Salisbury, aged 20.
92 Sqn	Spitfire I	R6616	See above: aged 21.
	F/O J F Drummond	+	
92 Sqn	Spitfire I	X4553 'C'	Crash-landed after above action. A/c badly
	Sgt W T Ellis	Safe	damaged and SoC.
238 Sqn	Hurricane I	P3984	Patrol. Baled out after combat at 1300, with Me109
	P/O R F T Doe DFC	Wounded	over Warmwell. Wounded in leg and shoulder.
249 Sqn	Hurricane I	V7537	Patrol. Killed in crash, at Cooling, Kent. Thought due
	Sgt E A Bayley	+	to oxygen failure, 1545. Later excavation showed bullet
			strikes, so he may have been picked off by JG2. Aged 29.
312 Sqn	Hurricane I	L1547	Patrol. Caught fire in the air, baled out but drowned in
	Sgt O Hanzlíček	+	the River Mersey. Buried Liverpool, aged 29.

11 October 1940

41 Sqn	Spitfire I	X4052	Patrol. Baled out after colliding with X4554 but
	F/O D H O'Neill	+	parachute failed; 1625. Buried Mitcham, Surrey, aged 25.
41 Sqn	Spitfire I	X4554	See above. Baled out safely. See 6 July 1941.
	Sgt L R Carter	Safe	
41 Sqn	Spitfire I	P9447	Shot down by Me109 near Maidstone at 1630 but did
	P/O J G Lecky	+	not survive. Aged 19.
66 Sqn	Spitfire I	X4562	Patrol. Shot down by Me109 of JG51 flown by Werner
	P/O J H T Pickering	Injured	Mölders, 1115, over Canterbury. See 30 August 1940.
72 Sqn	Spitfire I	K9870	Patrol. Baled out after being shot up and wounded by
	P/O P D Pool	Wounded	Me109 off Deal at 2000 hrs. See 19 August 1942.

73 Sqn	Hurricane I Sgt R Plenderleith	V6676 Wounded	Patrol. Baled out with burn injuries by Me109 over Frindsbury, Kent, at 1110.
253 Sqn	Hurricane I P/O L C Murch	V6570 Injured	Patrol. Baled out with broken arm following combat over Tunbridge Wells, 1200. See 3 September 1940.
421 Flt	Spitfire IIa Sgt C A H Ayling	P7303 +	Patrol. Shot down in combat near Newchurch, Kent, at 1600. See 7 June 1940. Aged 28.
611 Sqn	Spitfire IIa Sgt K C Pattison	P7323 DoW	Patrol. Shot down in combat near Kidderminster with Do17. Died 13 October – aged 27.

12 October 1940

72 Sqn	Spitfire I P/O H R Case	P9338 +	Patrol. Crashed near Folkestone at 0920, cause unknown. Aged 24.
92 Sqn	Spitfire I P/O A J S Pattinson	X4591 +	Patrol. Shot down by ME109 at 1640 over Hawkinge. Buried Poole, aged 21. See 23 September 1940.
145 Sqn	Hurricane I Sgt P Thorpe	P3896 Injured	Patrol. Baled out after attack by Me109 over Coghurst, near Hastings, 1020.
145 Sqn	Hurricane I P/O P W Rabone	V7251 Safe	Force-landed with battle damage after scrap with Me109s at 1030 over Dungeness. New Zealander. A/c repaired.
145 Sqn	Hurricane I Sgt J V Wadham	V7426 +	Patrol. Shot down in above action. Buried Newport, IoW, aged 21.
219 Sqn	Blenheim If Sgt G M Head P/O R V Baron	L1113 Safe +	Night patrol. Baled out due to engine trouble, but Baron's' chute failed. He was 40-years-old.
249 Sqn	Hurricane I Adj G C Perrin	V7313 Wounded	Patrol. Baled out after combat with Me109 over Sussex at 0950. French pilot.
257 Sqn	Hurricane I P/O C F A Capon	V7298 Wounded	Patrol. Baled out after combat over Dungeness with Me109 at 1700.
421 Flt	Spitfire IIa F/L C P Green	P7441 Wounded	Patrol. Baled out at 20,000 ft after attack by Me109 over Kent. Hit in neck and arm. See 23 May 1940.
605 Sqn	Hurricane I Sgt P R C McIntosh	P3022 +	Patrol. Missing after combat with many Me109s over Romney Marsh at 1230. Family members found his body in crashed aircraft near Littlestone Golf Course. Buried Shirley, Surrey, aged 20.

13 October 1940

17 Sqn	Hurricane I P/O J K Ross	P3536 Wounded	Patrol. Shot down by British AA fire over Chatham area and baled out at 1350.
29 Sqn	Blenheim If Sgt R E Stevens Sgt O K Sly AC2 A Jackson	L6637 + + +	Patrol. Shot down in error at 1800, by Hurricanes off Point of Aire, Wirral. Stevens and Sly NKGs, both aged 20; Jackson's body recovered, buried Mexborough, Yorks, aged 29.
66 Sqn	Spitfire I Sgt H Cook	X4543 Safe	Patrol. Crash-landed Hornchurch after combat over Maidstone. SoC.

14 October 1940

605 Sqn	Hurricane I F/O R Hope	P3107 +	Patrol. Chased He111 into Inner Artillery Zone (IAZ) and hit a balloon cable, or hit by AA fire, 1250 am. Aged 26. See 28 September 1940.

15 October 1940

41 Sqn	Spitfire I Sgt P D Lloyd	X4178 +	Patrol. Shot down by Me109 of JG51 off North Kent coast at 1900. Body washed ashore on 27 October. Aged 23.

46 Sqn	Hurricane I P/O P S Gunning	N2480 +	Patrol. Shot down by Me109 over Thames Estuary at 1305. Aged 29.
46 Sqn	Hurricane I F/S E E Williams	V6550 +	Shot down by Me109 over Thames Estuary at 1430. NKG, aged 28.
46 Sqn	Hurricane I Sgt A T Gooderham	V6789 Wounded	Baled out slightly burned at 1440, after combat with Me109 in above action. See 2 November 1940.
92 Sqn	Spitfire I Sgt K B Parker	R6838 +	Patrol. Shot down by Me109, 1440, over Thames Estuary. Body washed ashore on Dutch coast and buried at Terschelling. Aged 25.
92 Sqn	Spitfire I F/L C B F Kingcome DFC	X4418 Wounded	Baled out after combat with Me109 at 1145, over Thames Estuary.
92 Sqn	Spitfire I P/O J W Lund	R6642 Safe	Ditto. Rescued from the sea. See 2 October 1941.
145 Sqn	Hurricane I P/O J J Macháček	V7337 Wounded	Patrol. Baled out after combat with Me109 over Christchurch at 1300. Leg wound. Czech pilot. See 8 July 1941.
229 Sqn	Hurricane I S/L A J Banham	P3124 Wounded	Patrol. Baled out with burn injuries after combat with Me109 at 1300, over Christchurch Bay. See 26 August 1940.
302 Sqn	Hurricane I Sgt M Wedzik	P2752 'R' Safe	Patrol. Baled out during combat with Me109 over north Kent at 1130.
421 Flt	Spitfire IIa Sgt M A W Lee	P7444 Wounded	Patrol. Damaged in forced landing after attack by Me109 at 1100. A/c repaired.
501 Sqn	Hurricane I Sgt S A Fenemore	V6722 +	Patrol. Shot down by Me109 over Redhill at 0815. Aged 20.
605 Sqn	Hurricane I F/L I J Muirhead DFC	N2546 +	Patrol. Shot down my Me109 over Maidstone at 1145. Baled out but too low. See 26 May and 7 October 1940. Aged 27.

16 October 1940

249 Sqn	Hurricane I P/O K T Lofts	V6878 Safe	Patrol. Force-landed near Tenterden, Kent, 1130, after combat with Do215. See 15 September 1940. A/c repaired.

17 October 1940

66 Sqn	Spitfire I P/O H W Reilly	R6800 'N' +	Patrol. Shot down by Me109 of JG51 – Werner Mölders – at 1525 over Westerham, Kent. Canadian, age 22.
74 Sqn	Spitfire IIa F/O A L Ricalton	P7360 +	Patrol. Shot down by Me109 over Maidstone at 1540. Aged 26.
213 Sqn	Hurricane I P/O R Atkinson	P3174 'G' +	Patrol. Shot down by Me109 at 1630, near Ashford, Kent. Aged 19.
242 Sqn	Hurricane I P/O N N Campbell	V6575 +	Patrol. Crashed into the sea during attack on Do17 off Yarmouth, 0900. Body recovered. Canadian, aged 27.

20 October 1940

74 Sqn	Spitfire IIa Sgt T B Kirk	P7370 Wounded	Patrol. Baled out badly wounded at 1455, after combat with Me109 over Maidstone. Died of his injuries on 22 July 1941, aged 22.
74 Sqn	Spitfire IIa Sgt C G Hilken	P7426 Wounded	Ditto. See also 21 April and 27 June 1941.
74 Sqn	Spitfire IIa P/O B V Draper	P7355 Safe	Patrol. Force-landed near Tonbridge after combat with Me109 at 1300. A/c repaired.

248 Sqn	Blenheim IVf	P6952 'X'	Recce sortie. Engaged off coast of Norway, 0930, and shot
	F/L G M Baird	PoW	shot down. Pilot Nav New Zealanders, Stalag Luft III.
	W/O D L Burton	PoW	Copcutt NKG, aged 20. Wood, wounded, later
	Sgt R Copcutt	+	Stalag Luft III.
	W/O S V Wood	PoW	
248 Sqn	Blenheim IVf	L9453 'Z'	Recce sortie. Missing off Norwegian coast searching for
	P/O S R Gane	+	P6952. NKGs; Gane and Green both aged 20.
	P/O M D Green	+	
	Sgt N J Stocks	+	

22 October 1940

46 Sqn	Hurricane I	R4074	Patrol. Shot down over Dungeness by fighters at 1650.
	Sgt J P Morrison	+	Aged 25.
74 Sqn	Spitfire IIa	P7431	Patrol. Shot down by Me109 over South Nutfield,
	F/O P C B StJohn	+	Surrey, 1530. Buried Amersham, aged 23.
74 Sqn	Spitfire IIa	P7364	Ditto. Baled out. New Zealander.
	P/O R L Spurdle	Safe	
257 Sqn	Hurricane I	R4195	Patrol. Hit by AA fire during fight with Me109s over
	P/O N B Heywood	+	Folkestone, 1645. Buried Manchester, aged 22.
257 Sqn	Hurricane I	V6851	Shot down by Me109 over at 1650, over Folkestone.
	Sgt R H B Fraser	+	Aged 20.
605 Sqn	Hurricane I	V6783	Patrol. Crash-landed near Dorking following combat
	P/O J A Milne	Wounded	with Me109 at 1430. Hospitalised with a fractured hip.
			Canadian.

25 October 1940

46 Sqn	Hurricane I	V6804	Patrol. Crashed onto a house in Romford returning
	P/O W B Pattullo	DoI	to base. Died the next day. Aged 21.
66 Sqn	Spitfire I	X4170	Patrol. Baled out after combat with Me109s over
	F/O R W Oxspring	Safe	Tunbridge Wells, 0900.
145 Sqn	Hurricane I	P3926 'Y'	Patrol. Force-landed near Brightling, Kent, at 1200.
	P/O R D Yule	Wounded	Leg wound. A/c Repaired. New Zealand pilot.
249 Sqn	Hurricane I	P3615	Patrol. Baled out after combat with Me109 over Linton,
	Sgt J M B Beard	Wounded	Kent at 1200. See 7 September 1940.
249 Sqn	Hurricane I	V7409	Wounded in combat with Me109, hit in left arm, leg and
	Sgt H J Bouquillard	Wounded	head. Force-landed on Rochester airfield. See 11 March
			1941.
302 Sqn	Hurricane I	V7593 'V'	Patrol. Failed to return from sortie over the Channel
	F/L F Jastrzębski	+	at 1050. Body washed up at Sylt. Aged 34.
501 Sqn	Hurricane I	N2438	Patrol. Shot down by Me109 over Cranbrook at 1515.
	P/O V R Snell	Safe	
501 Sqn	Hurricane I	P2903	Patrol. Collided with V6806 during combat with
	P/O V Goth	+	Me109s over Tenterden, Kent, at 1525. Czech, aged 25.
501 Sqn	Hurricane I	V6806	Collided with P2903 while attacking Me109s and baled
	P/O K W MacKenzie DFC	Safe	out. See 7 October 1940 and 29 September 1941.
603 Sqn	Spitfire I	P7365 'W'	Patrol. Baled out after combat with Me109s near Brede,
	P/O J F Soden	Injured	Sussex. See 16 August 1940.
603 Sqn	Spitfire I	P7309	Shot down by Me109, baled out at 1020 over
	P/O P Olver	Sl/WIA	Hastings, a/c crashed at Brede, Sussex.

603 Sqn	Spitfire I P/O L Martel	P7350 Wounded	Hit by cannon-shell, pilot wounded by splinters to left leg and body. A/c repaired. Polish pilot. This Spitfire is now flying with the Battle of Britain Memorial flight (2007).

26 October 1940

222 Sqn	Spitfire I Sgt P O Davis	R6773 Safe	Patrol. Crash-landed following engine fire at 1745. A/c repaired.
229 Sqn	Hurricane I P/O D B H McHardy	V6704 PoW	Patrol. Shot down off French coast at 130, by Me109, after attacking an He59. Dulag Luft and Stalag Luft III.
229 Sqn	Hurricane I F/O G M Simpson	W6669 +	Ditto. NKG, aged 21. New Zealander.
602 Sqn	Spitfire I Sgt D W Elcome	R6839 +	Patrol. Failed to return, 1230. NKG, aged 21.
605 Sqn	Hurricane I F/O C W Passy	P3737 Safe	Patrol. Written off in forced-landing at Marks Cross, Sussex, 1235, after engine problem, chasing Me109. See 15 August and 1 December 1940.
605 Sqn	Hurricane I F/O J C F Hayter	P2916 Safe	Baled out after combat with Me109 at 1545. New Zealander.

27 October 1940

66 Sqn	Spitfire IIa P/O J R Mather	P7539 +	Patrol. Crashed, possibly oxygen failure. Buried Ifield, Sussex, aged 25. See 18 September 1940.
74 Sqn	Spitfire IIa Sgt J A Scott	P7526 +	Patrol. Shot down by Me109 over Maidstone at 0900. Aged 22.
92 Sqn	Spitfire I Sgt D E Kingaby	R6721 Safe	Patrol. Written off in forced-landing near Leatherhead, 1445.
145 Sqn	Hurricane I F/O D G S Honor	V7422 Safe	Patrol. Forced-landing at 1220 near Hastings, having run out of fuel while in combat. A/c repaired.
145 Sqn	Hurricane I Sgt D B Sykes	N2494 Safe	Ditto. See 7 November 1940. A/c repaired.
145 Sqn	Hurricane I P/O A R I G Jottard	P3167 +	Patrol. Shot down by Me109 off the Isle of Wight at 1715. NKG, aged 28. Belgian pilot.
145 Sqn	Hurricane I Sgt J K Haire	V6888 Safe	Crash-landed during above action, on the sands at Bembridge, 1715. See 6 November 1940.
145 Sqn	Hurricane I P/O F Weber	V7592 Safe	Ditto. Baled out into the sea and rescued by MTB. Czech pilot.
222 Sqn	Spitfire I P/O E F Edsall	X4548 Injured	Patrol. Ran out of fuel after combat at 1800, and written off in crash landing near Hailsham. See 31 August and 20 September 1940.
603 Sqn	Spitfire IIa F/O C W Goldsmith	P7439 DoW	Patrol. Shot down by Me109 of JG51 south of Maidstone at 1405 and died the next day. Buried Hornchurch, aged 23.
603 Sqn	Spitfire IIa P/O R B Dewey	P7365 +	Ditto. Buried Hornchurch, aged 19.
605 Sqn	Hurricane I F/O A Ingle	V7599 'U' Safe	Patrol. Written off in forced-landing due to battle damage, at Barcombe, Sussex, 0940. Pilot very slightly injured. See 1 December 1940, 1 June and 11 September 1943.
609 Sqn	Spitfire I P/O P A Baillon	P9503 Safe	Patrol. Baled out over Andover, 1150, after combat. See also 28 November 1940.

610 Sqn	Spitfire I ?	N3264 ?	Damaged by Me109, crash-landed near Manston, Kent. Written off.

29 October 1940

1 Sqn	Hurricane I Sgt W T Page	P3318 Safe	Patrol. Forced-landing at 1730 near Peterborough, after combat with Do17. A/c repaired.
1 Sqn	Hurricane I P/O E Čižak	V7302 Safe	Ditto. Crash-landed at Wittering with battle damage. Czech. A/c repaired.
19 Sqn	Spitfire IIa Sub-Lt(A) A G Blake	P7423 +	Patrol. Shot down by Me109 near Chelmsford at 1715. Aged 23.
46 Sqn	Hurricane I Sgt H E Black	P3053 DoW	Patrol. Shot down by Me109 near Ashford, Kent, and died on 9 November 1940. Buried Ibstock, aged 26.
213 Sqn	Hurricane I P/O R R Hutley	V7622 +	Patrol. Baled out off Selsey, after combat at 1445, but picked up dead. Buried Tangmere, aged 22.
257 Sqn	Hurricane I Sgt A G Girdwood	V6852 +	Patrol. Shot down taking off from North Weald by Me109 of LG2, at 1640 Buried Paisley. See 18 August 1940.
257 Sqn	Hurricane I P/O F Surma	P3893 Safe	Patrol. Baled out after combat with Me109 over Bobbingworth, Essex, at 1700. Polish pilot. See 8 November 1941.
302 Sqn	Hurricane I F/L J A Thomson	P3085 'A' Injured	Patrol. Baled out after colliding with another Hurricane over Brooklands at 1530.
302 Sqn	Hurricane I F/O J Czerny	V6923 'U' Safe	Collided with P3085 and crash-landed. Repaired.
310 Sqn	Hurricane I P/O E Fechtner DFC	P3889 'S' +	Patrol. Collided with P3707 (slightly damaged) near Duxford at 1510. Buried Brookwood, aged 24.
501 Sqn	Hurricane I Sgt P O'Bryne	V7595 Safe	Patrol. Crashed near Leatherhead at 1415, cause unknown. A/C repaired.
615 Sqn	Hurricane I P/O N D Edmond	V6785 Wounded	Patrol. Damaged in combat at 1245. Canadian. See 20 April 1941.

30 October 1940

41 Sqn	Spitfire IIa P/O G G F Draper	P7282 Injured	Patrol. Written off after crash after a combat over Ashford at 1600. See August 1941.
41 Sqn	Spitfire IIa Sgt L A Garvey	P7375 +	Ditto. Shot down by Me109. Buried Wilton Cemetery, Birmingham, aged 26.
222 Sqn	Spitfire I P/O A E Davies	N3119 +	Patrol. Shot down by Me109 over Crowhurst, Sussex, 1210. Aged 23.
222 Sqn	Spitfire I P/O H P M Edridge	K9939 +	Wrecked crash-landing after above action. Died after rescue from burning wreck. See 30 August 1940.
249 Sqn	Hurricane I P/O W H Millington	V7536 +	Patrol. Shot down over Channel at 1300 in action with Me109. NKG, aged 23.
602 Sqn	Spitfire I Sgt W B Smith	X4542 Wounded	Patrol. Written off in forced-landing near Lydd at 1620, following attack by Me109.

After the Battle – November to December 1940

The fourth and final phase of the Battle of Britain ended officially at the close of October. However, Fighter Command had still to contend with the hit-and-run tactics used by the Luftwaffe during the final weeks of this momentous year. With the winter weather approaching and with their bombers having taken a severe mauling over the summer, the Luftwaffe resorted mainly to fighter sweeps, with *Jabo* Me109s carrying bombs which were dropped almost indiscriminately, but were enough of a threat to have Fighter Command try to engage them. This period was a most trying time for the RAF fighter pilots, playing a deadly game of hide-and-seek in the cloudy skies over southern England, especially during November.

1 November 1940

46 Sqn	Hurricane I Sgt R E deCannert d'Hamale	V7616 +	Patrol. Crashed at Acrise, Kent, after combat with Me109s at 1300. Aged 19. Belgian pilot.
74 Sqn	Spitfire IIa F/L W H Nelson	P7312 +	Patrol. Shot down by Me109 at 1400 over Stanford, Kent. NKG, 23-year-old Canadian.
74 Sqn	Spitfire IIa Sgt H J Soars	P7523 Wounded	Baled out in above action.
92 Sqn	Spitfire I P/O C H Saunders	X4555 Safe	Patrol. Shot down in combat east of Eastchurch and crash-landed. A/c repaired.
213 Sqn	Hurricane I P/O B A Wlasnowolski	N2608 'V' +	Patrol. Shot down by Me109 over Portsmouth, pm. Polish pilot, aged 23.
310 Sqn	Hurricane I P/O F Vindis	P8809 'T' Safe	Patrol. Crashed at Sudbury, Suffolk, cause unknown, returning to base.
501 Sqn	Hurricane I Sgt M S Marcinkowski	V7405 +	Patrol. Failed to return from sortie over the Channel. NKG, aged 21. Polish.
605 Sqn	Hurricane I S/L A A McKellar DSO DFC*	V6879 +	Patrol. Crashed 0815 after fight with Me109s, near Addisham. Buried Glasgow, aged 28.

2 November 1940

310 Sqn	Hurricane I Sgt J Kominek	L1842 'Z' Safe	Patrol. Baled out after aircraft caught fire over Sheppey.

3 November 1940

111 Sqn	Hurricane I Sgt B Olewinski	V6560 +	Patrol. Shot down by return fire from He111 over North Sea, pm. Polish pilot; NKG, aged 21.

5 November 1940

19 Sqn	Spitfire IIa P/O F Hradil	P7545 +	Patrol. Shot down by Me109, pm, off Southend. Body recovered a week later, buried Southend. Czech, aged 28.
238 Sqn	Hurricane I P/O B B Considine	V6792 Wounded	Patrol. Baled out after combat over Bournemouth, Dorset, pm. Irish.
238 Sqn	Hurricane I Sgt J Jeka	V7535 Wounded	Ditto. Polish pilot. See 21 May 1944.
242 Sqn	Hurricane I P/O N Hart	P2806 +	Patrol. Shot down off Sheerness pm, by Me109. Canadian; NKG, aged 25.
310 Sqn	Hurricane I Sgt M Jiroudek	V7588 'B' Safe	Patrol. Shot down over Sittingbourne, pm, by British AA fire and wrecked.
310 Sqn	Hurricane I Sgt F Mlejnecy	V7597 'D' Sl/inj	Damaged in attack by Me109 over Thames Estuary, pm. Crash-landed and turned over at base, Cat B.

310 Sqn	Hurricane I Sgt R Půda	V6619 'V' Safe	Baled out in above action.
310 Sqn	Hurricane I F/L J Jefferies DFC	R4089 Safe	Damaged in above action, made belly landing at Hornchurch.
310 Sqn	Hurricane I Sgt A Dvořák	P2795 Safe	Damaged in this action and crashed at Fowlmere. A/c repaired.
603 Sqn	Spitfire IIa Sgt P H R R Terry	P7509 Wounded	Patrol. Damaged by Me109, pm, over Canterbury. Damage Cat 2, but repaired.
616 Sqn	Spitfire I F/L C A T Jones	X4055 Wounded	Patrol. Badly wounded in the elbow in attack on He111 of KG53 off Spurn Head, 1730. A/c damaged.

6 November 1940

145 Sqn	Hurricane I P/O J K Haire	V6627 +	Patrol. Shot down pm, over the Isle of Wight, probably by Helmut Wick of JG2. Baled out too low. Buried Belfast, aged 20.
145 Sqn	Hurricane I Sgt J Weber	R4177 Safe	Shot down and baled out in the same action.
213 Sqn	Hurricane I Sgt H H Adair	V7602 +	Patrol. Shot down over Portsmouth by Me109, pm – Helmut Wick of JG2. Remains found in excavation of of a/c in 1979. Aged 23.
238 Sqn	Hurricane I P/O J Tillett	V6814 +	Patrol. Shot down by Me109 pm, over Fareham, by JG2.

7 November 1940

145 Sqn	Hurricane I F/L R W Bungay	V6889 Injured	Patrol. Baled out over Isle of Wight, in combat with Me109 of JG2, 1430. Knee injury. Australian.
145 Sqn	Hurricane I F/O A N C Weir DFC	P2720 +	Shot down by Me109 off the Isle of Wight by JG2, 1430. NKG, aged 21.
145 Sqn	Hurricane I Sgt J McConnell	P8816 Injured	Ditto. Baled out.
145 Sqn	Hurricane I P/O J H Ashton	P2770 Safe	Ditto. Crash-landed near Ashley, IoW. A/c repaired.
145 Sqn	Hurricane I Sgt D B Sykes	P2924 Injured	Ditto. Crash-landed near Ventnor, Isle of Wight. See 27 October 1940.
249 Sqn	Hurricane I P/O T F Neil DFC	V7676 'J' Safe	Patrol. Baled out after collision with G/C F V Beamish over Kent, pm.

8 November 1940

46 Sqn	Hurricane I P/O W R Farley	V6922 Injured	Patrol. Shot down by Me109, baled out and broke leg on landing at Marden, Kent.
257 Sqn	Hurricane I Sgt A D Page	V6870 +	Patrol. Shot down by Me109 over Kent, pm. Buried Folkestone, aged 21.
302 Sqn	Hurricane I Sgt W Korsarz	P3538 'J' +	Patrol. Shot down by Me109 over Mayfield, pm. Buried Northwood, aged 32.
302 Sqn	Hurricane I Sgt E J A Nowakiewicz	P3935 'D' Wounded	Shot-up by 109 and crash-landed at Detling – wheels-up.
501 Sqn	Hurricane I Sgt H C Grove	V6805 +	Patrol. Baled out after attack by Me109s but parachute failed. Aged 29.
603 Sqn	Spitfire IIa F/O M T Kirkwood	P7285 +	Patrol. Shot down by Me109s off Deal, pm. NKG.

| 605 Sqn | Hurricane I
P/O C Tarkowski | N2649
Safe | Patrol. Wrecked in forced-landing at Staplehurst, following Me109 combat, pm. Polish. |
| 615 Sqn | Hurricane I
P/O L N Landels | V7652
Injured | Patrol. Wrecked in forced-landing at Challock, Kent, after combat with Me109. |

11 November 1940

17 Sqn	Hurricane I P/O D H Wissler	V7570 +	Patrol. Shot down attacking a Ju87 over Thames Estuary, midday. NKG. See 24 September 1940.
17 Sqn	Hurricane I Sgt R D Hogg	P2794 +	Ditto. Buried Bedford, aged 22.
66 Sqn	Spitfire II F/L H R Allen	X4255 Safe	Fuel tank exploded over Channel returning from sortie over French coast. Crash-landed Hawkinge. A/C damaged.

14 November 1940

| 74 Sqn | Spitfire IIa
P/O W Armstrong | P7386
Safe | Patrol. Baled out in combat over Dover, 1400. |
| 238 Sqn | Hurricane I
P/O W Rózycki | P3618
Safe | Patrol. Written off in crash at Stockbridge, Hants. Polish. |

15 November 1940

19 Sqn	Spitfire IIa Sgt H A C Roden	P7420 DoI	Hit a tree attempting to force-land following combat with Me110s off Harwich. Died on 16 November, aged 24.
264 Sqn	Defiant I P/O W R A Knocker P/O F A Toombs	N1547 Safe DoI	Patrol. Engine cut, hit a tree on the approach to Rochford, and exploded. Toombs badly burned and died later.
605 Sqn	Hurricane I P/O C Gauze	V6951 +	Patrol. Shot down over Kent, 0930, by Me109s, and ditched. Polish. Buried Whyteleafe, Surrey, aged 22.
605 Sqn	Hurricane I P/O R E Jones	P2560 Safe	Ditto. Baled out over North Foreland.

16 November 1940

| 25 Sqn | Blenheim If
Sgt P L T Winter
Sgt A J Theasby
Sgt A L Romanis | L6679
+
+
+ | Night patrol. Crashed near Billericay,
Essex.
Aged 23.
Aged 24. |
| 234 Sqn | Spitfire I
Sgt H Sharpley | X4027
+ | Patrol. Went into the sea off Porth, Cornwall, on interception sortie. NKG. |

17 November 1940

17 Sqn	Hurricane I F/O M B Czernin DFC	V7500 'D' Safe	Patrol. Shot down by Adolf Galland of JG26 while attacking Me110 near Bredfield, Suffolk. Baled out 0920. See 16 May 1940.
92 Sqn	Spitfire I Sgt J W Allison	N3229 Safe	Patrol. Damaged in forced-landing after combat over Eastbourne, pm. A/c repaired.
257 Sqn	Hurricane I Sgt B Henson	N2342 +	Patrol. Shot down by JG26 (Galland) east of Harwich, 0925. Body was recovered, buried Cambridge.

21 November 1940

| 603 Sqn | Spitfire IIa
Sgt R E Plant | P7387
+ | Patrol. Collided with He111 of KG53 at 1235 over Faversham, Kent. Buried Stoke, Coventry, aged 21. |

27 November 1940

74 Sqn	Spitfire IIa P/O P Chesters	P7306 Wounded	Patrol. Baled out in combat with JG51 over Chatham, 1535. See 10 April 1941.
421 Flt	Spitfire IIa P/O K A Lawrence	P7499 Injured	Weather recce. Baled out after hits by Me109 of JG26 over Ramsgate, at 0825. Broken right leg and right arm dislocated. New Zealand pilot.

28 November 1940

64 Sqn	Spitfire I P/O W N C Salmond	K9950 Safe	Patrol. Baled out after aircraft caught fire near Tunbridge Wells.
66 Sqn	Spitfire IIa F/O H R Allen	P7492 Safe	Patrol. Baled out following collision with P7491 over Edenbridge, Kent. See 14 February 1941.
66 Sqn	Spitfire IIa Sgt P H Willcocks	P7491 +	See above. Aged 21.
152 Sqn	Spitfire I P/O A R Watson	R6597 +	Patrol. Baled out in combat with Me109s but parachute torn on aircraft and he fell to his death. Aged 19.
152 Sqn	Spitfire I Sgt Z Klein	P9427 +	Shot down by Me109 off Dorset coast into the Channel. NKG, aged 22; Polish.
213 Sqn	Hurricane I Sgt H J R Barrow	V6691 +	Patrol. Shot down by Me109 of JG2 at 1510 over Tangmere. Went into the sea and body washed up on French coast. Aged 21.

Belgian P/O Count R G C de Hemricourt de Grunne, killed in action on 21 May 1941. He had become an ace during the Spanish Civil War and had flown with 32 Squadron during the Battle of Britain – WIA 18 August.

P/O W J Sandman, 74 Squadron, shot down and made a prisoner on 27 June 1941.

249 Sqn	Hurricane I P/O P H V Wells	V6729 Wounded	Patrol. Baled out and burned after combat with Me109 of JG26 – Adolf Galland – over Kent, pm. See 7 September 1940.
501 Sqn	Hurricane X Sgt L J Patterson	P5189 +	Patrol. Shot down by Me109 of JG51 off Hastings, pm. NKG, aged 23.
602 Sqn	Spitfire I P/O A Lyall	N3242 +	Patrol. Baled out too low following combat with Me109 over Isle of Wight at 1410. Aged 27.
609 Sqn	Spitfire I P/O P A Baillon	R6631 +	Shot down by Helmut Wick, JG2, off IoW, 1615. Buried Bayeux, France, aged 26. See 27 October 1940.
609 Sqn	Spitfire I F/L J C Dundas DFC*	X4586 'O' +	Patrol. Shot down by Me109 of JG2 (Rudolf Pflanz) off Isle of Wight at 1615. NKG, aged 24.

29 November 1940

249 Sqn	Hurricane I P/O R G A Barclay DFC	V6692 Wounded	Patrol. Baled out after attack by Me109 of JG26 over Tunbridge Wells, am. Wounded in leg, ankle and elbow. See 20 September 1941.
603 Sqn	Spitfire IIa P/O W P H Rafter	P7449 +	Patrol. Dived into the ground south of Broomfield, cause unknown. Age 19.

30 November 1940

46 Sqn	Hurricane I P/O C F Ambrose	P3429 Safe	Patrol. Baled out after combat with Me109 over Ashford, 1330. See 4 September 1940.
46 Sqn	Hurricane I Sgt N M S Walker	V7202 +	Ditto.

1 December 1940

65 Sqn	Hurricane I F/O J T Strang	P9454 Safe	Patrol. Baled out, a/c caught fire over Mayfield. New Zealand pilot.
253 Sqn	Hurricane I Sgt S Kita	P3678 Injured	Patrol. Shot down, crash-landed at Falmer, Sussex. SoC. Polish.
605 Sqn	Hurricane II F/O P L Parrott DFC	Z2323 Safe	Patrol. Baled out after attack by Me109 over East Hoathly, Sussex. See 26 May 1940.
605 Sqn	Hurricane I F/L A Ingle	V7609 Wounded	Ditto. See 27 October 1940, 1 June and 11 September 1943.
605 Sqn	Hurricane I F/O C W Passy	V7055 Wounded	Ditto. See 15 August & 26 October 1940.
605 Sqn	Hurricane I Sgt H N Howes DFM	V6844 Safe	Crash-landed at Gravesend after this action. A/c repaired.

2 December 1940

501 Sqn	Hurricane I P/O R C Dafforn	V6919 Wounded	Patrol. Written off in forced landing at Detling, after combat with Me109. See 18 August 1940.

5 December 1940

64 Sqn	Spitfire IIa Sgt C L Hopgood	P9450 +	Patrol. Shot down by Me109 over Kent coast. Buried Boulogne, aged 22.
249 Sqn	Hurricane I Sgt G A Stroud	V7677 Wounded	Patrol. Baled out after combat with Me109 of JG1 north of Rye. Burn injuries.

10 December 1940

17 Sqn	Hurricane I P/O L W Stevens	V7079 Wounded	Patrol. Damaged in forced-landing near Butley, Suffolk, having been hit by AA fire. A/c repaired. See 21 May 1941.

12 December 1940

65 Sqn	Spitfire I P/O W H Franklin DFM*	R6978 +	Patrol. Shot down in combat with Ju88 of 4(F)/121 near Selsey, 1420. NKG, aged 29.
65 Sqn	Spitfire I Sgt M H E Hine	R6982 +	Ditto. NKG, aged 24.
602 Sqn	Spitfire I Sgt A L Edy	X4658 Safe	Patrol. Shot down by Me109 near Folkestone and crash-landed. SoC. Canadian.

29 December 1940

263 Sqn	Whirlwind I F/L W O L Smith	P6978 +	Escort. Collided over Dartmoor in bad weather.
263 Sqn	Whirlwind I P/O D Vine	P6975 +	Ditto.

Chapter 6

Taking the Offensive, 1941

The New Year found Fighter Command still on the defensive. As far as anyone knew for certain, as soon as the winter weather improved in the coming spring, the 'Battle of Britain' would continue. However, the Luftwaffe's main thrust now was night bombing, which Fighter Command was ill-equipped to counter. While Blenheim fighters and the new Beaufighter, now equipped with Air Interception (AI) radar, were available, their numbers were small and the Command had to rely too on single-seat day fighters operating at night, supplemented by Defiants which had been relegated to night work after their failure to survive in daylight.

As the year progressed, and no major daylight assault came from the Germans, the RAF began to take the offensive, although the Luftwaffe fighter force still attempted to dominate the south-east corner of England and the Channel with fighter patrols and sweeps. However, the RAF had had time to lick its wounds of the previous summer and autumn; new pilots were arriving at the squadrons, and Fighter Command HQ felt capable of taking the air war to the Germans across the Channel.

1 January 1941

| 111 Sqn | Hurricane I | V6875 | Patrol. Damaged by Ju88 rear gunner and written off in |
| | S/L A J Bigger | Safe | crash-landing at Montrose. |

3/4 January 1941

23 Sqn	Blenheim If	L6781 'X'	Night intruder sortie. Failed to return.
	S/L V G F Coleman	PoW	Stalag Luft III.
	F/S D W Mathews	+	NKG, aged 30.
	Sgt H I MacRory	+	NKG, aged 21.

9/10 January 1941

23 Sqn	Blenheim If	L1226	Night intruder sortie near Beauvais area.
	Sgt R W Jones	PoW	Missing. Kopernikus Camp.
	Sgt G E Bessell	PoW	Kopernikus Camp.
	Sgt R W Cullen	PoW	Various – including Stalag Luft 6.
307 Sqn	Defiant I	N3401	Night patrol. Wreckage found in sea but circumstances
	Sgt A Joda	+	unknown. Merioneth, Wales.
	Sgt W Gandurski	+	

10 January 1941

74 Sqn	Spitfire IIa	P7561	Anti-shipping strike. Wrecked in crash-landing at
	Sgt L E Freese	+	Detling after running out of fuel. Died later, aged 24.
249 Sqn	Hurricane I	P3579	Circus 1. Baled out and wounded, rescued near Dover.
	P/O W W McConnell	Wounded	See 14 February 1944.

12 January 1941

242 Sqn	Hurricane I	P2961	Rhubarb. Shot down by Me109. NKG, aged 22.
	F/O W M McKnight DFC*	+	Canadian.
242 Sqn	Hurricane I	V7203	Rhubarb. Shot down by Me109. NKG, aged 27.
	P/O J B Latta DFC	+	

16 January 1941

32 Sqn	Hurricane I	P2984	Night patrol. Baled out after combat with He111 near
	F/O J P Falkowski	Injured	Portsmouth. Broke left leg on landing. Polish.
234 Sqn	Spitfire IIa	X4428	Patrol. Lost during combat with Ju88 over Plymouth.
	P/O G W Rogers	+	NKG, aged 24.

234 Sqn	Spitfire I P/O W L Beech	N3191 +	Patrol. Crashed near Truro returning from sortie; aircraft written off.

20 January 1941

43 Sqn	Hurricane I P/O Tufnell	P3775 Injured	Patrol. Crashed off Dundee after combat with Ju88, lost an eye.

2 February 1941

74 Sqn	Spitfire IIa S/L E J C Michelmore	P7741 +	Sweep. Attached to 74, flying No. 2 to S/L A G Malan, shot down by Me109s of 1/LG2. Aged 25.
605 Sqn	Hurricane II Sgt H W Pettit	Z2308 +	Battle climb. Drifted over North Sea and shot down by Me109. NKG, aged 20.
605 Sqn	Hurricane II Sgt K H Jones	Z2329 PoW	Ditto. Landed on German airfield in error; set a/c on fire with Very pistol. Stalag Luft 6, Heydekrug.

5 February 1941

1 Sqn (RCAF)	Hurricane I F/O R G Lewis	P3920 +	Circus 3. Baled out after attack by Me109 over the Channel but was not rescued. NKG, aged 30.
56 Sqn	Hurricane I Sgt R C Jones	P3123 +	Circus 3. Missing. Buried at Wimille, France, aged 24.
65 Sqn	Spitfire IIa P/O G Hill	P7665 'L' PoW	*Rajshahi*. Circus 3. Shot down by Me109 near St Omer. Colditz.
65 Sqn	Spitfire IIa Sgt H C Orchard	P7733 +	Circus 3. Shot down by Me109. Buried Neufchatel-Hardelot, aged 24.
610 Sqn	Spitfire I Sgt H D Denchfield	N3249 PoW	Circus 3. Shot down by Walter Oesau of I/JG3. Stalag Luft 6.
611 Sqn	Spitfire IIa P/O H S Sadler	X4547 +	Circus 3. Shot down over the sea by Me109. NKG, aged 24.
615 Sqn	Hurricane I Sgt O M Jenkins	V6980 +	Circus 3. Shot down over Calais. Buried Bellebrune, France.
615 Sqn	Hurricane I P/O S Czternastek	V7598 'U' +	Circus 3. Collided over Dover with V6618. Polish.
615 Sqn	Hurricane I P/O B Wydrowski	V6618 Safe	Baled out after colliding with V7598. Polish pilot.

8 February 1941

242 Sqn	Hurricane I P/O L E Cryderman	V6823 +	Patrol. Ditched after combat with Do17 off Clacton, but not found. NKG, Canadian.
263 Sqn	Whirlwind I P/O K A G Graham	P6969 'V' +	Interception. In combat with Ar196, 0930. Crashed south of Start Point, Devon. NKG, aged 20.

10 February 1941

46 Sqn	Hurricane II P/O C H Hedley	V7594 +	Roadstead. FTR, near Calais.
46 Sqn	Hurricane II Sgt D J Steadman	V7443 Wounded	Roadstead. Shot down by Me109; crash-landed on a sandbank and swam ashore to safety.
249 Sqn	Hurricane I P/O W L Davis	V7171 PoW	Circus 4. Shot down by Me109 of I/LG2, wounded. Early pm.
601 Sqn	Hurricane I P/O R C Lawson	V6630 +	Roadstead. Seen to crash into the sea. NKG, aged 21.

601 Sqn	Hurricane I Sgt F Mares	V7236 Safe	Roadstead. Damaged in force-landing near Martlesham Heath. A/c repaired. See 12 April 1941. Czech pilot.

11 February 1941

66 Sqn	Spitfire IIa P/O S Baker	P7568 +	Sweep. Shot down by Me109 of LG2 off Boulogne. NKG, aged 21.
66 Sqn	Spitfire IIa P/O P R Mildren	P7520 +	Ditto. Buried Boulogne.

13/14 February 1941

306 Sqn	Hurricane I P/O B Bielkiewicz	P3069 'Y' +	Night patrol. Crashed after hitting a tree, landing at Buntingsdale LG (landing ground).

14 February 1941

66 Sqn	Spitfire IIa P/O J Lawson-Brown	P7522 Safe	Patrol. Damaged by Me109 over SE England, and crash-landed. Repaired.
66 Sqn	Spitfire IIa P/O D A Maxwell	P7541 +	Ditto. Crashed into the sea. NKG, aged 24.
66 Sqn	Spitfire IIa Sgt C A Parsons	P7670 Wounded	Ditto. Slightly damaged. See 20 August 1941.
66 Sqn	Spitfire IIa F/L H R Allen	P7504 Wounded	Ditto. Force-landed at Biggin Hill. Hit in right arm. A/c repaired. See 28 November 1940.

15 February 1941

66 Sqn	Spitfire IIa Sgt Pearce	P7670 Wounded	Patrol. Crash-landed at Manston after combat with Me109s. A/c repaired.
71 Sqn	Hurricane I P/O V C Keough	V7606 +	Patrol. Lost during combat with Do17 off Skegness. American. NKG, 29.
615 Sqn	Hurricane I F/O D G A Stewart	P3231 +	Rhubarb. Shot down at Zeebrugge. Buried Adegem, Belgium, aged 27. Canadian.
615 Sqn	Hurricane I Sgt A C Fotheringham	V7651 PoW	Rhubarb. Force-landed near Koksijde Belgium. Stalag Luft 6.

17 February 1941

91 Sqn	Spitfire IIa F/O J J O'Meara	? Safe	Crash-landed near Folkestone after combat with Me109. Cat 2 damage.

20 February 1941

41 Sqn	Spitfire IIa Sgt J McAdam	P7302 +	Patrol. Shot down by Werner Mölders of JG51, 1550. See 7 and 24 September 1940. Picked up dead from the sea; Buried Island Magee, Co Antrim, aged 21.
41 Sqn	Spitfire IIa Sgt R A Angus	P7322 +	Ditto. Baled out but not found. NKG, Aged 21.

22 February 1941

605 Sqn	Hurricane IIA P/O J H Rothwell	Z2347 +	Patrol. Crashed near Littlehampton, possible oxygen problem, Buried at Poynings, Sussex, aged 20.

23 February 1941

64 Sqn	Spitfire IIa P/O L Hawkins	P7778 +	Convoy patrol. Believed to have collided with P7852.
64 Sqn	Spitfire IIa P/O J G Pippet	P7852 +	See above. NKG, aged 21.

24 February 1941

74 Sqn	Spitfire IIa Sgt N Morrison	P7618 +	Failed to return from patrol. Buried Glasgow, aged 26.
74 Sqn	Spitfire IIa Sgt J A Rogowski	P7559 Injured	Patrol. Crash-landed at Eastbourne, suffering scalp injury. A/c repaired. Polish pilot.
257 Sqn	Hurricane X P/O E H Atkins	P5186 +	Patrol. Lost in combat with Ju88 off Happisburgh, Norfolk, 1045. NKG, aged 24. Canadian.

25 February 1941

| 611 Sqn | Spitfire IIa
P/O D A Stanley | X4592 'S'
+ | *St. George.* Escort. Shot down off Gravelines by
Werner Mölders, JG51. NKG, aged 19. |

26 February 1941

54 Sqn	Spitfire IIa Sgt H Squire	P7443 'E' PoW	Circus 5. Shot down by I/LG2 near Calais.
56 Sqn	Hurricane IIA Sgt A Turner	Z2755 +	Patrol. Shot down into the Channel by JG51. NKG, aged 23.
256 Sqn	Defiant I F/L S F F Johnson Sgt C S Lewis	N3520 + Safe	Dusk patrol. Ran short of fuel; gunner baled out but pilot crashed attempting to land at Collingbourne, Wilts. Aged 25.
615 Sqn	Hurricane IIA S/L R A Holmwood	Z2354 +	Patrol. Shot down off Dover by JG51.

Sgt J L McCairns of 616 Squadron was brought down on 6 July 1941 to become a prisoner. Escaped and returned to England via Spain in April 1942. Awarded the MM, he returned to flying and won the DFC and 2 Bars, plus the French *Croix de Guerre*, by the war's end.

Sgt W G Lockhart, 74 Squadron, shot down 6 July 1941; he escaped and evaded, returning to England via Spain. Later DSO DFC & Bar, killed in action on 28 April 1944 as a W/C and OC 7 Squadron.

615 Sqn	Hurricane IIA P/O C N Foxley-Norris	Z2754 Safe	Ditto. Baled out 25,000 feet.
615 Sqn	Hurricane IIA P/O D H Hone	Z2698 Injured	Ditto. Crash-landed at Tenterden. A/c repaired. See 26 August 1940.
615 Sqn	Hurricane IIA Adj G C Perrin	? Safe	Ditto. Shot down, crash-landed. French pilot. See 12 October 1940.

1 March 1941

74 Sqn	Spitfire IIa S/L C A Wood	P3752 Wounded	Patrol. Crash-landed after attack by Me109 of I/LG2. A/c repaired.
234 Sqn	Spitfire I Sgt C H Bell	N3101 +	Failed to return from convoy patrol off the Scilly Isles. NKG.

3 March 1941

54 Sqn	Spitfire IIa P/O J C Lockwood	P7300 +	Patrol. Shot down by Me109 of JG51 near Maidstone, Kent. Aged 22.

3/4 March 1941

23 Sqn	Blenheim If Sgt J S Rose Sgt T F Nicholas Sgt R A Walker	L1453 + + +	Intruder sortie. Believed shot down by flak near Guines. Rose buried in Guines, aged 25.

5 March 1941

610 Sqn	Spitfire IIa P/O M C W Ormond	P7752 PoW	*The Warden of London.* Circus 6. Shot down by Me109 of JG51 near Boulogne. New Zealander.
610 Sqn	Spitfire IIa P/O R E Owen	P7596 +	Ditto. Over the Channel.
610 Sqn	Spitfire IIa P/O N G Drever	P8027 PoW	Ditto. Stalag Luft III.
610 Sqn	Spitfire IIa Sgt S Hamer	P7501 +	Ditto. Killed trying to crash-land at Wilmington, Sussex. A/c repaired.

8 March 1941

266 Sqn	Spitfire IIa F/O F P Ferris	X4594 +	*Andhradesa (Madras).* Interception. Shot down by Ju88 off Skegness, at 1015. Buried Chawton, Hamps.

10 March 1941

54 Sqn	Spitfire IIa Sgt J F Cooper	P7371 +	Sweep. Shot down off Le Tréport by Me109 of JG51, 1535.
616 Sqn	Spitfire II Sgt B Bingley	P7662 +	Interception. Crashed near Wiston, Sussex. Probably oxygen failure.

10/11 March 1941

23 Sqn	Blenheim If Sgt V H Skillen Sgt F H Abbott Sgt R R J Nute	L1340 'X' + + +	Intruder. Collided with He111 over Amiens-Glisy. All buried Amiens St Pierre, aged 24, 22 and 23.

11 March 1941

263 Sqn	Whirlwind I P/O H H Kitchener	P6985 'J' Wounded	Patrol. Hit by fire from Ju88 at 1710, off Cornwall and seriously injured in crash-landing.

| 615 Sqn | Hurricane IIA
Adj H J Bouquillard | Z2757
+ | Patrol. Shot down by Me109 near Tilbury, evening.
French, aged 32. See 25 October 1940. |

12 March 1941

54 Sqn	Spitfire IIa Sgt A A Burtenshaw	P7689 +	Patrol. Believed shot down by Me109 near Maidstone, pm. Snodland Cemetery.
74 Sqn	Spitfire IIa Sgt J N Glendinning	P7506 +	Patrol. Shot down by Me109 of JG51 – Werner Mölders – crashing at Ivychurch, Kent, pm. Aged 28.
91 Sqn	Spitfire IIa Sgt J Mann	P7693 Sl/WIA	Patrol. Shot down by JG51, crash-landed Dungeness, pm, a/c repaired. See 4 April 1941.

12/13 March 1941

| 96 Sqn | Defiant I
F/O V Vesely
Sgt Heycock | N1803
Wounded
Safe | Night patrol. Hit during attack on He111 over
Liverpool. Aircraft was repaired. Czech pilot. |

13 March 1941

| 64 Sqn | Spitfire IIa
S/L A R D MacDonell DFC | P7555
PoW | Circus. Baled out after attack by Me109 of JG51 –
Werner Mölders – near Calais, pm. Stalag Luft III. |
| 611 Sqn | Spitfire IIa
Sgt A S Darling | P7368
Safe | Circus. Crash-landed at Dungeness after combat with
JG51, pm. See 26 April 1941. A/c repaired. |

14 March 1941

| 263 Sqn | Whirlwind I
P/O P G Thornton-Brown | P6988
Injured | Convoy patrol. Crash-landed at Portreath due to poor
weather, and seriously injured. See 21 December 1943. |

18 March 1941

| 17 Sqn | Hurricane IIA
Sgt L H Bartlett | Z2704
Wounded | Patrol. Baled out near Uckfield, Sussex, after attack by
Me109 of I/JG51, am. |
| 17 Sqn | Hurricane IIA
Sgt A J Hughes | Z2670
Wounded | Ditto. |

19 March 1941

1 Sqn	Hurricane IIA Sgt J Stefan	Z2810 Safe	Convoy patrol. Crash-landed after attack by Me109 of I/LG2, late pm, and SoC. Czech pilot.
1 Sqn	Hurricane IIA P/O A Kershaw	Z2759 +	Ditto. Baled out over Hastings but parachute failed. Aged 21.
610 Sqn	Spitfire IIa Sgt Hale	? Wounded	Patrol. Attacked by Me109 of III/JG53 and crash-landed at Hailsham.

27 March 1941

74 Sqn	Spitfire IIa P/O A H Smith	P7328 +	Patrol. Shot down by Me109 off Dungeness, 1100.
609 Sqn	Spitfire IIa Sgt P H A MacSherry	P7785 +	Interception. Shot down by Me109 of I/LG2, SW of Dungeness 1630.
315 Sqn			This squadron based at Speke, near Liverpool, lost four Hurricanes and three pilots this day over the sea. It started out as a practice flight but in the air turned into a convoy patrol during which these losses occurred:
	Hurricane I P/O T Hoyden	V7656 +	Crashed into the sea.
	Hurricane I F/L W Szulkowski	V7188 +	Collided with V7187.
	Hurricane I Sgt E Paterek	V7187 +	Collided with V7188.

	Hurricane I F/O K Wolinski	P3936 Safe	Ran out of fuel, baled out – rescued.

30 March 1941

| 229 Sqn | Hurricane I
P/O J M F Dewar | V6872
+ | Failed to return from patrol. Possibly collided with W9307. NKG, aged 24. |
| 229 Sqn | Hurricane I
P/O R A L DuVivier | W9307
+ | See above. |

1 April 1941

| 263 Sqn | Whirlwind I
F/L D A C Crooks DFC | P6989
+ | Patrol. Shot down by rear gunner of Do215 off the Lizard, Cornwall, late pm. Canadian. |

3 April 1941

| 242 Sqn | Hurricane IIA
F/L H N Tamblyn DFC | Z2692
+ | Convoy patrol. Shot down by return fire from Me110 off Norfolk coast at 0905. Died from exposure before being found. Buried Ipswich, aged 23. Canadian. |

4 April 1941

91 Sqn	Spitfire IIa Sgt J Mann	P7783 Injured	Interception. Shot down by Me109 of JG26, crash-landed Hawkinge and burned out. Pilot burned. See 12 March 1941.
91 Sqn	Spitfire IIa Sgt A W P Spears	P7565 Wounded	Ditto. Shot down by Adolf Galland of JG26. See 30 August 1940.
79 Sqn	Hurricane I P/O J J Robinson	P3661 +	Dusk patrol. Crashed into the sea off Linley Head, Pembrokeshire.

7 April 1941

| 249 Sqn | Hurricane IIA
Sgt R E N Wynn | Z2663
+ | Convoy patrol. Crashed Ongar, Essex, on return. See 2 September 1940. |

8/9 April 1941

| 29 Sqn | Beaufighter I
F/L G P Gibson DFC
Sgt R Bell (219 Sqn) | R2250
Safe
Wounded | Patrol. Shot-up by Ju88 when landing at Wellingore, 2348 hrs. Slight A/c damage – repaired. Gibson later won the VC on the Dams raid, OC 617 Sqn. |

9 April 1941

| 64 Sqn | Spitfire IIa
P/O J H Rowden | P7784
+ | Rhubarb. Crashed on French coast after attack by Me109 of II/JG51. Buried Dunkirk. |

9/10 April 1941

| 23 Sqn | Blenheim If
P/O G A Simpson
Sgt H C J Brewer
Sgt T G F Nicholls | L8616 'M'
+
+
+ | Intruder. Shot down by flak, Avelin. All buried Avelin, France. Simpson aged 23, Nicholls 26. |
| 257 Sqn | Hurricane I
Sgt L R Truman | V6611
+ | Patrol. Shot down by Do17 intruder of I/NJG2, while landing at Coltishall; crashed and killed as he attempted to bale out. |

10 April 1941

| 74 Sqn | Spitfire IIa
P/O P Chesters | P7854
+ | Interception. Crashed flying victory roll over Manston after shooting down a Me109 of JG51. Buried Southend, aged 21. |
| 312 Sqn | Hurricane IIA
F/L A A M Dawbarn | V7066
+ | Patrol. Shot down by EA gunner off Aberdeen, 1430. NKG. |

11 April 1941

92 Sqn	Spitfire IIa Sgt T G Gaskell	X4062 +	Patrol. Shot down into the Channel by Me109 of III/JG51, pm. NKG, 20.

12 April 1941

303 Sqn	Spitfire IIa S/L Z K Henneberg DFC	P8029 'P' +	Rhubarb. Shot down by flak from Montreuil airfield, 1725. Ditched and seen in the sea but not rescued. NKG, aged 29.
601 Sqn	Hurricane IIA Sgt F Mares	Z2803 Wounded	Rhubarb. Hit in combat with Me109 of III/JG51. A/c repaired. See 10 February 1941. Czech pilot.

13 April 1941

303 Sqn	Spitfire IIa F/L W Łapkowski	P7567 'X' Wounded	ASR sortie. Shot-up by Me109 off Le Touquet. A/c repaired. See 6 September 1940 and 2 July 1941.

13/14 April 1941

87 Sqn	Hurricane I Sgt R T G Stirling	P3593 PoW	Night patrol. Became lost and baled out over Guernsey. Kopernikus camp.

15 April 1941

266 Sqn	Spitfire IIa W/C W E Coope	P7901 Safe	Channel patrol. Crash-landed at Manston after combat with Galland of JG26. A/c repaired. See 4 November 1939 and 4 June 1941.
266 Sqn	Spitfire IIa Sgt H Whewell	P8014 Wounded	Ditto. Crash-landed at Hawkinge. A/c repaired.
266 Sqn	Spitfire IIa Sgt R G V Barraclough	P7544 Wounded	Ditto. Crash-landed after combat with JG26. A/c repaired.
610 Sqn	Spitfire IIa P/O A R Ross	P7684 +	*Belfast.* Failed to return from patrol and combat with Ju88 off the Isle of Wight. Buried Surbiton, aged 21.
615 Sqn	Hurricane IIA P/O P W Dunning-White	Z2410 Safe	Channel patrol. Baled out 1020, over Dymchurch after combat with Me109 of I/JG51. Rescued by ASR launch.
615 Sqn	Hurricane IIA S/Lt P M Blaize	Z2694 +	Ditto. Shot down off Dover. French pilot.

16 April 1941

303 Sqn	Spitfire IIa P/O B Mierzwa	P7819 'S' +	Circus 8. Shot down by Me109 from JG53, near Dungeness. Aged 22.
303 Sqn	Spitfire IIa P/O M Waszkiewicz	P8039 'R' +	Ditto.
303 Sqn	Spitfire IIa P/O W S Strzembosz	P7385 Wounded	Ditto. Damaged but repaired.
601 Sqn	Hurricane IIB S/L J A O'Neill DFC	Z3090 Wounded	Escort. Baled out following attack by Me109 of JG51 off Dungeness. Rescued by HSL 143.
601 Sqn	Hurricane IIA W/C G A L Manton	Z2576 Wounded	Ditto. Crash-landed Dungeness. (Northolt Wing Leader). Repaired.
601 Sqn	Hurricane IIA G/C T N McEvoy	Z2492 Wounded	Ditto – crash-landed at Llydd. (Northolt Station Commander).

16/17 April 1941

264 Sqn	Defiant I F/O W R A Knocker Sgt O A Hardy	N3369 Safe Safe	Night patrol. Hit by AA fire over Crowborough and baled out.

19 April 1941

| 74 Sqn | Spitfire IIa
P/O E W G Churches | P7381
+ | Channel patrol. Shot down by Me109 of JG53, 1800 hrs.
NKG, aged 19. New Zealander. |

20 April 1941

54 Sqn	Spitfire IIa P/O C Colebrook	P7833 +	*Portadown.* Patrol. Shot down by Me109 of JG51, 2635, off Clacton. NKG.
54 Sqn	Spitfire IIa P/O J Stokoe	P7666 'Z' Safe	*Royal Observer Corps.* Baled out and rescued following combat with JG51. See 2 September 1940.
91 Sqn	Spitfire IIa Sgt E E Sykes RCAF	P7351 Safe	Patrol. Shot down by Me109, ditched off Sandgate and swam ashore with slight wounds. See 15 June 1942.
242 Sqn	Hurricane IIA S/L W P F Treacy DSO	Z2887 +	Patrol. Collided with Z2632 over the Channel, trying to avoid enemy a/x. Buried Boulogne. See 25 and 27 May 1940.
242 Sqn	Hurricane IIA F/O N D Edmund	Z2632 'A' +	See above: also 29 October 1940. Canadian, buried North Weald.
242 Sqn	Hurricane IIA F/O O E Lang	Z2634 +	Also collided with Z2887 over the sea in the above action.

602 Squadron pilots in 1940. Fourth from the left is P/O T G L Ritchie, who was shot down and killed on 21 July 1941. S/L A A McKeller DSO DFC*, second from left, was killed in action on 1 November 1940. To his left is F/O W H Coverley, killed in action 7 September 1940, while far right is F/L P J Ferguson, wounded 18 August 1940. F/L D MacF Jack stands far left. Other pilot is unknown.

303 Sqn	Spitfire IIa Sgt M Pavlović	P7859 'V' +	*Rainscombe*. Patrol. Shot down by H-J Joppien, JG51, over Le Touquet. Aged 25.

21 April 1940

74 Sqn	Spitfire IIa Sgt G G Hilken	P7614 Wounded	Patrol. Baled out after attack by JG51 Me109. See 20 October 1940 and 27 June 1941.
616 Sqn	Spitfire IIa Sgt R L Sellars	P7812 +	Patrol. Baled out over the Channel but not recovered. NKG, aged 23.

23 April 1941

242 Sqn	Hurricane IIA Sgt A J M David	Z2513 +	Convoy patrol off Clacton. Failed to return. NKG, aged 20.

24 April 1941

91 Sqn	Spitfire IIa P/O Peall	P7531 Safe	Shipping recce. Baled out over Channel after attack by I/LG2. Rescued by Margate lifeboat. Rhodesian.
616 Sqn	Spitfire IIa Sgt T F McDevette	P7736 +	Rhubarb. Shot down by flak during strafing attack Maupertus airfield at 1435. NKG.

26 April 1941

56 Sqn	Hurricane IIA P/O T F Guest	Z2763 PoW	Sweep. Shot down by JG51 over the French coast. Stalag Luft III.
91 Sqn	Spitfire IIa Sgt A S Darling	P7615 +	Shipping recce. Shot down by ME109 of II/JG51. See 13 March 1941.
302 Sqn	Hurricane IIA Sgt T Nastorowicz	Z2814 'K' +	Channel patrol. Crashed into the sea probably due to oxygen problem. Aged 26.

28 April 1941

611 Sqn	Spitfire IIa P/O A E Pennings	P7774 +	Rhubarb. Shot down by Me109 of JG1, am. Dutch pilot.

29 April 1941

72 Sqn	Spitfire IIa Sgt B Collyer	P8231 +	Interception. Lost in combat with Ju88 of 1(F)/120 over North Sea am.
609 Sqn	Spitfire IIa Sgt G C Bennett	P7669 +	Roadstead. Shot down by Me109 of JG51 off Calais. See 31 May 1940.

1/2 May 1941

604 Sqn	Beaufighter I F/O I K S Joll Sgt A A O'Leary	R2091 Safe Wounded	Night sortie. Damaged in action with He111 near Sopley, Dorset. O'Leary suffered five bullet wounds in the leg. but still aided his pilot to return to base – awarded DFM, A/c repaired.

3 May 1941

615 Sqn	Hurricane I Adj C P Guerin	V7163 +	Convoy patrol. Crashed near ships attempting to ditch and went down with the a/c, SW of Valley, Anglesey. French pilot.

Chapter 7

The Shooting Season, Summer 1941

Throughout the spring of 1941, both fighter forces had continued to test each other over the Channel and Southern England. As the weather improved the RAF began to strengthen its intention to take the war to the Luftwaffe over the northern areas of France, Belgium and Holland. For its part, the Luftwaffe intensified its night attacks upon Britain, culminating in raids against London in early May. There was also an operation called 'Channel Stop' implemented, its intention to deny the Germans free use of the Channel. In this, the RAF took its share of the actions against shipping off the French coast, and supporting light bombers attacking ships and ports along this same stretch of water.

3/4 May 1941

222 Sqn	Spitfire IIa P/O B P Klee	P7699 'K' +	*Zanzibar III.* Night sortie. Shot down by Ju88 intruder from I/NJG2, 0100, near Coltishall. Buried Worcester, aged 20.

4 May 1941

601 Sqn	Hurricane IIB F/L H C Mayers DFC	Z3087 Safe	Patrol. Shot down by Werner Mölders of JG51, off Deal. Rescued. See 13 August and 7 October 1940.
601 Sqn	Hurricane IIA Sgt C W J Fearn	Z2574 Wounded	ASR search. Attacked by Me109 of II/JG53, wheels-up crash-landing at Manston. A/c repaired.

4/5 May 1941

257 Sqn	Hurricane I Sgt R J Parrott	P3866 +	Night sortie. Shot down by intruder of I/NJG2, over Duxford while landing. Buried Whittlesford, Cambs. Aged 25.

5 May 1941

616 Sqn	Spitfire IIa F/O L H Casson	P7753 'X' Safe	*Pamperp 1.* Interception. Baled out near Littlehampton after combat with Ju88 near Tangmere, 0725. See 1 September 1940 and 9 August 1941.

6 May 1941

74 Sqn	Spitfire IIa P/O J Howard	P7928 'N' +	*Deven Squadron.* Roadstead. Shot down by Me109 from JG51, 1405. Buried Marquise, France, aged 22.
74 Sqn	Spitfire IIa Sgt A D Arnott	P8364 PoW	*Sirinam.* Ditto. Kopernikus camp.
74 Sqn	Spitfire IIa Sgt A F Wilson	P7537 Safe	Ditto. Baled out as engine caught fire over southern England on return.
601 Sqn	Hurricane IIA Sgt Briggs	Z2743 Safe	ASR escort. Baled out and rescued after attack by Werner Mölders of JG51, off Dover at noon.

6/7 May 1941

29 Sqn	Beaufighter If W/C S C Widdows DFC Sgt B Ryall	R2260 Wounded +	Night sortie. Damaged in combat with Ju88 over the Channel. AI operator baled out and was lost.

7 May 1941

54 Sqn	Spitfire IIa Sgt H K Hall	P8178 +	Roadstead. Missing over the Channel after combat with Me109, am. NKG.

611 Sqn Sgt J L Claxton	Spitfire IIa	P7817 +	Roadstead. Shot down off Deal by Me109 am. NKG, aged 26.

7/8 May 1941

256 Sqn S/L G H Gatheral F/O D S Wallen	Defiant I	N3500 'B' Safe Safe	Night sortie. Baled out near Widnes after combat with Ju88 over Birkenhead, 0110.
604 Sqn Sgt Wright Sgt Vaughan	Beaufighter If	R2101 Safe Safe	Night sortie. Baled out after successful combat with Ju88 off Portland – rescued.

8 May 1941

302 Sqn S/L P Łaguna	Hurricane IIB	Z3435 Safe	Patrol. Baled out after combat with Me109 of JG51, evening. See 27 June 1941.
302 Sqn Sgt M B Domagala	Hurricane IIA	Z2523 Safe	Ditto.
302 Sqn F/L Z J Kinel	Hurricane IIB	Z3095 'N' +	Ditto. Shot down by Me109. Buried at Northwood.
616 Sqn F/O H S L Dundas	Spitfire IIa	P7827 'A' Safe	Channel patrol. Cat B damage, crash landed at Hawkinge.

9 May 1941

92 Sqn P/O Maitland-Thompson	Spitfire IIa	R6908 Wounded	Patrol. Crash-landed and SoC after combat with Me109s of JG5, evening.
303 Sqn P/O J E L Zumbach	Spitfire IIa	P7962 'A' Safe	*Inspiration.* Channel patrol. Baled out over Dover after combat with Me109 of III/JG3.
609 Sqn Sgt R T D Mercer	Spitfire IIa	P7305 +	Channel patrol. Crashed onto the beach near St Margaret's Bay after combat with JG53, 1735, hitting and exploding a mine.

9/10 May 1941

600 Sqn F/O R S Woodward Sgt A J Lipscombe	Beaufighter If	T4641 Safe Safe	Night sortie. Baled out after attack by 'friendly' Beaufighter of 604 Sqn near Warwick.

10/11 May 1941

1 Sqn Sgt F Bęhal	Hurricane IIA	Z2921 +	Night sortie. Shot down in combat with He111 and crashed near Sanderstead, Surrey. Aged 29. Czech.

11 May 1941

504 Sqn F/L B E G White	Hurricane IIA	V7175 Wounded	Interception. Crash-landed near Wellington, Somerset, after combat with Me109 of JG2. Leg wounds.

13 May 1941

234 Sqn P/O N H Goodall	Spitfire IIa	P7779 +	Channel sweep. Collided pm, with P7317.
234 Sqn Sgt E L Stoodley	Spitfire IIa	P7317 +	Ditto. Seen to bale out but no trace. NKG.
504 Sqn P/O H N Hunt	Hurricane I	V6730 +	Convoy patrol. Crashed off Lyme Regis. Canadian. NKG, aged 22.

16 May 1941

74 Sqn P/O W J Sandman	Spitfire IIa	P8363 Safe	*Banka.* Roadstead. Damaged in combat with JG51 over Broadstairs. SoC 27 May.

16/17 May 1941

600 Sqn	Beaufighter If S/L C A Pritchard Sgt Gledhill	X7544 Injured Wounded	Night sortie. Baled out during combat with Ju88, over Berkswell, Coventry, around midnight. Pilot suffered burns while Gledhill was hit in leg by bullet.

17 May 1941

54 Sqn	Spitfire IIa Sgt E J Kean RNZAF	P7833 +	Patrol. Shot down over Maidstone by Wilhelm Balthasar of JG2, 1805. Buried Hornchurch, aged 28.
71 Sqn	Hurricane IIB F/O S M Kolendorski,	Z3186 +	Interception. Shot down by Me109 of G53 off Clacton, J1810. American. Buried Rockanje, Netherlands, after body washed ashore 13 August 1941.

19 May 1941

234 Sqn	Spitfire IIa P/O A S Harker DFM	P7922 Safe	*Man & Metal*. Convoy patrol. Baled out near Portland after attack by Me109 of JG2, 1150, and rescued.
306 Sqn	Hurricane IIB P/O K Rutkowski	Z3065 Safe	Patrol. Baled out after attack by JG52 at noon, and rescued.
306 Sqn	Hurricane IIA P/O J A Czapiewski	Z2456 +	Patrol. Shot down into the sea by JG52.
306 Sqn	Hurricane IIB Sgt B Kroczynski	Z2965 Wounded	Patrol. Baled out wounded in the above action.

21 May 1941

1 Sqn	Hurricane IIA F/L J C E Robinson	X2764 +	Circus. Shot down by Me109 of JG51 over the Pas de Calais. NKG, aged 23.
56 Sqn	Hurricane IIA Sgt G V Hoyle	Z2587 +	Sweep. Shot down by Me109. NKG.
145 Sqn	Spitfire IIa F/L L W Stevens	P7493 +	Patrol. Collided with P7737 on return from op. See 5 December 1940.
145 Sqn	Spitfire IIa F/O D W Owen RCAF	P7737 +	Ditto. Above Tangmere.
242 Sqn	Hurricane IIA P/O D K Oak-Rhind	Z2511 +	Sweep. Shot down by Me109 off Gravelines.
258 Sqn	Hurricane IIB S/L W G Clouston DFC	Z3250 'V' Wounded	Circus. Attacked and damaged by Me109.
258 Sqn	Hurricane IIA P/O R A R White RNZAF	Z2699 PoW	Circus. FTR. Stalag Luft III.
258 Sqn	Hurricane II F/O V B de la Perrelle	'D' Wounded	Circus. Shot-up by Me109. See 11 June 1941.
302 Sqn	Hurricane IIA Sgt M Rytka	Z2423 Evaded	Circus. Shot down, evaded and got back to UK via Gibraltar three months later. (KIFA 5 December 1942, DFC MBE)
609 Sqn	Spitfire IIa P/O R G C de H de Grunne	P7436 'M' +	Circus. A/c broke up during air fight over the Channel, 1715. See 18 August 1940.

31 May 1941

253 Sqn	Hurricane II Sgt H M Cox	V7235 +	Convoy patrol. Crashed SE Brough Head, Orkney, pm. Cause unknown. Buried Orkney, aged 20.

4 June 1941

54 Sqn	Spitfire V F/L D G Gribble DFC	R7275 +	Roadstead. Shot down by Me109 of II/JG53, baled out 12 miles off English coast, but not found. NKG, aged 21.
266 Sqn	Spitfire IIa W/C W E Coope	P8034 +	Sweep. Dived into the sea, reason unknown. NKG. See 14 November 1939 and 14 April 1941.
303 Sqn	Spitfire IIa P/O B Klosin	P8205 Wounded	Roadstead. Hit by Me109, crash-landed at Crowbridge, Kent. SoC.
609 Sqn	Spitfire IIa F/L J Curchin DFC	P7292 +	ASR search. Believed collided with Me109 of Stab JG3 over Channel, searching for F/L Gribble. NKG, aged 23.

7 June 1941

603 Sqn	Spitfire Va P/O R J Burleigh	W3111 +	Channel patrol. Shot down by Me109 from III. JG53 near Boulogne, and buried there.

9 June 1941

74 Sqn	Spitfire Vb P/O W W Burgon	W3186 +	*Oswald Finney II.* Channel patrol. Shot down by Me109 of JG25, in Straits of Dover. NKG.

10 June 1941

32 Sqn	Hurricane IIA P/O M Remy*	Z2832 'M'	Interception. Crash-landed Ireland after combat with He111 of Wekusta 51, and interned. A/c became Irish Air Corps No. 94, but returned to RAF in 1943. *Pilot's real name, Roger Motte (later Air Comm Indochina – KIFA October 1962). French.
601 Sqn	Hurricane IIB F/L G F Gregory	Z3026 +	Rhubarb. Probably flak. Buried at Samer, France, aged 22.
601 Sqn	Hurricane IIB Sgt R W Scales	Z3264 PoW	Rhubarb – FTR. Stalag Luft 4.

11 June 1941

247 Sqn	Hurricane I Sgt D C Ross	W9260 +	Night patrol. Crashed into the sea off Cornwall in poor visibility. Body recovered and buried at sea.
258 Sqn	Hurricane IIB F/O V B de la Parelle	Z3170 Wounded	Rhubarb. Shot up by Me109 of JG26 but returned to Martlesham Heath. See 21 May 1941.
258 Sqn	Hurricane IIB F/O W T Everist RNZAF	Z3269 'E' +	*Conqueror.* FTR after fight with JG26 over Channel. NKG, aged 23.
609 Sqn	Spitfire IIa Sgt G A Chestnut RCAF	P8654 'L' +	*Flintshire.* Channel patrol. Damaged Me109 of JG26; crashed into cliffs at Ramsgate trying to make Manston. 1705 hrs.

13/14 June 1941

85 Sqn	Havoc I (DB-7) Sgt T C E Berkely Sgt R Carr	AX848 'K' + +	Night sortie. Shot down attacking a He111 of KG4 off Thames Estuary. NKGs, aged 23 and 26 respectively.

16 June 1941

1 Sqn	Hurricane IIB Sgt A Nasswetter	Z3460 DoW	Patrol. Shot down into the Channel by 2/JG26 1830; died next day. Czech pilot, aged 21.
54 Sqn	Spitfire Va P/O G Grant-Govern	R7295 'U' Safe	*The Pastures.* Scramble. Baled out after attack by Me109 of JG26, late pm. Rescued by RN launch.
74 Sqn	Spitfire I S/L J C Mungo-Park DFC	W3174 Safe	*Oswald Finney.* Damaged by Me109; crash-landed at Hawkinge, SoC. See 27 June 1941.

91 Sqn	Spitfire IIa P/O D H Gage	W3126 +	ASR escort. Shot down by Me109 over the Channel. NKG, aged 23.
258 Sqn	Hurricane IIB F/L A M Campbell	Z3073 'C' Safe	Circus 13. Baled out over Channel and rescued after combat with JG26.
258 Sqn	Hurricane IIB P/O Dunn	Z3339 'B' Missing	Ditto. Galland and Oblt H-J Westphal each claimed one Hurricane, pm.

17 June 1941

56 Sqn	Hurricane IIA P/O P E M Robinson	Z2812 +	Circus 14. Shot down by Me109, evening. Buried, St Andrew's churchyard, North Weald, aged 27.
56 Sqn	Hurricane IIA F/L F W Higginson DFM	Z2575 'L' PoW	Circus 14, shot down by Me109 of JG26. Evaded, captured and later escaped back to England via Spain. See 16 August 1940.
56 Sqn	Hurricane IIB Sgt R D Carvill	Z3329 +	Ditto. NKG.
56 Sqn	Hurricane IIA P/O P A Harris	Z2664 'O' +	Ditto. NKG, aged 20.
74 Sqn	Spitfire Va P/O H F Parkes	R7278 PoW	Circus 14. Shot down by JG26.
74 Sqn	Spitfire IIa P/O R J E Boulding	W3251 PoW	Ditto. Stalag Luft III.
234 Sqn	Spitfire IIa Sgt J F Armitage	P7569 +	Roadstead. Shot down by Me109, mid-pm. NKG.
242 Sqn	Hurricane IIC S/L E T Smith	Z3246 PoW	Circus 14. Shot down by JG26. Stalag Luft 6.
242 Sqn	Hurricane IIA F/L B A Rogers	Z2888 +	Ditto. Shot down by Me109. Buried at Ambleteuse, France, aged 23.
242 Sqn	Hurricane IIa F/O J Bryks	Z2508 PoW	Ditto. NW Béthune. Colditz. Czech. (MBE).
303 Sqn	Spitfire IIa P/O J Bondar	P8641 Wounded	Ditto. Hit in the leg by fire from Me109 of JG26. Crash-landed at Northolt on return. A/c repaired.

18 June 1941

145 Sqn	Spitfire IIb Sgt K Palmer	P8254 PoW	Circus 15. Shot down by JG26.
145 Sqn	Spitfire IIb Sgt G M Turnbull	P8328 PoW	*The Transpitter.* Ditto. Adolf Galland and Gustav Sprick – each claimed one. Stalag Luft III camp.
258 Sqn	Hurricane IIB P/O W W Anderson	Z3331 +	Circus 15. Hit by AA fire.
609 Sqn	Spitfire Vb P/O S J Hill	W3211 'H' +	*Norman Merrett.* Circus 15. Shot-up by Me109 over Channel and crashed into the cliffs near Dover. Buried at Folkestone.

21 June 1941

1 Sqn	Hurricane IIB P/O V A Kopecky	Z2909 Safe	Circus 16. Shot down by Me109 of JG26 over sea and ditched off Folkestone. Rescued. Czech pilot. See 18 December 1941.
1 Sqn	Hurricane IIB P/O N Moranz	Z3461 PoW	Ditto. FTR. Gustav Sprick and Ltn J Naumann each claimed one. Stalag Luft III. American Eagle.
92 Sqn	Spitfire V Sgt G W Aston	R6923 Safe	Circus 16. Baled out over the sea and rescued. See 26 June 1941.

Sqn	Aircraft	Serial	Notes
145 Sqn	Spitfire IIb F/L M A Newling DFC	P8339 Safe	Circus 16. Cat B damage by Me109. See 18 May 1940 and 6 July 1941.
145 Sqn	Spitfire IIb Sgt F J Twitchett	P8341 Sl/WIA	Ditto. Cat B damage over Channel. Both A/c in combat with JG26.
257 Sqn	Hurricane IIB S/L R R S Tuck DSO DFC**	Z3152 Safe	Patrol. Shot down by Me109 and rescued from North Sea by a coal barge, pm. See 18 and 25 August 1940 and 28 January 1942.
603 Sqn	Spitfire V F/O D Stewart-Clark	R7345 Wounded	Circus 17. Crash-landed on Goodwin Sands after attack by Me109 of JG26 Josef Priller. See 3 September 1940 and 19 September 1941.
616 Sqn	Spitfire IIa P/O E P S Brown	P7730 +	*Pemba I.* Circus 16. Shot down by Adolf Galland, JG26 (69th victory), over Boulogne, 1940.

On 22 June 1941, Germany attacked the Soviet Union in Operation Barbarossa. For the Luftwaffe fighter arm it meant that defence on the Western Front was left to two fighter Jagdgeschwaders: JG2 to the south of the River Seine to Cherbourg, and JG26 north of the Seine to Holland. Once this became known to the British, the recently instigated policy of increasing pressure over northern France became paramount, as it was the only way Britain could give any support to her new ally, Russia. For their part, the Jagdwaffe fighter pilots were directed to attack everything the RAF mounted, whereas in the past few months, they had often ignored pure fighter sweeps, and only engaged formations that included bombers.

Therefore, for the rest of 1941 the light bombers of 2 Group Bomber Command, sometimes supported by four-engined Stirlings, Fighter Command continued to press operational sorties in the form of Circus, Roadstead, Ramrod and Rhubarb, as well as fighter sweeps in order to maintain pressure in the West. The night raids on Britain had fallen off dramatically since mid-May 1941, the main reason now becoming clear, but the RAF continued to maintain night-fighter operations, including intruder sorties over German bases in France and Belgium.

Another important feature was the introduction of one-man rubber dinghies, given to fighter pilots in the early summer of 1941. Until then, the only life support for a man coming down into the sea was his Mae West life jacket. Life expectancy in a cold sea was sometimes counted in minutes; unless found and rescued very quickly, chances of survival were very slim indeed. With the arrival of the 'K' type dinghy many lives were saved, and rescue could still be successful after several days, provided the man was unwounded and fit enough to get into his dinghy. The first recorded rescue of a fighter pilot using this new apparatus was 16 June 1941. Bomber and Coastal Command crews, of course, had used larger dinghies since the war began but it was not deemed necessary for Fighter Command, as it was believed they would mainly be operating over land on defensive sorties – until, that is, France fell.

Sgt S W R Mabbett of 611 Squadron, killed in action by JG2, 21 July 1941.

22 June 1941

609 Sqn	Spitfire Vb P/O F X E de Spirlet	W3116 'T' Wounded	Circus 18. Shot down by Me109 off Dover; baled out and rescued. Belgian pilot.
609 Sqn	Spitfire IIa Sgt T C Rigler	W3215 Safe	Circus 18. Damaged but repaired.
611 Sqn	Spitfire Va F/O P S C Pollard	R7209 +	Circus 16. This aircraft claimed by JG26 at 1600s. Buried Dunkirk.

23 June 1941

92 Sqn	Spitfire V Sgt H Bowen-Morris	R6761 WIA/PoW	Escort. Shot down over France, pm, and seriously wounded, losing right arm. Repatriated in October 1943.
485 Sqn (RNZAF)	Spitfire IIa Sgt R J Bullen	P7975 +	*Spirit of Taranaki*. Sweep, shot down by Me109 off French coast, SW of Boulogne, pm. NKG, aged 29.
303 Sqn	Spitfire IIb P/O B M Gladych	P8330 'D' Wounded	*Batavia*. Escort. Rammed/collided with Me109, crash-landed near Ramsgate. SoC 3 July 1941.
603 Sqn	Spitfire V F/O W A Douglas	W3110 Wounded	Circus 19. Injured by cannon shell splinters, pm. A/c repaired.
616 Sqn	Spitfire IIa Sgt D W Beedham	P7435 Safe	Circus 19. Baled out into the Channel when out of fuel – rescued.

24 June 1941

603 Sqn	Spitfire V F/O K J McKelvie	W3121 +	Circus 21. FTR, pm.
603 Sqn	Spitfire V Sgt D P Lamb	W3364 Wounded	Ditto. Force-landed at Walmer. See 9 December 1941. A/c repaired.
611 Sqn	Spitfire Vb F/L T F A Buys	R7349 +	Circus 21, FTR, pm. Dutch pilot.

25 June 1941

54 Sqn	Spitfire V W/C J R Kayll DSO DFC	R7259 PoW	Circus 23. Hornchurch Wing Leader. Shot down by Me109 near St Omer, am. Stalag Luft III.
54 Sqn	Spitfire Vb Sgt J D Beresford	W3323 PoW	*The New Forest*. Ditto. Stalag Luft III as F/L.
54 Sqn	Spitfire V P/O K E Knox	R7222 Wounded	Ditto. A/c damaged but repaired. See 5 July 1941.
92 Sqn	Spitfire Vb P/O T S Wade	W3264 Wounded	Sweep. Hit by Me109; damaged but repaired. See 28 July and 19 August 1940.
303 Sqn	Spitfire IIb P/O S Paderewski	P8672 'F' +	Circus 23. FTR.
610 Sqn	Spitfire IIb P/O J R Scott	P8399 'O' PoW/WIA	Circus 23, FTR, pm. Stalag Luft III.
610 Sqn	Spitfire IIb Sgt Davies	'V' Wounded	Circus 23 – hit in the leg, pm.
616 Sqn	Spitfire IIb Sgt J A H Jenks	P8272 +	Circus 23. Shot down over St Omer by Me109 pm. Buried at Boulogne, aged 25.
616 Sqn	Spitfire IIb Sgt R L Brewer RNZAF	P7327 +	Ditto. NKG, aged 29.

26 June 1941

92 Sqn	Spitfire Va Sgt G W Aston	P8532 PoW	Sweep. FTR, am. See 21 June 1941. Kopernikus camp.
145 Sqn	Spitfire IIb Sgt A MacBeth	P8314 PoW	Circus 24. Shot down by Me109 off Gravelines. Kopernikus camp.
603 Sqn	Spitfire V P/O C A Newman	R7272 +	Sweep. FTR am. Buried Bergen op Zoom, Holland, aged 24.

27 June 1941

19 Sqn	Spitfire IIb P/O M F Andrews	P7379 PoW	Sweep. Shot down by Me109, late pm and seen to crash-land. Stalag Luft III.
19 Sqn	Spitfire IIb P/O D M Cowley	P7813 PoW/WIA	Sweep. Shot down by Me109 late pm.
74 Sqn	Spitfire Vb S/L J C Mungo-Park DFC*	X4668 'E' +	Sweep. Shot down by I/JG26, 2100. Crashed and buried Adinkerke. See 16 June 1941.
74 Sqn	Spitfire Vb Sgt C G Hilken	W3252 PoW	Ditto. Shot down over St Omer. See 20 October 1940 and 21 April 1941. Stalag Luft III.
74 Sqn	Spitfire Vb P/O W J Sandman RNZAF	W3210 PoW	*Malta.* Ditto. Stalag Luft III.
266 Sqn	Spitfire IIa P/O S Cook	P8188 +	*North Borneo V.* Sweep, FTR late pm. Last seen leaking glycol after combat. Buried Dunkirk, aged 24.
266 Sqn	Spitfire IIa P/O W H Holland	P8185 PoW	Ditto. Shot down by Me109 St Omer. Stalag Luft III.
303 Sqn	Spitfire IIb W/C P Laguna	P8331 'M' +	*Sumatra.* Northolt Wing Leader. Hit and shot down by 88m flak near Hardelot, flying at 4000 m. Buried Pihen-les-Guines Cemetery. Aged 35. See 8 May 1941.

28 June 1941

303 Sqn	Spitfire IIb P/O W M Drecki	P8335 'R' Safe	*Semarang.* Circus 26. Shot down by Me109, baled out into the Channel, rescued by ASR.
303 Sqn	Spitfire IIb P/O J Bondar	P8346 'T' +	Ditto. Early am. By JG26, south of Lille. Buried Lille, aged 24.
306 Sqn	Hurricane IIB P/O J Żulikowski	AP516 'X' Evaded	Circus 26. FTR early am. Captured but escaped and returned via Spain.

29 June 1941

603 Sqn	Spitfire Va Sgt L E S Salt	R7270 +	*Nae Bother.* Circus. FTR, evening. Buried Pihen-les- Guines, aged 20.

30 June 1941

257 Sqn	Hurricane IIB Sgt V Uher	Z3163 +	Convoy patrol. Crashed into the sea 35 miles NE Happisburgh. Seen in his Mae West but not rescued. Czech, aged 26. NKG.

1 July 1941

91 Sqn	Spitfire V Sgt F A Thornber	R7340 +	Shipping recce, FTR, 0700.

2 July 1941

71 Sqn	Hurricane IIB P/O W I Hall	Z3094 PoW/WIA	Circus 29. Shot down by Me109 of JG26 – Rolf Pingel – 1300. American Eagle. Stalag Luft III.

74 Sqn	Spitfire Vb P/O S Z Krol	W3263 PoW	Sweep, pm. Was part of the Great Escape in March 1944, murdered c.12 April. Polish, aged 28.
74 Sqn	Spitfire Vb Sgt G T Evans RCAF	W3259 PoW	*Makesi.* Sweep, shot down near St Omer. Kopernikus camp.
145 Sqn	Spitfire IIb Sgt J G L Robillard	P8536 Evaded	Circus 29. Shot down by Me109 pm, at Cauchy-en-la-Tour. Returned to UK in October via Spain and Gibraltar.
303 Sqn	Spitfire IIb S/L W Łapkowski	P8596 'V' +	*Riouw.* Escort. Shot down over the Channel by Me109. Buried Belgium, aged 27. See 5 September 1940.
303 Sqn	Spitfire IIb Sgt M Wojciechowski	P8390 'U' Wounded	Escort. Damaged by Me109 over Channel; a/c repaired.
303 Sqn	Spitfire IIb Sgt R Górecki	P8463 'T' Safe	Ditto. Rescued 74 hours later.
303 Sqn	Spitfire IIb P/O W Strzembosz	P8329 'P' Wounded	Cat B damage; overturned on landing at Martlesham, and SoC.
308 Sqn	Spitfire IIa F/L E S Kawnik	P8525 'T' +	*Leigh.* Circus 29. FTR, am. NKG. Aged 28.
308 Sqn	Spitfire IIb Sgt P Kowala	P7536 'W' PoW	Ditto. Mühlberg (Elbe) camp.
308 Sqn	Spitfire IIb P/O B Kudrewicz	P7883 'E' Wounded	Ditto. A/c Cat 2 damage but repaired.

3 July 1941

74 Sqn	Spitfire V Sgt R H Cochrane	W3232 PoW/WIA	Sweep. FTR am. Kopernikus.
92 Sqn	Spitfire Vb S/Lt E de Cherade de Montbron	X4476 'S' PoW	Escort. Shot down and pretended to be a French-Canadian, rather than French.
266 Sqn	Spitfire IIb Sgt G W L Matthews	P8566 +	Sweep. Shot down by Me109 of JG26 pm. Buried at Dunkirk.
266 Sqn	Spitfire IIb Sgt R J Thoburn	P8173 PoW	*Alton & District.* Ditto. Kopernikus camp.
611 Sqn	Spitfire Va Sgt M K McHugh RNZAF	R7293 +	*Sans Tache.* Circus 30. Shot down by Me109 near St Omer. Aged 23.
616 Sqn	Spitfire IIa Sgt D B Crabtree	P7980 Evaded	Sweep. Shot down near Hazebrouck. Got home via Spain.

4 July 1941

54 Sqn	Spitfire Vb G/C H Broadhurst DFC AFC	W3244 Wounded	Circus 32. Hornchurch Wing Leader.
74 Sqn	Spitfire Va Sgt W G Henderson	W3258 +	Sweep pm. Shot down over Norrent-Fontes. Buried Longuenesse, France, aged 27.
603 Sqn	Spitfire Va F/O H A R Prowse	R7339 PoW	*Waverley.* Ditto. Stalag Luft III camp.
609 Sqn	Spitfire Va F/O A K Ogilvie DFC	X4664 PoW	Circus 32. Shot down by JG26 and baled out, wounded, near St Omer. Stalag Luft III.

4/5 July 1941

452 Sqn (RAAF)	Spitfire IIa Sgt A G Costello	P8085 +	Shot down by intruder from NJG/2, 0108, while attempting to land at North Coates.

124

5 July 1941

54 Sqn	Spitfire V P/O K E Knox	R7222 +	Circus 33. Shot down by Me109, pm. Buried Reingelst, Belg, aged 23. See 25 June 1941.
308 Sqn	Spitfire V Sgt S Krzyzagórski	P7314 Injured	Ditto. Baled out over Channel and rescued by ASR.
616 Sqn	Spitfire IIa F/L C H MacFie	P8651 PoW	*St Helens.* Sweep. Shot down near Lille by Me109 of JG26, early pm. Stalag Luft III camp.

6 July 1941

74 Sqn	Spitfire Vb P/O W M Skinner DFM	W3208 'U' PoW	*Eastbourne.* Circus 35. Shot down over France pm, by JG26. See 30 August 1940.
74 Sqn	Spitfire Vb Sgt L R Carter	W3176 +	Ditto. See 10 October 1940. NKG, aged 21.
74 Sqn	Spitfire Vb Sgt W G Lockhart	W3317 Evaded	Ditto. Shot down over Herly. Evaded capture and interned in Spain.
92 Sqn	Spitfire Vb Sgt C G Todd	W3331 +	*The King Rufus.* Escort Stirlings to Lille. Buried Dunkirk, aged 23.
145 Sqn	Spitfire Va F/L M A Newling DFC	W3336 +	Circus 35. Shot down near Lille pm. NKG. See 18 May 1940 and 21 June 1941.
611 Sqn	Spitfire Vb Sgt N J Smith	W3311 PoW	Ditto. Over Lille by Me109. Kopernikus camp.
616 Sqn	Spitfire IIa Sgt J A McCairns	P8500 PoW	Sweep. Crash-landed at Gravelines but later escaped from Stalag IXC and returned to UK via Spain: awarded MM.

7 July 1941

74 Sqn	Spitfire Vb Sgt C Stuart	W3172 Wounded	*Huddersfield II.* Sweep. Shot down into the sea and rescued.
145 Sqn	Spitfire Va Sgt G F Silvester	X4667 Wounded	*Huddersfield III.* Circus 37. Written off after landing. Battle damage.
609 Sqn	SpitfireVa Sgt G Evans	W3115 Wounded	Sweep. Baled out over the sea off Boulogne and rescued.

8 July 1941

92 Sqn	Spitfire IIa P/O P H Beake	W3265 Safe	Escort early pm. Baled out near the French coast and rescued.
145 Sqn	Spitfire Va P/O P R I Pine RCAF	R7263 PoW	*British B.R.C.* Circus 40 – FTR. Stalag Luft III. American pilot.
145 Sqn	Spitfire Va F/O J J Macháïek	R7218 +	*Retford.* Circus 40. Shot down pm. Czech, aged 26.
258 Sqn	Hurricane IIB P/O J G Duval	Z3346 'E' PoW	Circus 39 – FTR. Stalag Luft III.
303 Sqn	Spitfire IIb S/L T A Arentowicz	P8502 'C' +	*The Heart of England.* Shot down over Dunkirk pm. Aged 31.
303 Sqn	Spitfire IIb F/O W S Strzembosz	P8669 'M' +	Ditto. Buried Merville, aged 26.
303 Sqn	Spitfire IIb Sgt W Giermer	P8247 Wounded	Ditto. Returned wounded, A/C damaged but repaired.

308 Sqn	Spitfire IIa Sgt J Biel	P7845 'C' PoW	*Newfoundland*. Ditto. Lost over Lille pm. Stalag Luft I.
312 Sqn	Hurricane IIb Sgt J Mensik	Z3327 Evaded	Circus 39. Shot down by JG2 over Lisbourg, early am. Got back to UK via Spain and Gibraltar, in October 1941. (KIFA 68 Sqn, April 1943).
485 Sqn (RNZAF)	Spitfire IIa Sgt W N Hendry	P8470 'S' +	*Foremost*. Circus 39. Last seen off Gravelines, 0700. NKG, aged 23.
603 Sqn	Spitfire Va Sgt B H Wood	R7299 Sl/inj	ASR escort. Shot up by Me109 and force-landed near Canterbury; burnt out and SoC.
609 Sqn	Spitfire IIa Sgt J A Hughes-Rees	W3239 'N' Safe	Sweep. Ditched near Goodwin Sands after combat with Me109 at 0630. Rescued.
610 Sqn	Spitfire IIb P/O F G Horner	P8504 'F' PoW	Circus 40. Shot down over France. Stalag Luft III.
610 Sqn	Spitfire II P/O J R Stoop	P8534 'H' Wounded	Ditto. Came down in the sea and rescued. (serial suspect)
611 Sqn	Spitfire Va Sgt B W Feeley RNZAF	R7277 +	Sweep. FTR, pm. NKG, aged 23.

9 July 1941

54 Sqn	Spitfire Va P/O G H Batchelor	R7269 PoW	*Jamshedpur Golmuri I*. Circus. In combat with Me109s, pm. Died 15 April 1942: bone disease, in Oflag VIB prison camp, aged 23.
54 Sqn	Spitfire Va P/O N G Baxter	W3169 +	Ditto. Buried at Enquin sur Baillons, France, aged 25.
92 Sqn	Spitfire IIa P/O P L I Archer	R7195 Wounded	Sweep. A/c damaged by Me109, pm. Repaired. See 21 August 1941.
145 Sqn	Spitfire Va Sgt J K McFarlane	R7309 +	Circus 41. Shot down by Me109 pm.
312 Sqn	Hurricane IIB Sgt J Truhlar	Z3023 PoW	Circus 41. Shot down over St Omer, pm. Wistritz bei Teplitz PoW camp.
312 Sqn	Hurricane IIB W/C J R A Peel DFC	Z3069 Safe	Circus 41. Shot down into the sea and rescued. Kenley Wing Leader. See 11 July 1940.
611 Sqn	Spitfire Vb P/O R A Johnston	W3325 +	Circus 41. Shot down by Me109, St Omer. Buried at Pihen les Guines, France, aged 23.
616 Sqn	Spitfire IIa S/L E P P Gibbs	P8070 Evaded	Sweep. Came down 12 miles east of Le Touquet; returned to UK via Spain and Gibraltar.
616 Sqn	Spitfire IIa Sgt R A Morton	P8386 PoW	Sweep, lost near St Omer. Kopernikus camp.

10 July 1941

72 Sqn	Spitfire Vb Sgt A J Casey	P8600 +	*Lady Linlithgow*. Circus 32. Last seen in combat with Me109s, noon. NKG.
72 Sqn	Spitfire Vb F/O J M T Godlewski	W3411 +	Ditto. Polish pilot, NKG, aged 26.
72 Sqn	Spitfire Vb Sgt C L Harrison	P8604 +	*Jamshedpur Golmari II*. Ditto.
92 Sqn	Spitfire Vb Sgt G C Waldern RCAF	W3403 Safe	*The Dog's Fighter*. Escort. Baled out over the Channel and rescued after five hours. See 19 July 1941.
234 Sqn	Spitfire IIa Sgt I E Pearce	P8137 +	*Sarum & South Wilts Spitfire*. Sweep over Channel off Cherbourg, pm.

234 Sqn	Spitfire IIb Sgt H A Newman	P8659 Wounded	Ditto. A/C damaged but repaired. See 14 November 1941.
234 Sqn	Spitfire IIa W/C M V Blake DFC	P8015 Safe	Ditto. Ditched after combat with Me109 and paddled 12 hours before rescue. See 19 August 1942.
610 Sqn	Spitfire IIb P/O P Ward-Smith	P8523 'R' PoW	*Bansi.* Circus 42. Shot down by Me109. Stalag Luft III.
610 Sqn	Spitfire IIb Sgt H C D Blackman	P8374 'K' +	Ditto. Buried Maizières, aged 24.
610 Sqn	Spitfire IIb Sgt J E Anderson	P8520 'Q' PoW	*The Mendip Spitfire.* Circus 42.
611 Sqn	Spitfire Vb Sgt L Hemingway	P8539 +	Circus 42. FTR.

10/11 July 1941

255 Sqn	Defiant I Sgt J C Cox Sgt Fitzsimmons	T3995 Safe Wounded	Night sortie. In combat with He111 north of Hull, 0203. Gunner slightly wounded by return fire.

11 July 1941

54 Sqn	Spitfire Vb F/L P M Gardner DFC	P8754 PoW	Circus. Shot down by Me109, pm. Stalag Luft III.
92 Sqn	Spitfire Va P/O J Dougall	W3183 PoW	Escort. Shot down by Me109, pm. Stalag Luft I.
452 Sqn (RAAF)	Spitfire IIb Sgt A C Roberts	P7562 Evaded	Sweep. Baled out after combat with Me109. French Resistance got him back to UK via Spain and Gibraltar.
485 Sqn (RNZAF)	Spitfire IIa P/O C Stewart	P7773 'D' +	Sweep. Last seen over Cap Gris Nez pm. NKG, 24. See 24 August 1940.
611 Sqn	Spitfire Va Sgt D E Fair RNZAF	R7208 PoW	Circus to Lens. FTR, late pm. Kopernikus camp.

12 July 1941

54 Sqn	Spitfire Va Sgt F E Tulit	R7225 PoW	Circus. FTR, am. Kopernikus camp.
308 Sqn	Spitfire Va Sgt W Majchrzyk	P7629 Safe	Circus. Written off in crash-landing at Manston. Cat B damage.
308 Sqn	Spitfire IIa F/O C Wielgus	P7888 'B' +	*Sind VII.* Circus. Body recovered from the sea next day. Buried at Northwood, aged 28.
308 Sqn	Spitfire IIa Sgt E Watolski	P8140 Safe	*Nuflier.* Sweep. Ran out of fuel and written off in crash-landing near Hawkhurst, Kent, after hitting a tree.

14 July 1941

54 Sqn	Spitfire Vb Sgt J W Panter	R7264 PoW	*Brycheiniog.* Circus 48. Collided with Spitfire of 611 Sqn, am, over Boulogne. Kopernikus camp.
72 Sqn	Spitfire Vb Sgt W M Lamberton	R7219 PoW/WIA	Ditto. Shot down by Josef Priller of JG26 (40th victory). Kopernikus.
234 Sqn	Spitfire IIa Sgt A S Parker	P8656 Safe	*Nippy.* Sweep. Engine cut on return, force-landed West Knighton, Dorset, and written off.
501 Sqn	Spitfire IIa Sgt A Dvorak	P8074 Wounded	Escort. Wounded in combat with Me109.

F/Lt E S Lock DSO DFC*, 611 Squadron, failed to return from a rhubarb sortie on 3 August 1941.

603 Sqn	Spitfire Va Sgt A C Hunter	X4665 PoW/WIA	*Royal Scott*. Circus. Shot down by Me109 am. Kopernikus.
611 Sqn	Spitfire Vb F/O P G Dexter DFC	P8581 +	Circus 48. Collided with 54 Sqn A/C and crashed. Buried Samer, aged 23. South African.

17 July 1941

3 Sqn	Hurricane IIB Sgt D H Todd	Z3083 +	Rhubarb. FTR, pm.
54 Sqn	Spitfire Va Sgt F M Laing RNZAF	W3216 +	*Maidenhead & District*. Sweep. Crashed near Hawkinge pm, with combat damage. Buried Hornchurch, aged 29.
72 Sqn	Spitfire Vb P/O L B Fordham	P8544 +	Channel patrol. Shot down by flak; picked up dead from sea, 60 miles east of Deal in his dinghy. Canadian.
234 Sqn	Spitfire IIa Sgt R T Martin	P8395 PoW	*Spirit of Crewe*. ASR escort. FTR after combat with Me109s, pm. Kopernikus PoW camp.
308 Sqn	Spitfire IIa P/O J Szyszka	P8698 'E' +	Sweep. Sqn attacked by Me109s, evening, St Omer area – JG26. Buried Dunkirk, aged 24.
308 Sqn	Spitfire IIb P/O S Maciejewski	P8519 'W' PoW	Ditto. Stalag Luft III.
308 Sqn	Spitfire IIa Sgt T R Hegenbarth	P7500 'A' +	Ditto. Aged 23.

18 July 1941

222 Sqn	Spitfire V Sgt R W Jenkins	P8474 +	FTR pm. Buried Longuenesse.

19 July 1941

72 Sqn	Spitfire V Sgt R F Lewis	W3181 +	Circus 51, pm. FTR. JG26.
92 Sqn	Spitfire Vb Sgt C G Waldern RCAF	W3326 +	*Mesopotamia*. Sweep to Lille. NKG. See 10 July 1941.

21 July 1941

19 Sqn	Spitfire IIa F/O H Oxlin	P7547 +	Sweep. Shot down by Me109 near Montreuil, evening.
19 Sqn	Spitfire IIa P/O M D Tucker	P7890 +	Ditto, near St Omer.
19 Sqn	Spitfire IIa Sgt S F Brooker	P8579 Sl/WIA	Ditto. Slightly wounded; a/c repaired.
602 Sqn	Spitfire IIa F/L T G F Ritchie	P8478 +	Circus. Shot down by Me109. Buried Reningelst, Belgium. JG26.
609 Sqn	Spitfire V Sgt K W Bramble	W3307 +	Circus 54. Shot down by Me109 near Lille. Buried Merville.
611 Sqn	Spitfire Vb Sgt W E Grainger	W3329 +	*Spirit of Uruguay*. Ditto. NKG.
616 Sqn	Spitfire IIa Sgt F A Nelson	P8434 +	Escort. Shot-up by Me109 and went into the sea off Worthing.
616 Sqn	Spitfire Vb Sgt S W R Mabbett	P8690 DoW	Sweep – Circus 55. Combat with Me109 near St Omer, pm, by JG26. Belly-landed but died later. Buried Languenesse, aged 21.

22 July 1941

54 Sqn	Spitfire V P/O L J D Jones	R7303 PoW	Sweep, pm; FTR.
308 Sqn	Spitfire IIb F/O W Bozek	P8313 'P' +	Ditto. Aged 27.
308 Sqn	Spitfire IIb P/O M M Orzechowski	P8590 'U' +	Ditto. Aged 27.
603 Sqn	Spitfire Va P/O P J Delorme	W3369 +	Ditto – possible oxygen failure.

22/23 July 1941

3 Sqn	Hurricane IIB Sgt T J L McEnery	Z3503 +	Havoc Co-op. Crashed early on the 23rd, near Ramsey, Essex.

23 July 1941

54 Sqn	Spitfire Va P/O C Cookson	R7268 'M' +	*The Swan*. Circus 59. Buried at Pihen les Guines, shot down by Me109 near Hazebrouck.
54 Sqn	Spitfire Va P/O V D Page	W3437 Wounded	*Kaapstad II*. Circus 59. A/c damaged but repaired.
72 Sqn	Spitfire Va Sgt J W Perkins	W3256 PoW/WIA	*Lerumo*. Circus 60. Shot down over France. Stalag Luft VII.
111 Sqn	Spitfire II Sgt A H Gregory	P7750 +	Sweep. Collided with P7848 on return flight.

Sqn	Aircraft / Pilot	Serial / Fate	Notes
111 Sqn	Spitfire II Sgt T R Caldwell	P7848 Safe	Baled out after this collision. See 4 September 1941.
145 Sqn	Spitfire Va F/O D N Forde	P8712 Evaded	Sweep. Shot down by Me109. Returned to UK. See 27 May 1940.
306 Sqn	Spitfire IIb P/O J B Kosmowski	P8334 'E' +	*Rembang.* Circus. Buried Huberser Parish Cemetery, France, aged 25.
306 Sqn	Spitfire IIb P/O J K Maras	P8461 'R' +	Circus pm, FTR. Buried Pihen-les-Guines, aged 24.
306 Sqn	Spitfire IIb F/L W Nowak	P8247 'F' Injured	Circus. Baled out seriously injured but rescued from the sea.
306 Sqn	Spitfire IIb F/O K Pniak	P8465 'P' Safe	Circus. Ran out of fuel, crash-landed Richmond Park, Surrey. A/c written off. See 24 August 1940.
401 Sqn (RCAF)	Hurricane IIb Sgt G W Northcott	Z3228 'A' Injured	Sweep. Hit by Me109; force-landed near Rolvenden, Kent and turned over.
603 Sqn	Spitfire Va P/O H Blackall RCAF	R7341 +	ASR escort. Ditched following engine trouble, pm. Rescued but died later.
603 Sqn	Spitfire Va Sgt W J Jackman	R7227 PoW	*Port O'Leith.* Sweep pm, FTR. Kopernikus camp.
603 Sqn	Spitfire Va Sgt G W Tabor	W3184 +	Ditto. Buried at Languenesse, aged 21.
610 Sqn	Spitfire Vb Sgt L E Philpotts	W3427 Wounded	Sweep, evening.
611 Sqn	Spitfire Vb F/O J R G Sutton	W3246 +	*Devon Squadron.* Circus. Shot down near St Pol and buried there. Aged 21. (Previously W/C F S Stapleton's a/c Hornchurch Wing Leader.)

24 July 1941

Sqn	Aircraft / Pilot	Serial / Fate	Notes
72 Sqn	Spitfire Vb Sgt G F Breckon RNZAF	W3316 PoW/Inj	*City of Salford.* Circus 61, pm. Shot down near St Omer. Kopernikus PoW camp.
92 Sqn	Spitfire Va Sgt S H Vinter	W3381 +	Sweep. Shot down into the sea, pm.
152 Sqn	Spitfire IIa F/L E S Marrs DFC	P7881 +	Escort to Brest. Shot down by flak. Buried Brest, aged 20.
152 Sqn	Spitfire IIa Sgt J A Short	P8512 PoW	Ditto. Actual cause not known. Kopernikus camp.
257 Sqn	Hurricane IIb F/L T A F Elsdon DFC	Z3489 Wounded	Sweep. Injured in arm during fight with Me109s. Crash- landed at Hawkinge. See 10 August 1940.
308 Sqn	Spitfire IIb P/O W W Chciuk	P8327 'X' PoW	*Java.* Circus pm. FTR. Stalag Luft III.
315 Sqn	Spitfire IIb P/O J Czachowski	P7835 'S' +	*Ballymena.* Circus. (315 Sqn pilot flying with 308 Sqn.) Shot down near Guines on his first op. sortie. NKG, aged 25.
485 Sqn (RNZAF)	Spitfire IIa Sgt J Maney	P7831 'G' +	*Tasmania.* Escort. Seen to bale out north of Cherbourg after attack by Me109; not found. NKG, aged 23.

25 July 1941

Sqn	Aircraft / Pilot	Serial / Fate	Notes
234 Sqn	Spitfire IIb Sgt R C Hoornaert	P7984 Safe	Convoy patrol. Baled out three miles south of Exmouth and rescued. Belgian.

27 July 1941

| 242 Sqn | Hurricane IIB
Sgt G A Prosser RCAF | Z3563
+ | MTB escort. Missing after combat with Me109s, pm. |

31 July 1941

| 242 Sqn | Hurricane IIA
S/L W W Straight DFC | Z2906
Evaded | Roadstead, pm. Shot down by flak-ship. Captured by Vichy French but escaped back to UK via Gibraltar. American. |
| 609 Sqn | Spitfire Vb
Sgt R Boyd | W3187
Safe | *Lord Lloyd II*. Shot down by E-Boats off Calais and rescued. |

1 August 1941

| 242 Sqn | Hurricane IIA
Sgt M G A Chase-Casgrain RCAF | Z2986
+ | Roadstead. Shot down by Spitfire north of Dunkirk. NKG. |
| 247 Sqn | Hurricane IIA
P/O R R Price | Z2411 'Z'
+ | Night sortie. Collided with Do17 south of the Lizard at 2250. Both a/c crashed. |

2 August 1941

| 129 Sqn | Spitfire I
P/O D O Cunliffe | X4427
Safe | Interception. Shot-up during fight with Ju88 70 miles east of Spurn Head at 1600. Crash-landed Leconfield 1635. Repaired. |

3 August 1941

| 92 Sqn | Spitfire Va
P/O D A Bruce | W3245
Wounded | Roadstead. Hit by flak, crash-landed at Lympne. A/c repaired. See 2 October 1941. |

Four pilots of 73 Sqn in France 1940 (L to R): L S Pilkington DFM (KIA 20 September 1941 with 111 Sqn), H G Paul DFC, N Orton DFC* (KIA 17 September 1941 with 54 Sqn), and E J Kain DFC who died in a flying accident on 7 June 1940.

611 Sqn	Spitfire Vb F/L E S Lock DSO DFC*	W3257 +	Rhubarb. Went down to strafe some soldiers near Calais and not seen again. NKG.

4 August 1941

118 Sqn	Spitfire IIb Sgt C W H Smith	P8516 +	Convoy patrol. Crashed into a hill on return, near Owermoigne, Dorset, pm.
257 Sqn	Hurricane IIB F/L K W Tait DFC	Z3164 +	Shipping recce. Baled out after fight with Ju88 45 miles east of Winterton, Norfolk, 1721. NKG, aged 22. New Zealander.

5 August 1941

603 Sqn	Spitfire V P/O N H C Keable	X4663 +	Circus. FTR, 1910. Washed ashore 30 August, buried Noordwijk, Holland aged 22.

5/6 August 1941

25 Sqn	Beaufighter If F/L T H Worth RNVR Sgt F P Nekludow	R2157 + +	Night patrol. FTR. NKGs. Aged 37. Aged 20.

6 August 1941

87 Sqn	Hurricane IIB G/C E J L Hope AFC	Z3224 +	Rhubarb. Shot down by ground fire during late evening strike on airfield at Maupertus. Buried Cherbourg, aged 42.
501 Sqn	Spitfire IIa Sgt A Beacham	P7731 +	Channel patrol. Lost off Cherbourg pm. NKG, aged 20.

7 August 1941

19 Sqn	Spitfire IIa P/O H B Milman	P7924 DoI	*Venture.* Circus. Crashed pm, near Charing Hill on return and died of his injuries on the 9 August.
19 Sqn	Spitfire IIa F/S S Plzak	P7771 +	Circus, evening. FTR. Polish.
41 Sqn	Spitfire Vb F/L G G F Draper	W3635 PoW	Sweep. Shot down near Lille, baled out over Merville; evening. See 30 October 1940. Stalag Luft III.
92 Sqn	Spitfire Vb Sgt C H Howard RNZAF	W3568 PoW/WIA	Escort, midday. FTR.
92 Sqn	Spitfire Vb Sgt G P Hickman	R7161 Injured	Ditto. Crash-landed near Deal pm. A/c repaired. See 20 September 1941.
222 Sqn	Spitfire IIb Sgt Maskery	P8591 Safe	ASR escort. Shot-up by two Me109s am; force-landed at Minster. A/c repaired.
257 Sqn	Hurricane IIB Sgt P Cowan	Z3744 Sl/WIA	Sweep. Hit and slightly wounded in the leg; A/c Cat 2 damage, repaired.
308 Sqn	Spitfire IIa P/O L Stapel	P8094 +	*On Target.* Sweep. FTR, evening. NKG, aged 22.
308 Sqn	Spitfire IIa Sgt Z Brózda	P8573 +	Ditto. Buried Longuenesse, aged 22.
401 Sqn (RCAF)	Hurricane IIB P/O T K Coupland	Z3344 +	Sweep. Shot down by Me109, pm. Buried Dunkirk, aged 21.
485 Sqn (RNZAF)	Spitfire IIa Sgt C S V Goodwin	P7594 'G' PoW	Circus 67. FTR, am. Kopernikus camp.
602 Sqn	Spitfire IIa P/O F K Thornton	P8719 PoW	Circus 67. FTR, am. Stalag Luft III.

610 Sqn	Spitfire Vb Sgt F McWatt	R7298 'A' Sl/WIA	Ditto. Slightly wounded, crash-landed at Friston. A/c Cat 2 – repaired.
611 Sqn	Spitfire Vb Sgt A P Holdsworth	P8756 PoW	Ditto. Lost near St Omer. Stalag Luft VI.
611 Sqn	Spitfire Vb Sgt G A Mason	W3523 Injured	Ditto. Shot-up by Me109 over France and force-landed near Deal, hitting a mine. Badly injured and A/c SoC. See 5 September 1942 and 24 September 1943.

9 August 1941

111 Sqn	Spitfire IIa P/O B W B Squires	P8198 +	Sweep. FTR, evening. Body washed ashore 30 August. Buried Bergen op Zoom, Holland.
315 Sqn	Spitfire IIa F/O J M Czerniak	P8506 'B' +	Circus 69. FTR. NKG, aged 28.
315 Sqn	Spitfire IIb F/O A Niewiara	P8696 'H' +	*Dilwar*. Ditto. Shot down by Me109. Buried Boulogne, aged 23.
315 Sqn	Spitfire Vb P/O E Fiedorczuk	P8670 'S' Safe	*Second City of London Textile*. Ditto. Damaged over St Omer, crash-landed short of fuel at Little Waldingfield, Suffolk, and A/c written off. All claimed by JG2.
403 Sqn (RCAF)	Spitfire V P/O D M Waldon	R7266 'J' +	*Jamshedpur Golmuri II*. Circus 68. Shot down by 6/JG26 and died later that day; buried Longuenesse, aged 27.
452 Sqn (RAAF)	Spitfire IIa P/O J H O'Byrne	P7682 PoW	Circus 68. Shot down am near to Coubronne. Stalag Luft III.
452 Sqn (RAAF)	Spitfire IIa Sgt G B Chapman	P7590 +	Ditto, over Salperwick. Buried at Longuenesse.
452 Sqn (RAAF)	Spitfire IIa Sgt G B Hayden	P8361 +	*Krakatau*. Ditto, over Quercamps. Buried at Longuenesse, aged 19.
609 Sqn	Spitfire Vb P/O A Nitelet	W3254 Evaded	Circus 68. Shot down by JG26 over Thiembronne, wounded. Captured but escaped, returning via Spain. Belgian pilot.
616 Sqn	Spitfire Vb W/C D R S Bader DSO* DFC*	W3185 'DB' PoW	*Lord Lloyd I*. Circus 68. Baled out over France during combat with JG26. Believed came down at Blaringhem. Tangmere Wing Leader. Stalag Luft III and Colditz.
616 Sqn	Spitfire Vb F/L L H Casson DFC	W3458 PoW	*Mirfield*. Circus 68. Shot down by Gerhard Schopfel, III/JG26 and crash-landed at Les Attaques, near Marquise 1145. Stalag Luft III.

10 August 1941

242 Sqn	Hurricane IIC S/Lt R de la Fite de Pellepont	Z3840 +	Roadstead. Hit by ship's flak near Gravelines, am. Also claimed by JG26. French pilot.

12 August 1941

19 Sqn	Spitfire IIa P/O J L Calvert	P7693 +	Circus 77. Shot down by Me109 of I/JG26. See 12 March 1941.
41 Sqn	Spitfire Va Sgt A L Bull RAAF	R7274 PoW	*West Riding*. Shot down west of Hazebrouck. Kopernikus camp.
41 Sqn	Spitfire Va Sgt R L Chapman	R7210 PoW	*City of Liverpool IV*. Shot down near Hazebrouck. Kopernikus camp.
54 Sqn	Spitfire IIb P/O R Powling	P7756 Sl/WIA	Circus. Slightly wounded am. A/C Cat 2 and repaired.

66 Sqn	Spitfire IIb Sgt Stevens	P7787 PoW	Sweep, noon. Shot down SW of Breskens.
152 Sqn	Spitfire IIa Sgt G D White	P8446 +	Sweep. Shot down by flak near Antwerp, noon. Buried Vlissingen, aged 24.
222 Sqn	Spitfire IIb Sgt J Christie	P8541 +	Escort. Shot down by Me109, am. Terlincthun Cemetery, aged 28.
485 Sqn (RNZAF)	Spitfire IIa Sgt W H Russell	P7970 'D' PoW	Circus. Shot down and lost an arm.
485 Sqn (RNZAF)	Spitfire IIa Sgt G M Porter	P7788 'E' +	Circus. FTR, evening. NKG, aged 24.
602 Sqn	Spitfire Vb Sgt H J Bell-Walker	AB844 PoW/WIA	Circus. Shot down by Me109, flying No. 2 to S/L A C Deere DFC. See 14 and 18 September 1940. Stalag Luft III.
611 Sqn	Spitfire Vb P/O R van der Honert	P8780 Sl/WIA	Circus 69. Hit by flak and wounded but RTB. A/c repaired. Belgian.

14 August 1941

3 Sqn	Hurricane IIC Sgt F Holt	Z3184 +	Intruder sortie to Le Touquet area 0317 – FTR. NKG, aged 25.
41 Sqn	Spitfire Vb F/L A L Winskill	W3447 Evaded	Sweep. Shot down by Me109 and returned via Spain and Gibraltar in December. JG26.
145 Sqn	Spitfire IIa ?	P8310 ?	Escort. FTR.
306 Sqn	Spitfire IIa S/L J Zaremba	P8466 'Z' +	Circus. FTR pm. Buried Dunkirk, aged 32.
306 Sqn	Spitfire IIa P/O W Choms	P8473 'P' +	Ditto. Buried Dunkirk, aged 28.
306 Sqn	Spitfire IIa Sgt S Zięba	P8462 'M' DoW	Ditto. Died of wounds, 23 August. Buried Hardinghen, aged 22.
308 Sqn	Spitfire IIa P/O J B Kremski	P8310 +	Sweep. FTR pm. Aged 26. All Polish losses claimed by JG26.
485 Sqn (RNZAF)	Spitfire IIa P/O J F Knight	P7822 Sl/WIA	Circus. Slightly wounded in the leg, pm. A/c repaired. See 21 September 1941.
616 Sqn	Spitfire Vb Sgt L M McKee	W3514 Evaded	Sweep. Baled out SE of Calais and returned via Spain and Gibraltar in December. JG26.

16 August 1941

306 Sqn	Spitfire IIb Sgt S M A Franczak	P8524 'A' PoW	*Mauritius.* Circus pm. Shot down by Me109 near St Omer. Stalag Luft III.
602 Sqn	Spitfire Vb Sgt C A Booty	P8793 +	*Slamat.* Ditto. Buried Pihen les Guines, aged 22.
609 Sqn	Spitfire Vb P/O D L Cropper	P8745 +	Sweep. Shot down by Stab/JG26 1845. Buried Pihen les Guines.
611 Sqn	Spitfire Vb P/O E J Lamb	W3567 +	Sweep. Shot down into the Channel by Me109, am. NKG.

17 August 1941

242 Sqn	Hurricane IIB P/O K M Hicks	Z3845 +	Roadstead. Shot down by Me109, evening.
242 Sqn	Hurricane IIB Sgt E A Redfern	Z3454 +	Ditto. Buried Etaples, aged 27.

18 August 1941

41 Sqn	Spitfire Va P/O M G Williams	R7217 PoW	*Onward.* Sweep. Shot down by Me109 near Armentieres, although possibly also collided with R7291 in the fight.
41 Sqn	Spitfire Va Sgt R D Jury	R7291 +	*Trustworthy.* See above.
92 Sqn	Spitfire Va Sgt G E Hann	R7346 +	Sweep. FTR, pm.

19 August 1941

71 Sqn	Hurricane IIB P/O V W Olson	Z3494 +	Sweep. Shot down into the Channel; body washed up 14 September and buried Vlissingen, Holland, aged 28. American Eagle.
111 Sqn	Spitfire IIa P/O J A Timmis	P7824 PoW	Sweep. FTR evening. Stalag Luft III.
111 Sqn	Spitfire IIa P/O G A Skelly	P8428 +	Ditto.
111 Sqn	Spitfire IIa Sgt J B M Vilandre RCAF	P7528 PoW	Ditto; Me109 near Hazebrouck. Stalag Luft IV.
111 Sqn	Spitfire IIa Sgt D J Connolly.	P7324 Wounded	Ditto. Cat 2 damage but repaired. All losses due to JG26.
222 Sqn	Spitfire IIb Sgt R Ptacek	P8244 'G' Evaded	*Wigan & District.* Shot down by Johannes Schmid, JG26 (24 vic). Baled out and returned to UK via Spain and Gibraltar. See 28 March 1942. Czech pilot.
242 Sqn	Hurricane IIB P/O J P McKechnie RAAF	Z3743 PoW	Shipping strike. FTR, pm. Stalag Luft III.
308 Sqn	Spitfire IIb Sgt A Pietrasiak	P8318 Evaded	Circus. Baled out and got back to UK via Spain and Gibraltar. See 29 November 1943.
308 Sqn	Spitfire IIb Sgt E Watolski	P8326 'F' Safe	Circus. Baled out over Channel and rescued.
403 Sqn (RCAF)	Spitfire Va P/O K H Anthony	R7342 'K' PoW	Circus 81. FTR, am. Stalag Luft III.
403 Sqn (RCAF)	Spitfire Va P/O N R D Dick	R7260 'R' Safe	*The Bristol Air Raid Warden.* Ditto. Baled out off Dover after combat with JG26; rescued. See 25 April 1942.
452 Sqn (RAAF)	Spitfire V P/O W D Eccleton	P8717 +	Circus 81. Shot down am by JG2. Buried Dunkirk, aged 25. New Zealander.
452 Sqn (RAAF)	Spitfire V Sgt R G Gazzard	AB785 +	Ditto. Buried Oostduinkerke, age 21.
452 Sqn (RAAF)	Spitfire V P/O N S Willis	AB794 Wounded	Ditto. A/c Cat 2 damage – repaired.
485 Sqn (RNZAF)	Spitfire IIa Sgt K C M Miller	P7977 'U' +	Circus 81. Shot down by JG2. NKG, aged 24.
609 Sqn	Spitfire Vb P/O V M Ortmans	W3241 'D' Safe	*L.P.E.* Baled out over Channel and rescued by HSL123. See also 27 September and 21 October 1941. Belgian pilot.

20 August 1941

66 Sqn	Spitfire IIa Sgt C A Parsons	P8435 +	*Morvi I.* Shot down by fighter off Dutch coast. See 14 February 1941.
66 Sqn	Spitfire IIa P/O S A Durrant	P7821 PoW	24 *Parganes II.* Escort – shot down by Me109 off Dutch coast. Stalag Luft VII.

21 August 1941

65 Sqn	Spitfire IIa Sgt W Kay	P7697 +	*Zanzibar.* Sweep. Missing after combat with Me109 pm. Buried Dunkirk, aged 21.
65 Sqn	Spitfire IIa Sgt H N Baxter	P8160 PoW	*The P.J. Spitfire.* Ditto, off Gravelines. Kopernikus camp.
92 Sqn	Spitfire V Sgt H S Harrison	P8747 +	Sweep. Crashed on take-off, 1250.
92 Sqn	Spitfire Vb Sgt J Aherne	W3409 +	*Peruvian Oil Fields.* Sweep, FTR.
92 Sqn	Spitfire Vb P/O P L I Archer	W3330 Sl/WIA	Sweep. Slightly wounded in legs during combat with Me109. A/c Cat 2 damage and repaired. See 9 July 1941.
130 Sqn	Spitfire IIa P/O H W Pickstone	P7904 PoW	Circus 82. Shot down by flak, 0725. Stalag Luft III.
130 Sqn	Spitfire IIa P/O W R Boyce	P8370 +	*Oldham.* Ditto. Shot down by Me109 returning from Ijmuiden. Aged 20.
403 Sqn (RCAF)	Spitfire V F/O D J McKenna	W3438 'G' DoW	*Kaapstad I.* Circus 83. Baled out but died of wounds 8 September. Buried Adegem, Belgium.
403 Sqn (RCAF)	Spitfire V S/L B G Morris	P8740 'E' PoW	Circus 84. FTR pm. Stalag Luft III.
403 Sqn (RCAF)	Spitfire Va Sgt C E McDonald	R7279 'S' PoW	*King's Messenger.* Ditto. American pilot.
603 Sqn	Spitfire Va P/O J A R Falconer	R7300 Sl/WIA	*Scottish Queen.* Circus. Slightly wounded, ditched off English coast am, rescued by two soldiers and then all three by launch. See 8 December 1941.
609 Sqn	Spitfire Vb Sgt E W Pollard	W3651 +	Circus. Shot down by Me109 near Dunkirk and buried there. Aged 21.
610 Sqn	Spitfire Vb F/L D Crowley-Milling DFC	W3455 'U' Evaded	Circus 91. Shot down by Me109 near Ergny, but returned to UK via Spain, in December.
610 Sqn	Spitfire Vb Sgt D Wright	W3504 'Z' PoW	Circus 91, FTR pm.
610 Sqn	Spitfire Vb Sgt W Raine	P8721 'P' +	Ditto. Buried Languenesse, aged 22.
610 Sqn	Spitfire Vb Sgt A W Black	W3434 'F' PoW	Ditto. Shot down near Le Trait. Kopernikus camp.

24 August 1941

302 Sqn	Hurricane IIB Sgt E Kropiwnicki	Z2913 'D' +	Convoy patrol. Engine trouble on return to Churchstanton, crashed near airfield, 1245. Buried at Taunton, aged 22.

26 August 1941

92 Sqn	Spitfire Vb P/O E W H Phillips	W3576 +	Sweep, FTR pm.
234 Sqn	Spitfire II Sgt C H Jacka	P8046 +	Strafe attack, FTR, am, Cherbourg area. Buried Cherbourg, aged 24.
242 Sqn	Hurricane IIB P/O H Quilliam	Z4001 +	Patrol. Shot down by flak off Calais attacking an E-boat. Buried Adegem, Belgium, 22.
611 Sqn	Spitfire Vb Sgt A E Gray	W3247 PoW/WIA	Circus 87. Shot down by Me109, evening, by Joachim Münchberg, 7/JG26 (49th vic). Stalag Luft VI.

27 August 1941

41 Sqn	Spitfire I Sgt W A Brew RAAF	R7304 'Q' PoW/WIA	Escort. Shot down by Me109 near Enguinegatte, St Omer and seriously injured. Kopernikus camp.
41 Sqn	Spitfire V Sgt H P D Morgan	R7223 +	*Portabello*. Sweep. FTR – body picked up off Dover, Buried in Folkestone Cemetery.
54 Sqn	Spitfire V Sgt G Ashurst	R7273 Wounded	Circus 86. Baled out over the sea and rescued.
71 Sqn	Spitfire IIa P/O W R Dunn	P7308 Wounded	Ditto. Hit in right leg and foot by Me109. A/C Cat 2 damage. American Eagle.
72 Sqn	Spitfire Vb F/O H Skalski	W3408 PoW/WIA	*Mr & Mrs Albert Ehrman*. Circus 85. Stalag Luft III. Polish pilot.
72 Sqn	Spitfire Vb Sgt J Rutherford RAAF	P8609 Safe	Circus 85. Baled out over the sea and rescued. (Died Canada 1942, shot in an accident.)
92 Sqn	Spitfire Vb Sgt E H Roff	W3319 'X' +	*Winchester & District*. Sweep. Seen in his dinghy off Dunkirk, am, but not rescued. NKG.
222 Sqn	Spitfire IIb F/L J C Martin	W3723 +	Circus. Buried Dunkirk. NKG, 27. New Zealander. (possible collision)
306 Sqn	Spitfire IIb P/O Z Radomski	P8324 'V' Wounded	Circus. Shot up by Me109, am, and crash-landed Deal. Lost a limb. A/c repaired.
402 Sqn (RCAF)	Hurricane IIB F/L T B Little	Z5001 +	Escort. Collided with Spitfire over the Channel am. Baled out but not recovered. See 222 Sqn above. See 11 September 1940.
402 Sqn (RCAF)	Hurricane IIB Sgt D W Jenkin	Z3424 +	Escort. Shot down am.
403 Sqn (RCAF)	Spitfire IIa F/L E C Cathels RAF	P8726 PoW	Circus 86. FTR, am. Stalag Luft III.
485 Sqn (RNZAF)	Spitfire Vb P/O W A Middleton	W3527 'M' +	*Spit Fighter*. Circus 85. Hit in combat, baled out too low SW of Calais. Buried Dunkirk, aged 22.
603 Sqn	Spitfire Va S/L M J Loudon	W3624 Wounded.	Circus. Damaged, Cat 2, am but repaired. See 19 July 1940.
610 Sqn	Spitfire Vb Sgt J E W Ballard	W3503 'Q' +	Sweep am, FTR. NKG, aged 23.

28 August 1941

19 Sqn	Spitfire IIa S/L W J Lawson DFC	P7995 +	Circus – evening. Shot down by 6/JG53 15 miles off Dutch coast. NKG, aged 28.
19 Sqn	Spitfire IIa F/L W Cunningham DFC	P8439 PoW	Circus. Shot down by flak, crash-landed on a Dutch beach. Stalag Luft III.
41 Sqn	Spitfire V Sgt W F Bodkin RCAF	R7255 +	Rhubarb to Le Havre area, pm. FTR.
152 Sqn	Spitfire IIa Sgt A Savidge	P7691 PoW	Circus. Shot down by JG53 over North Sea. Kopernikus camp.
247 Sqn	Hurricane II Sgt S O J Murphy RNZAF	BD857 PoW	Strike against Morlaix airfield. FTR. Kopernikus camp.

29 August 1941

19 Sqn	Spitfire IIb P/O P D G Stuart	P8668 +	ASR search. Looking for S/L Lawson and engaged by Me110s of 6/ZG76 over the sea, am.

19 Sqn	Spitfire IIb P/O P H Edmonds	P8243 +	Ditto. Buried Rockanje, Holland.
19 Sqn	Spitfire IIb Sgt G J Parkin	P8449 +	Ditto. NKG, aged 20.
19 Sqn	Spitfire IIb Sgt J W T Davies	P8255 +	Ditto. NKG, aged 20.
North Weald	Spitfire Vb W/C J W Gillan DFC* AFC	W3715 +	Sweep. FTR early am, leading Wing. A 111 Sqn machine. Buried Dunkirk, aged 34.
72 Sqn	Spitfire V Sgt P T Grisdale	P8713 +	Circus 88, am. Buried Zandvoorde, Belgium.
242 Sqn	Hurricane IIB P/O N J Lezemore	Z3557 +	Dawn patrol. Crashed at Westgate, Kent.
306 Sqn	Spitfire IIb S/L J K J Słoński-Ostoja	P8507 'Z' +	*Bermuda I.* Circus 88. Shot down by Me109, buried Dunkirk, aged 31.
308 Sqn	Spitfire IIb P/O J R Bettcher	P8311 'G' +	Circus 88. FTR, am. NKG, aged 26.
315 Sqn	Spitfire IIa F/L B Mickiewicz	P7606 'O' PoW	Ditto. Shot down by Me109 and Stalag Luft III.
485 Sqn (RNZAF)	Spitfire Vb Sgt L P Griffiths	W3643 'C' Safe	Ditto. Baled out over the sea and rescued.

30 August 1941

258 Sqn	Hurricane IIA S/L C A Wood	Z5121 'V' +	Convoy patrol. Ditched am. NKG.

**P/O V Ortmans DFC, a Belgian with 609 Squadron.
Prisoner of war on 21 October 1941.**

31 August 1941

41 Sqn	Spitfire V Sgt P Hind	R7307 PoW*	Sweep. Crashed in flames near Le Trait, evening. *Died 8 July 1942.
54 Sqn	Spitfire Vb F/L R Mottram	W3712 +	Sweep. FTR. Buried Merville, France. See also 18 September 1940.
92 Sqn	Spitfire Vb Sgt W F Kenwood RCAF	W3120 Safe	Convoy patrol. Baled out after losing his way near Brighton: evening.

31 August /1 September 1941

23 Sqn	Havoc I F/O D A Thomas F/S W D McAdam Sgt R S Bryer	AW404 PoW + +	Intruder to Gilze-Rijen A/F, Holland. Shot down and landed in the sea. Stalag Luft III. McAdam buried at Adegem, Belgium, aged 26. Bryer has NKG, aged 21.

1 September 1941

118 Sqn	Spitfire IIb P/O P J P Anderson	P8511 +	Ramrod. Shot down by flak NE of Cherbourg. Evening. NKG, aged 19.

4 September 1941

54 Sqn	Spitfire Vb P/O M M Evans	W3620 +	Circus 93. FTR, pm. NKG, aged 27.
54 Sqn	Spitfire Vb P/O J S Harris	AB808 +	Ditto. Buried Dunkirk, aged 24.
92 Sqn	Spitfire Vb P/O J E T Asselin RCAF	W3182 PoW	Sweep. FTR, pm. Stalag Luft III.
111 Sqn	Spitfire Vb Sgt T R Caldwell	W3451 Safe	Circus 93. Shot down by Me109 and baled out over Channel and rescued. See 23 July 1941.
222 Sqn	Spitfire Vb Sgt A O Sharples	AB801 PoW	Ditto. Kopernikus PoW camp.
222 Sqn	Spitfire Vb Sgt W B Rudd	W3124 PoW	Ditto. Kopernikus.
263 Sqn	Whirlwind I Sgt G L Buckwell	P7042 PoW/WIA	Escort. Shot down by Me109 off Cherbourg and baled out over the sea. Lamsdorf PoW camp.
308 Sqn	Spitfire IIb Sgt T M Kowalski	P8383 PoW	Sweep. Hit by flak and baled out. Kopernikus camp.
603 Sqn	Spitfire V Sgt G W McC Neil	W3711 Wounded	Circus 93. Wounded in left shoulder and foot. A/c Cat 2, repaired.
609 Sqn	Spitfire P/O W B Sanders	? 'L' Safe	Damaged in combat, crash-landed at Detling, out of fuel, hitting a gun emplacement. A/c SoC.

7 September 1941

71 Sqn	Spitfire V P/O H S Fenlaw	AB900 +	Sweep. Combat with Me109s pm. NKG. American Eagle.
71 Sqn	Spitfire V P/O W H Nicholls	AB909 PoW	Ditto. Stalag Luft III. American Eagle.
71 Sqn	Spitfire Vb F/O E Q Tobin	W3801 +	*Popocatapetl II.* Ditto, shot down by Me109. Buried Boulogne, aged 24. American Eagle.
71 Sqn	Spitfire Vb P/O F P Dowling	AB815 Sl/WIA	Ditto. A/c damaged but repaired. American Eagle.

7/8 September 1941

23 Sqn	Havoc I	BB905	Intruder to Lannion A/F. FTR.
	F/O P S B Ensor	+	Buried Lambezelle, Brest, aged 21.
	F/S P A Roberts DFM	+	Ditto, aged 23.
	F/S G D Oliver	+	Ditto, aged 26.

10 September 1941

242 Sqn	Hurricane II	BD767	Missing from Dawn patrol. Wreckage washed-up at
	Sgt P Y Reilly	+	Broadstairs. NKG.
263 Sqn	Whirlwind I	P7001	Strike. Shot down by flak pm, near Cherbourg, and
	P/O D W Mason	+	buried there, aged 23.

12 September 1941

257 Sqn	Hurricane IIB	Z3744	Patrol. FTR early pm. NKG, aged 27.
	F/L R A Jarvis	+	

15 September 1941

257 Sqn	Hurricane IIB	Z3322	Fighter strike. Shot down by Me109 of JG53 near Dutch
	Sgt P Cowen	+	coast. Buried Bergan, Netherlands.

16 September 1941

306 Sqn	Spitfire Vb	AB993 'S'	Sweep, evening. Shot down by Me109. Aged 26.
	Sgt S Wierprzkowicz	+	
315 Sqn	Spitfire Vb	AB923 'T'	Ditto. Near Boulogne. Both claimed by JG26. Aged 31.
	F/O K Woliński	+	

17 September 1941

54 Sqn	Spitfire Vb	W3772	*Moray.* Circus 95. Shot down by Me109 pm.
	S/L N Orton DFC*	+	NKG, aged 26. See 15 May 1940.
54 Sqn	Spitfire Vb	AB813	Ditto. Buried Dunkirk, aged 29.
	Sgt J D Draper RCAF	+	
54 Sqn	Spitfire Vb	W3109	Ditto, aged 20.
	Sgt R A Overson	+	
54 Sqn	Spitfire Vb	R7301	Ditto. Crash-landed Hornchurch. A/C repaired.
	Sgt W J Batchelor	Wounded	
54 Sqn	Spitfire Vb	W3653	*Doncaster.* Ditto. Collided with Me109, ditched and
	Sgt F L Preece	Wounded	rescued. All in action with JG26.
71 Sqn	Spitfire Vb	W3763 'L'	*Thane of Fife.* Circus 95, baled out over Channel and
	P/O W D Geiger	PoW	rescued by enemy E-boat. Stalag Luft III. American.
71 Sqn	Spitfire Vb	W3509	Ditto. Buried at Bergan after being washed ashore on
	P/O T P McGerty	+	20 October. American.
92 Sqn	Spitfire Vb	AB915	*Narayanganj.* Sweep. Baled out but drowned. Body
	P/O B Bartholomew*	+	recovered, buried in Brighton/Hove Jewish Cem.
			*Real name, B B Bloom.
92 Sqn	Spitfire Vb	W3709	Sweep. A/C Cat 2 damage, repaired.
	P/O E G Brettell	Wounded	See also 24 September 1942.
306 Sqn	Spitfire Vb	W3701 'G'	Circus 95. Shot down by Me109. Stalag Luft III.
	P/O C Daszuta	PoW	
308 Sqn	Spitfire Vb	W3524	Ditto. Collided with Me109 of JG26. Buried Longuenesse,
	P/O C Budzalek	+	aged 24.

602 Sqn	Spitfire Vb P/O A R Tidman	W3642 +	Circus pm. A 123 Sqn pilot. Body washed ashore 21 October, and buried at Bergen Op Zoom, Holland.
609 Sqn	Spitfire Vb P/O J A Atkinson	W3767 Safe	Escort. Shot-up by Me109 and baled out over the Channel and rescued.

18 September 1941

41 Sqn	Spitfire Vb Sgt W Palmer	AD126 Safe	Sweep. Damaged in combat and ditched off Freeston, rescued by HSL (High Speed Launch – rescue boat).
452 Sqn (RAAF)	Spitfire Vb P/O W D Willis	W3512 +	Circus 99. Shot down by Me109. Buried St Marie, Le Havre, aged 24.
452 Sqn (RAAF)	Spitfire Vb Sgt A R Stuart	P8703 PoW	Circus 99. Combat with Me109s. 7/JG26 pm. Stalag Luft VII.
452 Sqn (RAAF)	Spitfire Vb Sgt A K Try	W3508 PoW	Ditto. Stalag Luft IV.
452 Sqn (RAAF)	Spitfire Vb Sgt C F R Manning	W3600 +	Ditto.
485 Sqn (RNZAF)	Spitfire Vb Sgt A I Paget	AB903 +	*Otago II.* Shot down by Me109 on Circus 99. NKG, aged 24.
607 Sqn	Hurricane IIA P/O A J Beales	Z2388 PoW	Circus. Shot down over the Channel by Me109 – Joachim Müncheberg's 55th victory (JG26) pm. Stalag Luft III.
615 Sqn	Hurricane IIB P/O R M Hamilton	BD831 +	Roadstead off Blankenburge, FTR, am.
615 Sqn	Hurricane IIB P/O A H Milnes	BD787 Safe	Ditto. Baled out and rescued by HSL am.

19 September 1941

72 Sqn	Spitfire Vb F/L D Stewart-Clark	W3516 +	Shot down off Gravelines pm. Buried Pihen le Guines. See 30 September 1940 and 21 June 1941.

20 September 1941

92 Sqn	Spitfire Vb Sgt G P Hickman	W3179 PoW	Sweep pm. FTR. Lamsdorf camp. See 7 August 1941.
111 Sqn	Spitfire Vb F/L L S Pilkington DFM	AB962 +	Circus 100A, pm. FTR. JG26.
111 Sqn	Spitfire Vb Sgt D G Harwood	W3773 PoW	*Leyland U.D.C.* Ditto. Kopernikus camp.
452 Sqn (RAAF)	Spitfire Vb Sgt I A L Milne	AB841 PoW	Circus 100B, pm. FTR. Rescued from the sea. Kopernikus camp.
602 Sqn	Spitfire Vb Sgt C J Squibb	W3622 +	Ditto. Shot down near Abbeville.
602 Sqn	Spitfire Vb Sgt I M Brown RNZAF	P8787 +	*Hemel Hempstead.* Ditto. Body washed ashore in October. Buried, Leubringhen, NW Marquise, aged 27.
611 Sqn	Spitfire Vb F/L R G A Barclay DFC	W3816 'K' Evaded	*The Shopmate.* Circus 100A. Shot down by Me109 and crash-landed. Made way to Spain and returned to UK in December from Gibraltar.

21 September 1941

111 Sqn	Spitfire Vb Sgt R H Wharton	AB969 +	Circus 102. FTR, buried Dunkirk, aged 25.

111 Sqn	Spitfire Vb Sgt K J Haine	W3757 +	Ditto. Buried Merville, aged 22. JG26 claimed both, one by Adolf Galland – his 87th victory.
129 Sqn	Spitfire Vb S/L D L Armitage DFC	AD122 PoW	Circus. Baled out after attack by a Me109 of JG26.
129 Sqn	Spitfire Vb Sgt Drew	? Safe	Ditto. Rescued from the sea.
129 Sqn	Spitfire Vb Sgt C L MacDonald RCAF	P8752 +	Circus pm. Shot down by Me109 and buried Boulogne. Aged 22.
315 Sqn	Spitfire Vb S/L S Pietraszkiewicz	AB990 'A' PoW	Circus 101. Force-landed in France during combat with Me109s. Stalag Luft III.
315 Sqn	Spitfire Vb F/O T Nowak	AB927 'S' +	Ditto. Shot down by Me109 off Dover. Both claimed by 6/JG26. Aged 27.
485 Sqn (RNZAF)	Spitfire Vb P/O J F Knight	AB856 'E' PoW	*Wellington II.* Ditto. FTR, pm. See 14 August 1941.
602 Sqn	Spitfire Vb Sgt P V Bell	AB780 Evaded	Circus. Shot down by Me109 and returned to UK via Spain, in January 1942.
602 Sqn	Spitfire Vb Sgt A R Hedger	W3725 +	Circus pm, FTR. NKG, aged 21.
602 Sqn	Spitfire Vb P/O Osborne	P8790 Safe	Ditto. A/c written off.
603 Sqn	Spitfire Vb P/O G B Maclachan	W3460 Safe	*Cape Town VI.* Circus. Baled out after attack by Me109 of JG26 and rescued by HSL, pm.
607 Sqn	Hurricane IIA Sgt E A S Parris	Z2806 PoW	Circus. Shot down by Me109, pm. Kopernikus camp.
609 Sqn	Spitfire Vb P/O W B Sanders	W3315 'U' Injured	Circus. Ran out of fuel trying to land at Gravesend and crashed – written off.
616 Sqn	Spitfire Vb Sgt J C Carter	AB795 PoW	Circus. Lost 10 miles south of Le Touquet, pm.

22 September 1941

616 Sqn	Spitfire Vb P/O E H Burton	W3433 +	Collided south of Brighton with W3517. Canadian pilot.
616 Sqn	Spitfire Vb Sgt J B Slack	W3517 +	Ditto. Buried Paisley cem. Aged 29.

24 September 1941

124 Sqn	Spitfire Ia Sgt R H Pauley	X4108 +	Convoy patrol, am. Crashed near Orkney in low cloud.

25 September 1941

66 Sqn	Spitfire IIa Sgt F H M Green	P8270 +	Interception. FTR from engagement with EA, 40 miles off the Lizard, 1540. NKG.

27 September 1941

72 Sqn	Spitfire Vb Sgt A F Binns	AB843 +	Circus 103B, pm. FTR.
72 Sqn	Spitfire Vb Sgt J G Merrett RAAF	P8560 +	Ditto. Buried Vlissingen after being washed up on 23 October. Aged 25.
129 Sqn	Spitfire Vb Sgt J A Spence-Ross	W3824 PoW	*Holt II.* Ditto. Shot down by Me109. Rhodesian pilot. Kopernikus.

308 Sqn	Spitfire Vb Sgt E Watolski	W3940 PoW	*Madura II.* Circus, pm. FTR. Stalag Luft III.
402 Sqn (RCAF)	Hurricane IIB P/O S A Graham	Z5005 PoW	Circus pm. FTR. Stalag Luft III.
403 Sqn (RCAF)	Spitfire Vb S/L R A Lee Knight DFC	AD207 'C' +	Circus 103B, pm. Shot down by Me109 and buried at Dunkirk.
403 Sqn (RCAF)	Spitfire Vb Sgt McDonald	AB963 'E' Wounded	Ditto. Hit by flak; Cat 2 damage but repaired.
411 Sqn (RCAF)	Spitfire IIa Sgt J D McFarlane	P8172 Injured	Hit by flak near Le Touquet and baled out over Dungeness.
603 Sqn	Spitfire V Sgt W J Allard	R7221 PoW	Circus, pm. FTR. Stalag Luft III.
603 Sqn	Spitfire V Sgt W J Archibald RCAF	W3233 +	Ditto. Buried Dunkirk, aged 21.

Sgt A G Palmer DFM, 609 Squadron, killed in action 21 October 1941.

609 Sqn	Spitfire Vb P/O V M Ortmans	W3625 Safe	Circus. Ran out of fuel after combat and baled out off Dover; rescued by HSL 147. Belgian pilot. See also 19 August and 21 October 1941.
611 Sqn	Spitfire Vb Sgt G T Evans RCAF	W3442 PoW	Circus, pm. Lost near Hazebrouck. Kopernikus camp.
615 Sqn	Hurricane IIB P/O A D Roberts	Z3258 +	Jim Crow Sortie. FTR from Mardyck area, am.
616 Sqn	Spitfire Vb P/O R G Sutherland RCAF	W3334 +	*Progress I.* Sweep, pm, FTR. Buried Gamaches, France, aged 22.
616 Sqn	Spitfire Vb Sgt J G West DFM RNZAF	W3655 Safe	*Silver Grey.* Circus 103A. Damaged by FW190 of JG2 and baled out off Bexhill. Rescued.

28 September 1941

263 Sqn	Whirlwind I W/C A H Donaldson DFC AFC	P7044 Wounded	Strike against Morlaix Airfield. Cat 2 damage and pilot slightly wounded in both arms.

29 September 1941

247 Sqn	Hurricane IIB F/O K W Mackenzie DFC	BD832 PoW	Intruder. Ditched after being hit by flak attacking Lannion A/F. Paddled ashore and taken prisoner. Stalag Luft III, repatriated October 1944. See 7 and 25 October 1940.
247 Sqn	Hurricane IIB P/O S S Hordern	Z3561 Wounded	Ditto. Wounded in the leg and A/c damaged but repaired.
263 Sqn	Whirlwind I Sgt T Hunter	P7009 +	Strike, pm. Baled out over the sea near Plymouth as fuel ran out. Not found.
615 Sqn	Hurricane IIB Sgt C Chaloupka	Z3450 Safe	Rhubarb. Shot down by flak, baled out and rescued pm. See 6 October 1941. Czech pilot.

30 September 1941

118 Sqn	Spitfire Vb Sgt G A Painting	W3849 +	Shipping strike. Shot down by flak, pm, and crashed into the sea off Cherbourg. NKG, aged 17.

Chapter 8

Autumn and Winter 1941

1 October 1941

91 Sqn	Spitfire V P/O N P Warden	R7290 +	ASR escort. Shot down by Me109, 1350 hrs.
91 Sqn	Spitfire V Sgt G W Baker	W3422 +	Ditto. Buried at The Hague, Holland. Both claimed by JG26, Pips Priller credited with his 50th victory.

2 October 1941

92 Sqn	Spitfire Vb F/L J W Lund	W3459 +	Sweep. Combat with FW190s from JG2. See 15 October 1940.
92 Sqn	Spitfire Vb Sgt N H Edge	W3137 +	Ditto.
92 Sqn	Spitfire Vb Sgt K G Port	W3762 +	Ditto, over Le Tréport.
92 Sqn	Spitfire Vb P/O D A Bruce	W3657 Injured	Ditto. Shot-up and crash-landed near Ashford. A/C repaired. See 3 August 1941.

3 October 1941

54 Sqn	Spitfire Vb Sgt J C Ward	P7846 +	*Newfoundland III.* Circus 105. Fight with JG26. Buried at The Hague; body washed up 21 October. Aged 21. Johannes Schmid's 50th victory.
92 Sqn	Spitfire Vb Sgt H Cox	W3710 +	Circus 105, pm. FTR.
92 Sqn	Spitfire Vb Sgt G E F Woods-Scawen	AB779 'E' +	Ditto. Body washed ashore 20 October, buried at Noordwijk, Holland, aged 19.

5 October 1941

257 Sqn	Hurricane IIB S/L F J Soper DFC DFM	Z5045 +	Patrol. Lost in engagement with Ju88 off Suffolk coast, 1308. NKG, aged 28. See 17 May 1940.

6 October 1941

615 Sqn	Hurricane IIC Sgt C Chaloupka	Z3085 PoW	*Jim Crow.* FTR from sortie to Ostend area, am. See 29 September 1941. Czech pilot. Wistritz camp, near Teplitz.

12 October 1941

452 Sqn (RAAF)	Spitfire Vb Sgt K B Chisholm DFM	W3520 PoW	Sweep. Shot down off Berck and rescued by the Germans. Later escaped and awarded the MC.
602 Sqn	Spitfire Vb Sgt A E V Meredith	W3623 PoW	Sweep early pm, FTR. Lamsdorf PoW camp.

13 October 1941

41 Sqn	Spitfire V Sgt C J L Whiteford	R7258 +	Sweep, pm. FTR. Buried Aylesham Cemetery, aged 22.
41 Sqn	Spitfire Vb F/O L L Bache	AB826 +	Ditto. Buried Boulogne, aged 28.

65 Sqn	Spitfire Vb Sgt D H Warden	AB821 +	Circus 108A, pm. Shot down by Me109; buried Boulogne, aged 20.
71 Sqn	Spitfire Vb P/O G C Daniel RCAF	AD112 PoW/WIA	Circus, pm. Shot down and baled out into the sea; wounded in the leg. Stalag Luft III. Native American, aged 15!
129 Sqn	Spitfire Vb F/L R R MacPherson	P8542 +	*Violetta.* Sweep to Arcques. FTR following combat with Me109s, pm. NKG, aged 27.
129 Sqn	Spitfire Vb P/O G S Walker	AD721 +	Ditto. NKG, aged 24.
402 Sqn (RCAF)	Hurricane IIB F/L H S Crease	Z3421 PoW	Circus. Hit by flak and baled out over Busnes. Stalag Luft III.
411 Sqn (RCAF)	Spitfire Vb P/O R W McNair	P7679 'F' Safe	Sweep, pm. Shot down in combat with Me109. Rescued by HSL 24. See 27 July 1943.
452 Sqn (RAAF)	Spitfire Vb Sgt E P Jackson	AB852 +	Circus 108A. Shot down by Me109 on first mission.
452 Sqn (RAAF)	Spitfire Vb Sgt J R H Elphick	AD310 Safe	Ditto. Baled out over Channel and rescued.
602 Sqn	Spitfire Vb Sgt L L Ford RNZAF	W3897 PoW/WIA	*Nyasaland VII.* Circus 108A pm. Kopernikus camp.
602 Sqn	Spitfire Vb Sgt E Brayley	AB861 +	Ditto. Buried Longuenesse, age 20.
603 Sqn	Spitfire Vb Sgt A D Shuckburgh	X4389 +	Ditto. Buried Dunkirk, aged 23.

15 October 1941

234 Sq	Spitfire Vb Sgt H R Barnett	P8714 +	*Spirit of Warrington.* Ramrod 69. Shot down by Me109 off Le Havre, at 1230. NKG, aged 20.

16 October 1941

615 Sqn	Hurricane IIB F/O E S Aldous	Z3028 +	*Jim Crow.* Shot down by flak near Flushing. Buried Vlissingen, age 23. See also 28 September 1940.

17 October 1941

615 Sqn	Hurricane IIB S/L D E Gillam DFC AFC	? Sl/WIA	Armed recce. Slightly wounded in both feet by flak from Zeebrugge. A/c Cat 2 damage. See 2 September 1940 and 23 November 1941.

20 October 1941

71 Sqn	Spitfire Vb P/O O H Coen	AB827 Evaded	Rhubarb. Brought down by exploding train he was attacking. Walked to Portugal, then Spain; returned to UK December 1941.
234 Sqn	Spitfire Vb Sgt P H Fox	AD203 PoW	Rhubarb. Brought down by flak, pm, and crash-landed in France. Kopernikus. See 30 September 1940.

21 October 1941

65 Sqn	Spitfire Vb Sgt A H Johnson	AD267 PoW/WIA	Sweep am, FTR. Stalag Luft III.
65 Sqn	Spitfire Vb P/O D C Mitchell	W3633 Safe	Ditto. Shot down by Me109, baled out into the sea. Rescued after two hours in his dinghy.
129 Sqn	Spitfire Vb Sgt E Tucker	W3893 Sl/WIA	Ditto am. A/c damaged but repaired. Jamaican pilot.

303 Sqn	Spitfire Vb P/O R Łobarzewski	AB823 'Y' Safe	Sweep. Engine trouble during an air fight and caught fire. Baled out over Hawkinge.
401 Sqn (RCAF)	Spitfire Vb Sgt B F Whitson	AB863 POW/WIA	Sweep. Shot down by Me109, am. Stalag Luft IV.
485 Sqn (RNZAF)	Spitfire Vb Sgt A G McNeil	W3579 Wounded	Rodeo. Shot-up by Me109. Cat B damage but repaired; pilot arm wound. (KIFA February 1942)
603 Sqn	Spitfire Vb Sgt W McKelvie	W3123 +	Sweep. Collided with P/O S G H Fawkes over France and heard to say he was baling out. Buried at Dunkirk, aged 24.
603 Sqn	Spitfire Vb P/O S G H Fawkes	W3631 Safe	Ditto. Lost four feet from one wing and crash-landed in Kent. Repaired.
609 Sqn	Spitfire Vb F/O V M M Ortmans DFC	W3850 PoW	*Westmoreland.* Sweep. Shot down by FW190,1145. Rescued from the sea by the Germans. Belgian. See 19 August and 27 September 1941.
609 Sqn	Spitfire Vb Sgt A G Palmer DFM	AD136 'K' +	Ditto. Shot down by Me109 off Le Touquet. 1145. NKG.
609 Sqn	Spitfire Vb S/Lt M P C Choron	W3236 Safe	Ditto. Damaged by Me109 of JG26 and crash-landed near Rye, 1710. See also 10 April 1942.
611 Sqn	Spitfire Vb P/O J W Y Roeper-Bosch	W3227 +	Sweep am. Crashed into the sea off Boulogne. Buried Burck-sur-Mer.
611 Sqn	Spitfire Vb P/O J F Reeves	W3327 +	*Horsham & District.* ASR search pm. Reported to have collided with Smith, but both claimed by JG26, Adolf Galland gaining his 92nd victory.
611 Sqn	Spitfire Vb P/O N J Smith	W3515 +	Ditto. Lost over the Channel.

Spitfire Vb XR-C (AA855) 71 Eagle Squadron, crash-landed in France, 27 October 1941. P/O M W Fessler was taken prisoner.

24 October 1941

152 Sqn	Spitfire Vb Sgt F A Axe	P7680 +	Escort. Shot down 40 miles off the Dorset coast by Me109, 1437. NKG, aged 21.
315 Sqn	Spitfire Vb P/O E Fiedorczuk	W3761 'U' Wounded	Sweep. Seriously wounded in air fight. A/c Cat 2 but repaired.

25 October 1941

96 Sqn	Defiant I P/O J I Phoenix Sgt L H Seales	T3999 Safe Safe	Patrol. Hit goose-neck flare upon take-off, damaging tail and elevators. Climbed to 6000 ft and baled out near Wrexham, 2145.
125 Sqn	Defiant I Sgt C A G Dale Sgt Bayliss	T3985 + Safe	Night patrol. Hit balloon cable at Skewen, Swansea, 2203. AG baled out before crash. New Zealand pilot.

26 October 1941

72 Sqn	Spitfire Vb Sgt L Stock	AB822 +	Rodeo. Shot down off Dover by Me109. NKG.
245 Sqn	Hurricane IIB P/O B L G Hawkins	Z3470 PoW	Rhubarb, pm. Shot down by flak over Cherbourg area. Captured by Vichy French, escaped to UK October 1942.
253 Sqn	Hurricane IIB Sgt L G Horsfall	Z3918 +	Patrol. Crashed at Rothwell Park, near Caister, at 0705.

27 October 1941

71 Sqn	Spitfire Vb P/O M W Fessler	AA855 'C' PoW	Rhubarb, early am. Hit by debris from exploding train and forced to land. Stalag Luft III. American.
72 Sqn	Spitfire Vb Sgt F Falkiner RAAF	W3704 PoW/inj	*Qacha's Nek.* Rodeo, pm. Shot down by Me109 near Dunkirk and suffered burns to face and hands. Mühlhausen PoW camp.
152 Sqn	Spitfire Vb Sgt E O Grimesdick	P7901 +	Roadstead. Went down off Cromer at 1545 during encounter with Me109. See 15 April 1941 (P7901).
401 Sqn (RCAF)	Spitfire Vb F/O C A B Wallace	AB991 +	Sweep. Shot down by JG26, pm.
401 Sqn (RCAF)	Spitfire Vb P/O C W Floody	W3964 +	Ditto.
401 Sqn (RCAF)	Spitfire Vb P/O J A Small	AB983 +	*Singkawang.* Ditto. Buried Dunkirk, aged 24.
401 Sqn (RCAF)	Spitfire Vb Sgt B G Hodgkinson	W3955 PoW	Ditto. Adolf Galland's 93rd victory. Commissioned later. Hohen Fels PoW camp.
401 Sqn (RCAF)	Spitfire Vb Sgt S L Thompson	W3601 +	Ditto. Crashed at Deal and SoC.
401 Sqn (RCAF)	Spitfire Vb Sgt G B Whitney	W3452 Safe	*Midnight Sun.* Ditto. Baled out over Sandwich after combat with JG26. His parachute opened at 100ft.
611 Sqn	Spitfire Vb P/O A Carey-Hill	W3838 +	*Valpariso.* ASR escort. Shot down by Me109 of JG2. Buried Boulogne, aged 26.
615 Sqn	Hurricane IIB F/O C D Strickland	Z3826 +	Rhubarb, early am. Shot down by ground fire. Buried Credene Church Yard, Belgium.
615 Sqn	Hurricane IIC Sgt D A Potts	Z3464 +	Rhubarb, early am. FTR – body washed up 12 December, buried at Vlissingen, Holland. Aged 21.
615 Sqn	Hurricane IIC P/O C G Ford	Z3081 Wounded	Rhubarb. Cat 2 damage from flak, crash-landed at base, but repaired. Argentinian pilot.

28 October 1941

145 Sqn	Spitfire IIa P/O H L M Young	P8044 'J' +	*1st Canadian Division.* Convoy patrol. Crashed on return to Merston, 1730.
219 Sqn	Beaufighter 1f F/O J Kee Sgt T G F Dixon	R2131 + +	Dusk patrol. Stalled on take-off and crashed west of Merston.

29 October 1941

123 Sqn	Spitfire IIa Sgt W M Menzies	P8096 Safe	Scramble over Wick. Dazzled by flarepath lights and crash-landed at Casteltown, 2251. A/c repaired.

30 October 1941

137 Sqn	Whirlwind I F/O C A G Clarke	P7091 +	Rhubarb, am. Went down south of the Lizard, 1100. Rescued but died of his injuries.
263 Sqn	Whirlwind I F/O D Stein	P7015 +	Rhubarb, am. Brought down by flak attacking Morlaix A/F, crashed into the sea.

31 October 1941

85 Sqn	Havoc II W/C A T D Sanders DFC P/O S Austin DFM	AH520 'A' + +	Patrol. Crashed off Deal during fight with enemy aircraft, at 2010. NKGs. Sanders aged 28.
607 Sqn	Hurricane IIB Sgt A Zavoral	BE403 +	Ramrod. Brought down by flak, pm. Czech pilot, aged 24.
615 Sqn	Hurricane IIB P/O D W McCormack	Z3348 Wounded	Ramrod. Cat 2 damage from flak but repaired.
Kenley	Spitfire Vb W/C E N Ryder DFC*	W3579 'Q' PoW	*Southland II.* Circus 109. Kenley Wing Leader. Brought down by flak escorting Hurricanes attacking the Bourbourg Canal at Dunkirk. Stalag Luft III. A 485 RNZAF Sqn aircraft.

1 November 1941

71 Sqn	Spitfire Vb P/O A F Roscoe	AA857 Wounded	Escort, early pm. A/c Cat 2 damage, but repaired. American Eagle.

2 November 1941

234 Sqn	Spitfire Vb P/O B W Meyer	W3830 PoW	Shipping recce. Engine trouble; force-landed on Alderney Is, pm. Stalag Luft III. American pilot.
607 Sqn	Hurricane IIE Sgt W C Lees	BE425 +	Shipping recce, evening. Shot down by flak off Ostend.
615 Sqn	Hurricane IIB F/S J E Slade	BE144 +	Ditto.
615 Sqn	Hurricane IIC F/S A T Gooderham	Z3841 +	Ditto. See also 15 October 1940. NKG.

4 November 1941

501 Sqn	Spitfire Vb P/O E H L Shore	AA837 'E' PoW	*Harrogate.* Rhubarb. FTR from the St Lô area, evening. Engine trouble after attack by Me109. Crash-landed Normandy beach. Stalag Luft III.
607 Sqn	Hurricane IIE S/L G D Craig	BE418 PoW	Rhubarb, pm. Shot down by ground fire attacking airfield at Le Touquet. Stalag Luft III (MBE).

5 November 1941

611 Sqn	Spitfire Vb Sgt W P Dales	AB984 +	*West Borneo III.* Rhubarb, am. Shot down by Adolf Glunz, JG26, off coast at Gravelines. NKG, aged 22.

6 November 1941

263 Sqn	Whirlwind I Sgt J J Robinson	P6970 +	Rhubarb, am. Possibly hit the sea.
452 Sqn (RAAF)	Spitfire Vb Sgt E H Schrader	AD242 +	Escort. Shot down by FW190 of JG26 flown by Johannes Schmid (45th victory). In circling the crash-site, Schmid's wing hit the water and he was killed in the resulting crash.
452 Sqn (RAAF)	Spitfire Vb Sgt B M Geissman	AD430 +	Ditto. Shot down by Stab/JG26, pm. Both near Cap Gris Nez.
607 Sqn	Hurricane IIB P/O A Y McCombe	BE420 +	Ramrod, pm. Shot down by Me109 off Gravelines – JG26.

7 November 1941

72 Sqn	Spitfire Vb P/O H J Birkland RCAF	W3367 PoW	*Mafeteng*. Rodeo, pm. Shot down by JG26. Murdered after the Great Escape, from Stalag Luft III, *c*.31st March 1944. Aged 26.

7/8 November 1941

3 Sqn	Hurricane IIC Sgt C G Montgomery	BE152 PoW	Dover patrol. Midnight. FTR from Calais area. Stalag Luft IV.

8 November 1941

65 Sqn	Spitfire Vb Sgt S Štulíř	W3560 'R' +	Ramrod, am. FTR. Czech, aged 24.
72 Sqn	Spitfire Vb Sgt J E T Dykes	AB893 Safe	*Lilepe*. Ramrod. Baled out due to engine trouble and rescued 19 miles off Dungeness.
72 Sqn	Spitfire Vb P/O N E Bishop	W3511 +	Ramrod, pm. FTR.
72 Sqn	Spitfire Vb Sgt D R White RNZAF	AB855 +	*Swipem One*. Escort, midday. FTR. NKG, aged 24.
302 Sqn	Spitfire Vb P/O Z Gutowski	AB895 'C' PoW	*West Borneo V*. Escort, midday. Stalag Luft III.
308 Sqn	Spitfire Vb F/O F Surma	AB930 'J' +	Circus 110. Shot down by Me109 of JG26 off Dunkirk, midday. NKG, aged 25. See 29 October 1940.
315 Sqn	Spitfire Vb S/L W Szczęśniewski	W3944 'A' PoW	Circus 110, midday. Ran out of fuel. Stalag Luft III.
316 Sqn	Spitfire Vb S/L W Wilcewski	AD303 'M' PoW/WIA	Ditto. Shot down by flak and badly wounded in combat. Stalag Luft III.
401 Sqn (RCAF)	Spitfire Vb F/O J G Weir	AB922 PoW/WIA	*Liphamola*. Escort to Calais. Shot down, wounded, am. Wegschelde PoW camp. JG26.
401 Sqn (RCAF)	Spitfire Vb Sgt R W Gardner	AA925 +	Ditto. Buried Boulogne, aged 20. JG26.
412 Sqn (RCAF)	Spitfire Vb S/L C Bushell	W3959 +	Circus 110. Shot down by JG26, am.
412 Sqn (RCAF)	Spitfire Vb P/O K R E Denkman	W3952 +	Ditto.
412 Sqn (RCAF)	Spitfire Vb Sgt O F Pickells	AD270 +	Ditto.
452 Sqn (RAAF)	Spitfire Vb F/L K W Truscott DFC	AB842 Safe	*The Staffordian*. Ditto. Baled out and rescued east of Ramsgate.

F/O C D Strickland of 615 Squadron, brought down by ground fire on a rhubarb sortie, 27 October 1941.

452 Sqn (RAAF)	Spitfire Vb Sgt B P Dunstan	P8645 Safe	Ditto, off North Foreland, am.
501 Sqn	Spitfire Vb P/O W J H Greenaway	AD188 PoW	Escort. Shot down by Me109, pm. Stalag Luft III.
616 Sqn	Spitfire IIb W/C D R Scott AFC	P8701 +	Circus 110. Shot down by FW190. Buried Dunkirk, aged 33.

11 November 1941

65 Sqn	Spitfire Vb Sgt G D Morcom RNZAF	W3629 +	Ramrod, pm. Shot down by flak fire. Buried Janvel, nr Dieppe, aged 25.
234 Sqn	Spitfire Vb Sgt W E Sapsed	W3934 +	Sweep, pm. Buried Janvel, Dieppe.
402 Sqn (RCAF)	Hurricane IIB Sgt M R R Vair	BE472	Ramrod, pm. Buried Janvel, Dieppe.
607 Sqn	Hurricane IIB P/O L W Stevenson RNZAF	BE221 +	Ditto. Buried Janvel, Dieppe, aged 24.

15 November 1941

118 Sqn	Spitfire Vb Sgt H Alexander	W3706 +	Rhubarb, pm. Shot down by flak and last seen in the water off Marcouf. Buried Cherbourg, aged 26.
234 Sqn	Spitfire Vb Sgt H A Newman	AD326 +	Strike, am. Buried Calvados, France. See 10 July 1941.
609 Sqn	Spitfire Vb Sgt K N Laing RCAF	AD507 PoW	Sweep, pm. Shot down by flak near Calais. Stalag Luft VII.

17 November 1941

91 Sqn	Spitfire Vb P/O A W Black	AA731 'W' +	*Jim Crow*, early am. FTR. NKG, aged 25.

501 Sqn	Spitfire Vb Sgt R F C Dean	AD129 'K' +	Rhubarb, am. Buried Brevands, Fr.

19 November 1941

41 Sqn	Spitfire Vb S/L L M Gaunce DFC	AB858 +	Rhubarb. Shot down by Me109 off St Lô, pm. NKG aged 26. Canadian.

21 November 1941

401 Sqn (RCAF)	Spitfire Vb Sgt C R Golden	AD255 Injured	Convoy patrol, pm. Broke a leg in crash-landing at Manston.

22 November 1941

1 Sqn	Hurricane IIC Sgt L J Travis	BD940 +	Dusk scramble. Collided in poor visibility over the Isle of Wight.
1 Sqn	Hurricane IIC Sgt D P Perrin RNZAF	Z3899 Injured	See above; baled out.
401 Sqn (RCAF)	Spitfire Vb F/O H A Sprague	AD516 PoW	*Sir Robert*. Sweep, pm. Shot down in combat with Me109s and FW190s near Boulogne. JG26. Stalag Luft III.

23 November 1941

41 Sqn	Spitfire Vb Sgt D Fleming	R7213 +	Patrol, pm. Engine trouble, spun into the sea off Bognor.
315 Sqn	Spitfire Vb Sgt G Kosmanski	W3698 'Y' +	Ramrod XII, pm. Shot down by JG26. Buried Dunkirk, aged 23.
315 Sqn	Spitfire Vb F/O W Grudzinski	W3896 'F' +	*Nyasaland VI*. Ditto. NKG. Aged 24.
315 Sqn	Spitfire Vb P/O M Łukaszewicz	W3577 'W' +	Ditto. NKG, aged 25.
315 Sqn	Spitfire Vb Sgt M B B Staliński	AB937 'V' +	Ditto. Buried Dunkirk, aged 27.
315 Sqn	Spitfire Vb F/O J Grzech	AB934 'E' +	Ditto. Buried Dunkirk, aged 26.
315 Sqn	Spitfire Vb Sgt T Krieger	AB892 'H' Wounded	Ditto. A/c Cat 2 damage but later repaired.
615 Sqn	Hurricane IIB S/L D E Gillam DFC AFC	Z5078 Sl/WIA	Ramrod XII, pm. Hit by flak and baled out. Rescued by ASR launch.
615 Sqn	Hurricane IIB Sgt G Willis	Z3749 +	Ditto.
615 Sqn	Hurricane IIB Sgt F Zayzierski	BD937 Wounded	Ditto. Hit by flak and also brought back several inches of cable. Cat 2 damage but repaired. Canadian pilot.

24 November 1941

124 Sqn	Spitfire Vb P/O R B Gilman	R6722 Injured	Shipping recce, am. Collided in bad weather, landing at Shoreham. Repaired.
124 Sqn	Spitfire Vb F/L J Kulhánek	BL336 Injured	Ditto. Czech pilot. See 13 March 1942.

26 November 1941

74 Sqn	Spitfire IIa P/O A Williams	P7551 +	Interception. Shot down attacking three Ju88s, 1700, 20 miles west of St David's Head. Body washed up South Wales coast, 14 December.

From this point on, damaged aircraft categories changed. Until now Category 3 meant a total loss, while Category 2 was serious damage. From now, destroyed aircraft became Category E, damaged aircraft became Category B.

27 November 1941

91 Sqn	Spitfire Vb Sgt I W Downer RNZAF	? 'L' Safe	*Jim Crow*, am. Badly shot-up by a Me109 off Boulogne and A/c SoC after a wheels-up landing at RAF Hawkinge. See 29 December 1942.
607 Sqn	Hurricane IIB P/O K L Davies	BE508 +	Strike. Shot down into the sea by flak from Boulogne, pm.
607 Sqn	Hurricane IIB Sgt R Weir	BE504 +	Ditto. Flak and Me109s of JG26.
607 Sqn	Hurricane IIB Sgt W E Hovey RCAF	BE401 +	Ditto.

29 November 1941

132 Sqn	Spitfire I P/O D T McLaren	P9516 +	Convoy patrol. Crashed Tillymand Farm, Longhaven, pm.
317 Sqn	Spitfire Vb P/O K Wójcik	W3968 'H' +	Scramble. Crashed near Dartmoor in bad weather, am. Aged 24.
457 Sq (RAAF)	Spitfire IIa Sgt R T Brewin	P7445 +	Patrol, late am, Isle of Wight area. FTR. NKG, aged 25.

1 December 1941

317 Sqn	Spitfire Vb P/O W Pucek	AD372 Injured	Scramble. Overshot on landing at Exeter. Repaired.
457 Sqn (RAAF)	Spitfire IIa Sgt A L Gifford	P8380 Safe	Scramble. Hit a lorry on landing at Andreas; driver died of injuries. A/c repaired.
600 Sqn	Beaufighter II F/L J G Fletcher AFC Sgt E J F Grant	R2275 + +	Interception. Lost an engine and ditched off Land's End, early am. Pilot's (26) body later washed ashore, cremated Plymouth. Nav, NKG, 21.

5 December 1941

32 Sqn	Hurricane IIB S/L T Grier DFC	Z3237 +	Ramrod, pm. Shot down off Le Havre attacking ships. NKG, aged 23.
32 Sqn	Hurricane IIB Sgt W Fitch RCAF	BE582 +	Ditto. NKG.
32 Sqn	Hurricane IIB F/O A A S Law	Z4992 Wounded	Ditto. Flak damage, Cat B. A/c later repaired.
234 Sqn	Spitfire Vb P/O F R Clarke	AD427 +	Shipping recce early pm. FTR. Buried Dunkirk, aged 29.
234 Sqn	Spitfire Vb Sgt J H Walker	AA723 +	Ditto. NKG.
607 Sqn	Hurricane IIB Sgt J P Cravoisier	BE475 +	Strike, pm. Engaged by flak and fighters off Le Havre.
607 Sqn	Hurricane IIB Sgt A L Lewis RCAF	BE548 +	Ditto. NKG.

6 December 1941

615 Sqn	Hurricane IIB P/O A M Fisher	Z3499 +	Scramble late am. FTR from sortie near Angle. NKG.

7 December 1941

3 Sqn	Hurricane IIC P/O J D McVay RNZAF	Z3916 +	Convoy patrol. Crashed near Epping returning in bad weather. Aged 28.

121 Sqn	Spitfire Vb F/O R F Patterson RCAF	W3711 +	Rhubarb. FTR from Dutch coast. Buried Bredene Churchyard, east of Ostend. American pilot.

8 December 1941

72 Sqn	Spitfire Vb Sgt E G Enright RAAF	AA864 +	Ramrod, late am. FTR, shot down by JG26. NKG, aged 29.
72 Sqn	Spitfire Vb Sgt C L A Thompson	AA749 +	*Moshesh.* Ditto. NKG.
222 Sqn	Spitfire Vb P/O T K Robinson RAAF	AB805 +	Ditto. Buried Boulogne, aged 24.
255 Sqn	Beaufighter II W/C C M Windsor Sgt G P F Langdon	R2398 'A' + +	Patrol. Crashed on landing 2010. Brookwood Cemetery. Littleham Churchyard, aged 27.
315 Sqn	Spitfire Vb F/O B Groszewski	BL323 'W' +	Ramrod. Baled out and seen in his dinghy but not found by ASR. Buried Boulogne, aged 32.
410 Sqn (RCAF)	Defiant I F/L R L F Day F/S J J Townsend	V1137 Injured Injured	Interception. Struck trees coming in to land at Drem in poor visibility, 1900. Pilot seriously injured and Townsend received GM for pulling him out of the burning wreckage.
411 Sqn (RCAF)	Spitfire Vb P/O J R Coleman	AD264 +	*Paisley.* Ramrod. Went into the sea after combat with Me109, late am. Buried Pihen les Guines, aged 21.
411 Sqn (RCAF)	Spitfire Vb F/S D A Court	AA840 +	Ditto. NKG, aged 21.
452 Sqn (RAAF)	Spitfire Vb Sgt J M Emery	AB966 +	ASR escort. Lost in engagement with FW190s, pm.
603 Sqn	Spitfire Vb F/O S G H Fawkes	P8603 +	*Nabha I.* Circus, am. Shot down by fighters over Le Touquet. South African pilot, aged 23.
603 Sqn	Spitfire Vb F/O J A R Falconer	P8786 PoW	Circus, pm. FTR. Stalag Luft III.
603 Sqn	Spitfire Va Sgt H Bennett	R7333 PoW	Ditto – shot down over Le Touquet. Hohen Fels camp.

9 December 1941

603 Sqn	Spitfire Vb P/O D P Lamb	W3242 Safe	*Crispin of Leicester.* Convoy patrol. Baled out after engine trouble, and rescued by patrol boat off Clacton. Also see 24 June 1941.

12 December 1941

121 Sqn	Spitfire Vb P/O K LeR Holder	AA871 +	*Royal Tunbridge Wells.* Patrol, pm. Lost off Lincolnshire coast. Body found and buried Ipswich General Cemetery. American pilot.
253 Sqn	Hurricane IIA Lt J E Loken	Z3670 +	Dusk patrol. Crashed 1715. Norwegian.

13 December 1941

255 Sqn	Beaufighter II P/O P A Dale P/O H Friend	R2309 + Injured	Patrol. Hit trees coming in to land at Coltishall, 2119. Buried at Scottow Cemetery, aged 24.

14 December 1941

151 Sqn	Defiant II Sgt A I Mills Sgt R V Gazzard	AA429 + +	Convoy patrol. Crashed into the sea, reason unknown. NKG, aged 21. Buried Thornbury, Glos., aged 21.

15 December 1941

219 Sqn	Beaufighter I Sgt J P Ranger Sgt G Hunniford	R2154 + +	Dusk patrol. Crashed on return to Tangmere at 1940 hrs. Buried at Brookwood, aged 22. Nav, Irish, buried Seagoe Church of Ireland churchyard, aged 22.

15/16 December 1941

253 Sqn	Hurricane IIC F/L R P Stevens DSO DFC*	Z3465 +	Intruder to Gilze-Rijen A/F Holland. Buried Bergen op Zoom, aged 32.
600 Sqn	Beaufighter IIf F/L C G Imlay Sgt P G Pearce	R3212 + +	Interception. Lost during combat with He111 off Plymouth, 1000. Buried at St Brieuc, France aged 22. Pearce has NKG.

16 December 1941

411 Sqn (RCAF)	Spitfire Vb P/O G A Chamberlain	W3639 +	Shipping recce, pm. Shot down by fighters off Calais. NKG, aged 25.
411 Sqn (RCAF)	Spitfire Vb Sgt T D Holden	AD117 +	Ditto. Buried Pihen les Guines, aged 25. Both victims of JG26's Joachim Müncheberg, his 61st and 62nd kills.

18 December 1941

79 Sqn	Hurricane IIB Sgt G H N Davey	Z5151 +	Escort. Combat with fighters over Brest around noon. Buried at Brignonan, France, aged 27.
111 Sqn	Spitfire Vb F/O V Kopecky	AB798 Injured	Sweep. Crashed on take-off due to engine trouble – lost a leg. Czech.
316 Sqn	Spitfire Vb P/O T Dobrucki	W3941 'P' Injured	Sweep. Slightly injured in crash-landing near Exeter due to running out of fuel. Cat B, repaired.
603 Sqn	Spitfire Vb S/L R G Forshaw	P8796 Injured	Night interception. Crashed into the sea off Newburgh, Scotland, c.1830.

22 December 1941

79 Sqn	Hurricane IIB S/L C D S Smith DFC	Z5255 +	Patrol. Collided with He115 off south coast of Ireland, 1715. NKG, age 25.

23 December 1941

137 Sqn	Whirlwind I Sgt O'Neil	P7094 Injured	Patrol. A/c force-landed near airfield on return due to engine trouble; a/c Cat B, pilot slight injury to hand.

29 December 1941

485 Sqn (RNZAF)	Spitfire Vb P/O J J Palmer	AB853 'F' Wounded	Convoy patrol. Encounter with Ju88 and Me109s off Harwich. Baled out and rescued by HSL.

30 December 1941

234 Sqn	Spitfire Vb Sgt A E Joyce	AB854 'J' PoW	*Thaba Boshu.* Escort to Brest, pm. Shot down by fighters. Stalag Luft III; shot escaping and died on the operating table, 12 June 1943, aged 21.
306 Sqn	Spitfire Vb F/L S W Zieliński	W3945 'C'· +	Ditto. Seen to lose a wing in combat north of Brest. NKG, aged 36.
317 Sqn	Spitfire Vb Sgt T Baranowski	AD306 PoW	Ditto. Hohen Fels camp.

31 December 1941

130 Sqn	Spitfire Vb Sgt J Cox	BL286 +	Convoy patrol. Turned to investigate an approaching a/c off Falmouth, spun and crashed into the sea, 1430. NKG, aged 19.

Appendix A

Fighter Command Order of Battle 8 August 1940

Sqn	Aircraft	Code	Station	
No. 10 Group		**Headquarters:**	**Box, Wiltshire**	
87	Hurricane I	LK	Exeter	
213	Hurricane I	AK	Exeter	
92	Spitfire I	QJ	Pembrey	
234	Spitfire I	AZ	St Eval	
247	Gladiator I	ZY	Roborough	(one flight only)
238	Hurricane I	VK	Middle Wallop	Sector Station
609	Spitfire I	PR	Middle Wallop	
604	Blenheim If	NG	Middle Wallop	
152	Spitfire I	UM	Warmwell	
No. 11 Group		**Headquarters:**	**Uxbridge**	
17	Hurricane I	YB	Debden	Sector Station
25	Blenheim If	ZK	Martlesham Heath	
85	Hurricane I	VY	Martlesham Heath	
151	Hurricane I	DZ	North Weald	Sector Station
41	Spitfire I	EB	Hornchurch	Sector Station
54	Spitfire I	KL	Hornchurch	
65	Spitfire I	YT	Hornchurch	
74	Spitfire I	ZP	Hornchurch	
56	Hurricane I	US	Rochford	
43	Hurricane I	FT	Tangmere	Sector Station
601	Hurricane I	UF	Tangmere	
145	Hurricane I	ZX	Westhampnett	
64	Spitfire I	SH	Kenley	
615	Hurricane I	KW	Kenley	Sector Station
111	Hurricane I	JU	Croydon	
32	Hurricane I	LZ	Biggin Hill	Sector Station
610	Spitfire I	DW	Biggin Hill	
501	Hurricane I	SD	Gravesend	
1	Hurricane I	JX	Northolt	Sector Station
257	Hurricane I	DT	Northolt	
600	Blenheim If	BQ	Manston	
No. 12 Group		**Headquarters:**	**Watnall**	
19	Spitfire I	QV	Duxford	Sector Station
66	Spitfire I	LZ	Cotishall	
242	Hurricane I	LE	Cotishall	
73	Hurricane I	TP	Church Fenton	
249	Hurricane I	GN	Church Fenton	
616	Spitfire I	YQ	Leconfield	
229	Hurricane I	RE	Wittering	
266	Spitfire I	UO	Wittering	
222	Spitfire I	ZD	Kirton in Lindsey	
264	Defiant I	PS	Kirton in Lindsey	(one flight)
264	Defiant I	PS	Ringway	
29	Blenheim If	RO	Digby	
46	Hurricane I	PO	Digby	
611	Spitfire I	FY	Digby	
23	Blenheim If	YP	Collyweston	
No. 13 Group		**Headquarters:**	**Newcastle**	
72	Spitfire I	RN	Acklington	
79	Hurricane I	NV	Acklington	

605	Hurricane I	UP	Drem	
607	Hurricane I	AF	Usworth	
232	Hurricane I	EF	Turnhouse	
253	Hurricane I	SW	Turnhouse	
3	Hurricane I	QO	Wick	
603	Spitfire I	XT	Dyce	(one flight)
603	Spitfire I	XT	Montrose	(one flight)
232	Hurricane I	EF	Sumburgh	(one flight)
141	Defiant I	TW	Prestwick	
219	Blenheim If	FK	Catterick	
504	Hurricane I	TM	Castletown	
245	Hurricane I	DX	Aldergrove, NI	

Appendix B

Fighter Command Order of Battle January 1941

Sqn	Aircraft	Code	Station	
No. 9 Group Headquarters:		**Box,**	**Wiltshire**	
229	Hurricane I	RE	Speke	Sector Station
312	Hurricane I	DU	Speke	
96	Hurricane I	ZJ	Cranage	
307	Defiant I	EW	Jurby, IoM	
306	Hurricane I	UZ	Turnhill	Sector Station
No. 10 Group				
87	Hurricane I	LK	Charmy Down	Sector Station
501	Hurricane I	SD	Exeter	
504	Hurricane I	TM	Exeter	
263	Hurricane I	HE	Exeter	
32	Hurricane I	GZ	Middle Wallop	Sector Station
93	Havoc I	HN	Middle Wallop	
604	Beaufighter If	NG	Middle Wallop	
182	Spitfire I	UM	Warmwell	
609	Spitfire I	PR	Warmwell	
238	Hurricane I	VK	Chilbolton	
234	Spitfire I	AZ	St Eval	
79	Hurricane I	NV	Pembrey	
247	Hurricane I	ZY	Roborough	
No. 11 Group				
1	Hurricane I	JX	Northolt	Sector Station
601	Hurricane I	UF	Northolt	
41	Spitfire IIa	EB	Hornchurch	Sector Station
64	Spitfire I	SH	Hornchurch	
611	Spitfire I	FY	Hornchurch	
66	Spitfire IIa	LZ	Biggin Hill	Sector Station
74	Spitfire IIa	ZP	Biggin Hill	
92	Spitfire I	QJ	Biggin Hill	
421 Flt	Spitfire I	DL	Hawkinge	
141	Defiant I	TW	Gravesend	
253	Hurricane I	SW	Kenley	Sector Station
615	Hurricane I	KW	Kenley	
605	Hurricane IIa	UP	Croydon	
219	Beaufighter If	FK	Tangmere	Sector Station
65	Spitfire I	YT	Tangmere	
145	Hurricane I	SO	Tangmere	
302	Hurricane I	WX	Westhampnett	
610	Spitfire I	DW	Westhampnett	
23	Blenheim If	YP	Ford	

Sqn	Aircraft	Code	Station	
FIU	Blenheim If/Beaufighter If	ZQ	Ford	
56	Hurricane I	US	North Weald	Sector Station
249	Hurricane I	CN	North Weald	
264	Defiant I	PS	Gravesend	
17	Hurricane I	YB	Debden	Sector Station
249	Hurricane I	VY	Debden	
249	Hurricane I	LE	Debden	

No. 12 Group

Sqn	Aircraft	Code	Station	
19	Spitfire IIa	QV	Duxford	Sector Station
310	Hurricane I	NN	Duxford	
213	Hurricane I	AK	Church Fenton	Sector Station
303	Hurricane I	RF	Church Fenton	
222	Spitfire I	ZD	Coltishall	Sector Station
257	Hurricane I	DT	Coltishall	
151	Hurricane I	DZ	Wittering	Sector Station
266	Spitfire I	UO	Wittering	
25	Blenheim If	ZK	Wittering	
71	Hurricane I	XR	Kirton in Lindsey	Sector Station
255	Defiant I	YD	Kirton in Lindsey	
616	Spitfire I	YQ	Kirton in Lindsey	
46	Hurricane IIa	PO	Digby	Sector Station
29	Blenheim If	RO	Digby	
2 RCAF	Hurricane I	AE	Digby	
308	Hurricane I	ZF	Baginton	Sector Station

No. 13 Group

Sqn	Aircraft	Code	Station	
54	Spitfire I	KL	Catterick	Sector Station
600	Beaufighter	BQ	Catterick	
256	Defiant I	JT	Catterick	
43	Hurricane I	FT	Turnhouse	Sector Station
603	Spitfire IIa	XT	Turnhouse	
602	Spitfire I	LO	Prestwick	
245	Hurricane I	DX	Aldergrove, NI	Sector Station

No. 14 Group

Sqn	Aircraft	Code	Station	
111	Hurricane I	JU	Dyce	Sector Station
232	Hurricane I	EF	Elgin	
3	Hurricane I	QO	Castletown	
1 RCAF	Hurricane I	YO	Digby	
260	Hurricane I	ZT	Skitten	

Appendix C

Fighter Command Order of Battle 1 June 1941

Sqn	Aircraft	Code	Airfield	Sector Station

No. 9 Group

Sqn	Aircraft	Code	Airfield	Sector Station
302	Hurricane I	WX	Jurby, IoM	Ramsey
615	Hurricane I	KW	Valley	Valley
315	Hurricane I	PK	Speke	Speke
96	Hurricane I/Defiant I	ZJ	Crange	Speke
256	Hurricane I/Defiant I	JT	Squires Gate	Speke
403 RCAF	Tomahawk	KH	Ternhill	Ternhill
68	Blenheim If/Beaufighter If	WM	High Ercall	Ternhill
308	Spitfire IIa	ZF	Baginton	Baginton
605	Hurricane IIa	UP	Baginton	Baginton

No. 10 Group

32	Hurricane IIa	GZ	Angle	Pembrey
316	Hurricane I	SZ	Pembrey	Pembrey
79	Hurricane	NV	Pembrey	Pembrey
152	Spitfire IIa	UM	Portreath	Pembrey
247	Hurricane I	ZY	Portreath	Pembrey
66	Spitfire IIa	LZ	Portreath	Perranporth
501	Spitfire IIa	SD	Colerne	Colerne
600	Beaufighter If	BQ	Colerne	Colerne
263	Whirlwind I	HE	Filton	Colerne
87	Hurricane I	LK	Charmy Down	Colerne
307	Defiant I	EW	Exeter	Exeter
504	Hurricane I	TM	Exeter	Exeter
604	Beaufighter If	NG	Middle Wallop	Middle Wallop
93	Havoc	HN	Middle WAllop	Middle Wallop
118	Spitfire IIa	NK	Ibsley	Middle Wallop
234	Spitfire IIa	AZ	Warmwell	Middle Wallop

No. 11 Group

145	Spitfire IIa	ZX	Merston	Tangmere
616	Spitfire IIa	YQ	Westhampnett	Tangmere
610	Spitfire IIa	DW	Westhampnett	Tangmere
219	Beaufighter If	FK	Tangmere	Tangmere
23	Havoc	YP	Ford	Tangmere
FIU	Beaufighter			
	Havoc & Blenheim	ZQ	Ford	Tangmere
312	Hurricane IIa/IIb	DU	Kenley	Kenley
258	Hurricane IIa/IIb	ZT	Kenley	Kenley
1	Hurricane IIa/IIb	JX	Redhill	Kenley
609	Spitfire IIa	PR	Biggin Hill	Biggin Hill
92	Spitfire Vb	QJ	Biggin Hill	Biggin Hill
601	Hurricane IIb/IIc	UF	Manston	Biggin Hill
91	Spitfire Vb	DL	Hawkinge	Biggin Hill
74	Spitfire IIa/Vb	ZP	Gravesend	Biggin Hill
264	Defiant I	PS	Middle Wallop	Biggin Hill
29	Beaufighter If	RO	Middle Wallop	Biggin Hill
603	Spitfire Va	XT	Hornchurch	Hornchurch
54	Spitfire IIa/Va	KL	Hornchurch	Hornchurch
611	Spitfire Va	FY	Southend	Hornchurch
56	Hurricane IIa/IIb	US	North Weald	North Weald
242	Hurricane IIb/IIc	LE	Stapleford Tawney	North Weald
3	Hurricane IIb/IIc	QO	Martlesham	Debden
71	Hurricane IIa/IIc	XR	Martlesham	Debden
303	Spitfire IIb	RF	Northolt	Northolt
306	Hurricane IIa/IIc	UZ	Northolt	Northolt

No. 12 Group

19	Spitfire II	QV	Fowlmere	Duxford
310	Hurricane IIa	NN	Duxford	Duxford
222	Spitfire IIa/IIb	ZD	Coltishall	Coltishal
257	Hurricane I/IIc	DT	Coltishall	Coltishall
25	Beaufighter If	ZK	Wittering	Wittering
151	Hurricane I	DZ	Wittering	Wittering
266	Spitfire IIa	UO	Collyweston	Wittering
401 RCAF	Hurricane IIa/IIb	YO	Wellingore	Digby
402 RCAF	Hurricane IIa/IIb	AE	Coleby Grange	Digby
65	Spitfire IIA	YT	Kirton in Lindsey	Kirton in Lindsey
255	Defiant I	YD	Hibaldstow	Kirton in Lindsey
452 RAAF	Spitfire Ia/IIa	UD	Kirton in Lindsey	Kirton in Lindsey
485 RNZAF	Spitfire I	OU	Leconfield	Church Fenton

Appendix D

Night Fighter Squadrons
Operational or being formed, July 1941

Sqn	Aircraft	Code	Airfield	Sector Station
No. 9 Group				
68	Beaufighter If	WM	High Ercall	Hack Green
256	Defiant I	JT	Woodvale	Trewan Sands
456 RAAF	Defiant I	RX	Valley	(forming)
No. 10 Group				
604	Beaufighter If	NG	Middle Wallop	Sopley
307	Defiant I	EW	Exeter	Exminster
600	Beaufighter If	BQ	Charmy Down	Avebury
87	Hurricane I	LK	Charmy Down	Avebury
No. 11 Group				
85	Havoc	VY	Hundson	Foulness
29	Beaufighter If	RO	West Malling	Willesborough
264	Defiant I	PS	West Malling	Willesborough
219	Beaufighter If	FK	Tangmere	Wartling
23	Havoc	YP	Ford	Wartling
FIU	Beaufighter and Havoc	ZQ	Ford	Wartling
No. 12 Group				
255	Defiant I	YD	Kirton in Lindsey	Hampton Hill
400 RCAF	Defiant I	KP	Coleby Grange	Orby
25	Beaufighter If	ZK	Kingscliffe	Langtoft
151	Hurricane I	DZ	Kingscliffe	Langtoft
No. 13 Group				
141	Defiant I	TW	Ayr	St Quivox
406 RCAF	Beaufighter If	HU	Acklington	Northstead
410 RCAF	Defiant I	RA	Drem	(forming)

Appendix E

Wing Leaders 1941

Wing	Wing Leader	Dates
Biggin Hill	Wing Commander A G Malan DSO DFC	March 1941
	Wing Commander M L Robinson DSO DFC	August 1941
	Wing Commander J Rankin DSO DFC	September 1941
Kenley	Wing Commander J R A Peel DFC (a)	March 1941
	Wing Commander J A Kent DFC	July 1941
	Wing Commander E N Ryder DFC (b)	October 1941
	Wing Commander J R A Peel DFC (a)	December 1941
Hornchurch	Wing Commander A D Farquhar DFC (c)	March 1941
	Wing Commander J R Kayll DSO DFC (d)	June 1941
	Wing Commander F S Stapleton DSO DFC	July 1941
	Group Captain H Broadhurst DSO DFC AFC (e)	Summer 1941 (Acting)
Tangmere	Wing Commander D R S Bader DSO DFC (f)	March 1941
	Wing Commander H de C A Woodhouse DFC	August 1941
North Weald	Wing Commander R C Kellett DSO DFC (g)	March 1941
	Wing Commander J W Gillan DFC AFC (g)	July 1941
	Wing Commander F V Beamish DSO DFC AFC (h)	August 1941
Northolt	Wing Commander G A L Manton (i)	March 1941
	Wing Commander W Urbanowicz	April 1941
	Wing Commander J A Kent DFC	June 1941
	Wing Commander T Rolski	August 1941
Duxford	Wing Commander M N Crossley dfc (j)	March 1941
	Wing Commander R R S Tuckd DSO DFC (k)	July 1941
Middle Wallop	Wing Commander A H Boyd DSO DFC	August 1941
Wittering	Wing Commander P G Jameson DFC	June 1941
Debden	Wing Commander J R A Peel DSO DFC (a)	August 1941

(a) see 11 July and 9'July 1941
(b) see 3 April and 27 September 1940 and 31 October 1941
(c) see 22 February 1940
(d) see 25 June 1941
(e) see 25 June 1941
(f) see 4 July 1941
(g) see 29 August 1941
(h) see 7 November 1940
(i) see 16 April 1940
(j) see 18 and 24 August 1940
(k) see 18 and 25 August 1940 and 21 June 1941